JUSTICE OUTSIDE THE CITY

Insights on Contemporary Issues Series is an important collection of books which concentrate on a wide range of social geography and policy-related issues of direct concern to students, lecturers, policy-makers and opinion-formers.

All the books have been written by experts from the social science disciplines. They will bring together theoretical viewpoints and empirical data, in ways that allow the reader to evaluate contemporary issues, and to assist in the forecasting of future trends and developments.

Already published:
Johnston R J, Pattie C J & Allsopp J G : A Nation Dividing?

Forthcoming:
Gibb R, Wise M: 1992: A Europe for Whom?
Smith S J : Gender and Housing
Church A : Dockland Decline and Development
Smith C J : Urban Crisis

Justice Outside the City:

ACCESS TO LEGAL SERVICES IN RURAL BRITAIN

MARK BLACKSELL,
KIM ECONOMIDES
AND
CHARLES WATKINS

Longman
Scientific &
Technical

Longman Scientific and Technical
Longman Group UK Ltd,
Longman House, Burnt Mill, Harlow,
Essex CM20 2JE, England
and Associated Companies throughout the world.

Copublished in the United States with
John Wiley & Sons Inc., 605 Third Avenue, New York, NY 10158

© Longman Group UK Limited 1991

First published 1991

British Library Cataloguing in Publication Data
Blacksell, Mark
    Justice outside the city : access to legal services in
    rural Britain.
    1. Great Britain. Legal services
    I. Title II. Economides, Kim III. Watkins, Charles
    338.473441

    ISBN 0-582-04296-8

Set in 10/12pt Palatino

Produced by Longman Group (FE) Limited
Printed in Hong Kong

Contents

Preface

In the modern world legal services have become a social necessity, but like virtually all other forms of service one that is difficult to guarantee equally. The better-off and those living in towns and cities, where significant economies of scale are possible, tend to be well served, while those people living in rural areas, particularly if they happen to be poor, can be seriously deprived. The research on which this book is based has attempted to map out the structure of both private and public legal services in the rural UK and to ascertain the way in which they are used by the rural population. The bulk of the original survey work was undertaken in 1985 and 1986 in the counties of Cornwall and Devon in south-west England, but significant empirical studies were also undertaken in other parts of the country, notably Dyfed in Wales, Norfolk in England and Ross in Scotland. A further study was planned in Northern Ireland, but eventually a lack of resources meant that it had to be abandoned. Finally the whole of our work is firmly set within the more general context of rural legal service provision in North America, elsewhere in Western Europe, and other parts of the world which share European legal traditions (Economides and Blacksell, 1987).

The core of the research was funded by a grant from the Economic and Social Research Council (E00 232 054) and we should like to acknowledge formally here the invaluable support that this gave, enabling us to pursue our own independent research programme. The grant also provided the means to support fully one of us (CW) as a postdoctoral fellow for two and a half years.

In one form or other the work has extended over the greater part of the 1980s and, over such a period, there are inevitably many people who have contributed to the research. Alison Dixon was employed as a research assistant on the ESRC project throughout 1987. Sarah Blacksell worked on a parallel research project, funded by the Law Society, on Referrals to Solicitors in Rural Areas, during the first half of 1989. Andrew Clark and Felicity Harris are both now completing their doctorates at Exeter on allied topics and their research has been supported by two ESRC-linked studentships associated with our project. All these people have been closely involved at one time or another with the work and we want to put our grateful thanks to them on record.

More generally, we have received much help from Carole Willis at the Research Policy Planning Unit of the national Law Society in London and from the Devon and Exeter, the Plymouth and the Cornwall law societies locally. The latter assisted us enormously in the early stages of the research by helping to organise two seminars with local solicitors in Exeter and Camborne. The Lord Chancellor's Department has also assisted us on numerous occasions, not least when the Legal Aid Advisory Committee decided to make the theme of its 1986 conference the delivery of rural legal services and to base it at the University of Exeter. It is hard to express adequately our thanks to the CAB service. Nationally, NACAB has always generously facilitated access to its statistical records; regionally the Devon and Cornwall office, mainly in the persons of Jean Dunkley and Barry Williams, have always provided wise and unstinting help; and locally the Exeter CAB, in particular through the good offices of Cath Hunt, Sean Price and Lynda Sullivan, has enabled us all to gain first-hand experience of publicly funded advice services. Our work has also been much enhanced by a series of vii travel grants from the Canadian High Commission and from the British Academy, which have enabled us to extend the research to both Canada and the United States and to make valuable contacts with American researchers.

None of the research on which this book is based would have been possible without the generous co-operation of the solicitors, CAB managers, and residents of the parishes of Chulmleigh, Hartland and St Keverne, all of whom willingly gave their time to answering our questionnaires. We gratefully acknowledge the help of all concerned.

Individually, there are others we wish to thank. Neil Griffin and Bob Warner, solicitors in Devon and Cornwall respectively, gave most generously of their advice and time; Terry Bacon and Rodney Fry have designed and drawn the maps with their customary skill and efficiency; Anne Waters typed the final version of the manuscript; George Edwards of Waterlows the publishers provided the statistics on the distribution of solicitors; Elaine Kempson commented on much of the early survey work; Philip Lewis read and commented on the whole manuscript, Ron Johnston and Paul White, the series editors, have supported us throughout the latter stages of the work; the Departments of Geography and Law at the University of Exeter have provided us with the working environment that has made it possible for us to complete the research; and our families and friends have put up with our sometimes obsessive enthusiasm (and moments of despair) with a combination of amusement, tact and patience. We want to thank them all most warmly and we hope that the book is an adequate reflection of all their generosity. The final text is of course entirely our responsibility and we all blame each other for any shortcomings.

Mark Blacksell, Kim Economides and Charles Watkins
Exeter and Cirencester, Easter 1990.

List of Figures

Glossary

AJRBP   Access to Justice in Rural Britain Research Project
CAB(x)   Citizens' Advice Bureau(x)
COMAWIP   Cornwall Money Advice and Welfare Information Project
CPAG   The Child Poverty Action Group – a British anti-poverty charity
EDLCSG   The Exeter District Law Centre Steering Group
ESRC   The Economic and Social Research Council – one of the government-funded research councils
Green Form   A mechanism that allows solicitors to provide initial legal advice under the Legal Aid Scheme
HLA   Honorary legal adviser
Judicare   The name given to government-funded legal aid schemes in North America, staffed by private attorneys
LAG   The Legal Action Group – a British law reform pressure group
LCD   The Lord Chancellor's Department
LCF   The Law Centres' Federation
Legal Aid   Government-funded assistance for the cost of legal advice and representation
Legal Aid Board   The body that has administered Legal Aid in England and Wales since April 1989
Lord Chancellor's Legal Aid Advisory Committee   The body which annually advises the Lord Chancellor on the administration of the Legal Aid Scheme
LSC   The Legal Services Corporation – the body with responsibility for many federally funded public legal services in the United States
NACAB   The National Association of Citizens' Advice Bureaux

NCC   The National Consumer Council
NCSS   The National Council for Social Service
NCVO   The National Council of Voluntary Organisations
OEO   The Office of Economic Opportunity (USA)
PIRATE   Public Information in Rural Areas Technology Experiment
QRLS   The Queen's Rural Legal Services (Ontario, Canada)
RAIC   Rural Advice and Information Conference
RCLS   The Royal Commission on Legal Services
SACAB   The Scottish Association of Citizens' Advice Bureaux – now known as Citizens' Advice Scotland
SCC   The Scottish Consumer Council
Shelter   A national charity committed to combating homelessness

To The Memory Of Peter Ward (1953–1989)
Who Worked Against Poverty And For Justice

1.   Rural Justice

THE COUNTRY AND THE CITY

Law, and the Western legal tradition in particular, is often seen as a product of economic, political and cultural developments which are associated with the rise of the city. (Berman, 1983; Unger, 1976). Indeed, for Marx and Engels (1970: 69) the antithesis between town and country was of pivotal importance for an understanding of social transformation:

> The antagonism between town and country begins with the transition from barbarism to civilization, from tribe to State, from locality to nation, and runs through the whole history of civilization to the present day . . . . The existence of the town implies, at the same time, the necessity of administration, police, taxes etc.; in short, of the municipality, and thus of politics in general. Here first becomes manifest the division of the population into two great classes, which is directly based on the division of labour and on the instruments of production. (Harvey, 1973: 203–6)

Lewis Mumford (1961: 64) made this connection between legal development and the city while pointing to the anarchy which reigns beyond its boundaries:

> By putting power in some measure at the service of justice, the city, departing from the tedious archaic reign of the village, brought order more swiftly into its internal affairs; but it left an unguarded lawless wasteland in the area between cities, where no local god could exercise power or establish moral jurisdiction without colliding with another god.

This juxtaposition of the country and the city – the two traditional poles of life – is also to be found throughout literature which, as Raymond Williams (1973: 1) observed, has attached a number of images to these contrasting life-styles:

> On the country has gathered the idea of a natural way of life: of peace, innocence and simple virtue. On the city has gathered the idea of an achieved centre: of learning, communication, light. Powerful hostile associations have also developed: on the city as a place of noise, worldliness and ambition; on the country as a place of backwardness, ignorance, limitations. A contrast between country and city, as fundamental ways of life, reaches back to classical times.

The difficulty with such contrasts is that since they are largely rhetorical they may no longer accurately reflect contemporary reality. Given the redundant and often violent industrial wasteland within many of our modern cities it now seems inappropriate to describe the rapidly shrinking spaces between them as 'an unguarded lawless wasteland'. Law often has a presence in the village just as anarchy, in the form of urban riots and inner-city ghettos, finds expression in the metropolis. But this clearly has as much to do with changes in social structure as developments regarding legal behaviour. Close-knit communities are no longer seen as a peculiarly rural phenomenon (Buttel and Newby, 1980) and today it is possible to speak of the 'urban village'; similarly, the suburbanisation – even urbanisation – of agricultural communities has made many of the traditional and familiar stereotypes of village life obsolete, as Sarah Harper (1989: 179) argues: 'Rural zones are being socially, economically and physically restructured, research into the wider process behind this restructuring is clearly needed.'

While it is probable that law contributes to the process behind this 'rural *perestroika*', more directly, what kind of presence does it have outside the city? Ask any farmer and you will be told of the near-continual flow of laws and regulations which govern and intrude upon all aspects of rural life. Particularly during the post-war years planning laws have been passed to check urban sprawl while a host of environmental laws exist to protect the countryside from insensitive development and industrial pollution. As the 'green lobby' increases its influence throughout

Europe this trend can be expected to continue. Yet despite their ubiquity most laws can be traced back to their urban origins: the local town hall, Westminster or, more recently, Brussels. Moreover, disputes based upon such laws may ultimately be settled in the city before judges sitting in the superior courts. If the city then remains the cradle and grave of formal legal activity how do rural communities fit in with the modern legal system?

By focusing on the diverse impacts of the administration of justice in rural and remote areas we believe the concept of rural justice may point to some answers. However, the concept also raises interesting questions about whether these areas contain distinctive attitudes towards law and justice which shape the demands placed upon, and hence, to some extent, determine the nature of, rural legal services. Rural justice can therefore be seen both as part of the justice dispensed in the city as well as a local product of rural communities (Cooke, 1989a).

In this study we approach rural justice from the academic standpoints of law and geography, disciplines which have developed separately and yet share a number of common traditions (Economides, Blacksell and Watkins, 1986; Blacksell, Watkins and Economides, 1986; Blomley, 1989; Clark, 1989). We explore several themes which rural justice connects: legality, justice, local legal cultures, accessibility and rurality in an attempt to link theory with practice. By showing how the unequal distribution of legal resources is of concern to policymakers as well as to academic theorists our aim is to widen debates on the changing nature of legal services and the countryside. It is not enough simply to describe how rural areas are under-resourced with regard to legal services; we need also to ask the significance of this for changing professional, constitutional and ecological values, as well as legal and geographic theory. In our view, by establishing linkages between geographic principles of territorial or distributive justice and the administration of justice, rural justice contributes a number of valuable insights to ongoing debates within both law and geography.

RURAL JUSTICE AND THE LEGAL SERVICES DEBATE

Although in England and Wales policy on legal services continues to be dominated by London-based interest groups, for example the LCD, the Law Society, the Bar Council, NACAB, LCF, LAG, NCC and the new Legal Aid Board, all have shown increasing awareness of the problem of delivering legal services to rural areas. Indeed, rural legal services have often been at the centre of current debates on the future of the conveyancing market, fusion of the two branches of the profession and the 'franchising' of legal aid. As with the modernisation of the railways under Lord Beeching in the late 1950s, the issue has been one of rural accessibility: will rural communities pay a disproportionately high price for streamlining the administration of justice if, in the interests of economic efficiency, magistrates' courts and solicitors' branch offices in rural areas close down? As with other rural services, the problem has been defined in terms of how to sustain a satisfactory network of provision at reasonable expense.

The problem, however, has other dimensions which reach beyond mere physical accessibility. The quality of the services on offer, who provides them and how they are delivered focus attention away from the consumers of legal services towards the suppliers. Rural justice is a concept which also highlights a tension within the modern legal profession which may be expressed in terms of conflicting professional goals: the 'service ideal' versus the profit motive. Solicitors working as sole practitioners in rural areas may be portrayed as the last bastions of generalist, small-scale, legal practice and the custodians of true professional values. Certainly the closure of these outlets has implications not only for the rural communities they serve; the demise of this style of practice and its subordination to large, urban-based units of production could represent a major, and possibly an irreversible, shift in the nature of legal practice. Consumers of legal services stand to lose and gain from these developments. On the one hand, the 'personal touch' and human contact associated with small-scale practice will be threatened; on the other, economies of scale only possible in city practices mean that lawyers can acquire new skills in business management, information technology and marketing which should translate into faster, more efficient, more specialist and cheaper services for clients. The 'mega-firms' in the City are already rapidly adjusting in terms of legal technique and professional values and this trend is likely to continue until the advent of 'multi-disciplinary' and 'multinational' practices in the run-up to the unified, single, European Market in 1992; whether, and to what extent, rural and provincial practice can or should follow will be an issue we follow up later on.

Rural justice is not confined, however, to the services provided by solicitors working in rural areas. Although of central importance because of their widespread geographical distri-bution their work is, on the whole, limited in terms of the range of legal issues they habitually cover. Some of the slack is picked up by generalist advice agencies, or 'para-legals', such as Citizens' Advice Bureaux (CABx), but many issues containing a legal dimension appear to be dealt with by more informal methods within local communities. A further element within the concept of rural justice therefore concerns the question of indigenous attitudes towards dispute settlement. To what extent is the 'propensity to sue' in rural areas influenced by local customs and traditions? Does the existence of close-knit ongoing relationships in rural areas mean that there is a greater tendency to avoid courts and lawyers and substitute these for more informal methods of handling conflict? Or does the avoidance of formal litigation and adjudication result from the physical and social distance of courts and lawyers from rural communities? Whatever the reasons, can information technology overcome the barrier of physical distance which may prevent or inhibit these communities from having access to the legal system?

While answers to such questions are currently being sought (Clark, 1991; Harris, 1989) it is important to realise that the parameters of the debate on rural legal services remain narrowly circumscribed. The issues continue to be confined to how the sporadic and uneven distribution of legal services might be rectified. While the more important issue of quality of provision is gradually creeping on to the reform agenda, as seen for example in the debate on franchising Green Form Legal Aid work, this appears to have come about more as a result of a perceived threat to the network of Legal Aid supply points than the desire to improve the standards of rural legal services *per se*.

By introducing wider considerations into the debate rural justice may carry forward and inform the reform process which began as early as 1942 but did not get under way until the mid 1970s when the rural dimension to legal services finally surfaced (NCC, 1977; NCC/NCSS, 1978; Richards, 1989: 142–7).

Around this time several experiments were set up to investigate generalist information and advice services in rural areas as well as the needs they were supposed to meet (Roberts, 1978; Butcher, 1976; Brogden, 1978). By 1982 the Rural Advice and Information Conference, held in London, reported on and encouraged a further round of nationwide activity (RAIC, 1984; Elliott, 1984; Moseley and Packman, 1982; NCC, 1983; SCC, 1982, 1983). Local initiatives in Devon, such as the South Molton Community Information Project and the East Devon Mobile CAB, were typical of this activity. However, it was clear that essential as they were, generalist advice and information services had certain inherent limitations. While they were often able to diagnose and refer specialist legal problems, it was unlikely that such problems could always be resolved to the same degree of competence one would expect to find in the average solicitor. After all, solicitors themselves when confronted with problems outside their particular sphere of expertise often refer problems (Economides, Blacksell and Blacksell, 1991). The supplementary question of whether rural inhabitants had adequate access to *specialist* professional legal services therefore arose.

The question of the specialist dimension in rural legal services was by no means straightforward as it was not always clear that they could be distinguished from more generalist services. For certain categories of client and legal work, such as welfare rights claimants, generalist agencies were often able to offer a more expert and accessible service than that provided by solicitors, especially where they had back-up resources in the form of a welfare rights officer (Kempson, 1989). Indeed, it has not been unusual for solicitors themselves to employ para-legal welfare specialists or to make referrals to generalist para-legal agencies when issues of social welfare law come their way. Furthermore, because para-legal agencies have had fewer restraints imposed upon them by professional ethics and the market they have, in the past, enjoyed greater freedom than private practitioners in actively pursuing uneconomic work. This is now changing as para-legals become more professional through the monitoring and improvement of standards and as solicitors start to expand their markets through advertising and other marketing skills which inevitably modify traditional standards of professionalism. While specialist legal services can therefore no longer be equated with the work of the private legal profession it is still important that rural residents have access to the services of solicitors and barristers. Since the late 1970s it has been widely recognised that there is a 'rural problem' with regard to the accessibility of these services.

In 1979 the Benson Commission (RCLS, 1979, para. 8.38) first placed this specialist dimension to rural legal services on the reform agenda with the observation that

> Needs for legal services exist not only in the big cities. . . . They are also prevalent in rural areas, among a more widely scattered population. Such areas have suffered from the loss of a number of services, in particular public transport and of advice facilities generally. Solicitors' offices tend to be found only in the towns and are not always accessible to those who have need of their services.

Although in its report the Commission went on to recommend that 'measures should also be taken to meet rural needs', little positive action has been taken to improve the accessibility of rural legal services. The LCF have pointed to the absence of public legal services in sparsely populated areas (LCF, 1980) and the Lord Chancellor's Legal Aid Advisory Committee have also commented regularly on the difficulties faced by rural clients who seek the services of solicitors (LCD, 1983: para. 183; 1986a: paras 102–24; 1990: paras 36–7, 59). The absence of public legal services in rural areas means that the main plank of legal aid strategy since the 1970s – the 'mixed delivery system' – has not been in operation for rural communities. Recognition of the 'rural problem' in legal service delivery has not, however, led to any clear solution, even though several have been proposed.

The concept of a 'rural law centre' has been put forward (EDLCSG, 1981; Economides, 1982; LCD, 1983: para. 184) but so far none has been properly tried and tested in a rural area. The Benson Commission referred to the possibility of grants and loans to private practitioners in order to induce them into isolated rural areas (RCLS, 1979: paras 8.38, 16.23–9) and this idea has recently been picked up by the Legal Aid Board in its proposals for franchising the Green Form Scheme (Legal Aid Board, 1989: para. 34). Telephone advice and 'outreach' work by solicitors in satellite offices in rural locations have also been suggested as ways to tackle the barrier of physical distance (Legal Aid Board, 1989: para. 34; Marre, 1988, para. 7.102; Law Society, 1987: 8). While these and other solutions will be examined later, the point to emphasise now is that legal services policy in rural areas is essentially concerned with how to sustain, or transport, private professional legal services to rural communities. Presently these services are under threat from changes in the conveyancing market and government policy directed at rural magistrates' courts and the franchising of Legal Aid. The cumulative effect of measures designed to increase efficiency and competition in the market for legal services, along with proposals to privatise other rural services (Bell and Cloke, 1989) could either close down rural solicitors' firms altogether or else force them, through mergers and amalgamations, to concentrate resources in urban locations. In either case rural solicitors are under pressure to withdraw from rural communities.

The significance of such a development – for rural communities, the legal profession and other groups – is difficult to assess in the absence of a theory which explains how law functions in rural areas. Rural justice, we believe, may help fill this gap by increasing understanding of the theory and practice of law in rural society. By 'theory' we refer not to grand theory which might be used to predict human or social action; rather, for us, theory is an explanatory device to make sense of an interrelated set of characteristics – in this case, links which connect law with space. Rural justice contains a number of themes: legality, justice, local legal cultures – as well as accessibility and rurality. While these themes intersect at a number of different levels in debates on legal services, the countryside, and legal and geographic theory, we shall examine them as follows: legality, justice and local legal cultures will be considered within our discussion of legal services; while accessibility and rurality will be considered in the context of debates on the countryside. Our purpose, however, is not simply to test, exemplify or illustrate generalisations about rural justice; we aim also to deepen critical understanding of how law functions in rural areas, which should inform theoretical and policy developments affecting both legal services and rural society.

Legality

Unlike law, 'legality' suggests the possibility of a variety of systems for ordering and organising social networks beyond that of the state legal order (Sugarman, 1983). In this study we have had to move outside legal rules, or norms, and the activities of the formal legal system – the traditional focus of litigation, legal scholarship and legal education – in order to include within our conception of law a wide range of legal institutions (courts, tribunals and other informal mechanisms of dispute settlement), legal actors (judges, barristers, solicitors as well as 'para-legal' or generalist legal advisers) and the parties themselves. Legality redirects us away from positivist doctrinal analysis and focuses on an anthropological view of dispute processes.

It is an approach that is already very familiar in other areas of social analysis, where the nature of local–centre relations has been an issue of fierce debate in recent years (Massey, 1984; Sayer, 1989). There is now a widespread acceptance that social norms are mediated through, and changed by, local circumstances, though the precise nature of the processes at work is still an open question (Cooke, 1989b). Nevertheless, given our interest in the extent to which legal norms, often the products of highly centralised legal systems, penetrate and have relevance for rural society, the approach offered the prospect of a particularly promising way forward.

One important aspect of this approach is that law is seen in relative terms – it varies in space not merely across but also within the jurisdiction of states. As the anthropologist Geertz asserted, 'Like sailing, gardening, politics and poetry, law and ethnography are crafts of place: they work by the light of local knowledge' (1983: 167). Of course, sociological, comparative and historical jurisprudence has for some time demonstrated that differences exist between legal systems and the variety of customs found within them. More recently, under the labels of 'legal pluralism', 'delegalisation' and 'imposed law' (see Hooker, 1975; Galanter, 1980; Burman and Harrell-Bond, 1979), we find a similar tendency to uncover alternative normative orders which function outside, if not beyond the reach of, the official legal order. Much of this work assumes that the official legal order is a homogeneous entity which stands in contradistinction to the variety of 'private' orders which often are subordinated to it (Henry, 1983). Our understanding of legality, however, suggests that the state legal order may also be pluralist in that it responds to different kinds of local pressure and in so doing presents a variety of forms. Moreover, as part of the 'local state' (Dear, 1981), law may be autonomous, or semi-autonomous, from state activity at the national or transnational levels. Legal institutions such as the police, courts and the legal profession interact with local communities and inevitably reflect differences between them. As Sugarman (1983: 254) observes,

> The tensions and contradictions *within* the state order as between its different spheres and functions and the pressures this generates towards changes in the content and form of law, have tended to be neglected by historians, sociologists and lawyers.

While in agreement we would add that spatial variations, for example as between rural and urban areas, also need to be considered when explaining differences within the style, behaviour, and sphere of influence of legal institutions. By introducing a geographic perspective which links legality, locality and rurality, rural justice can shed light on a number of these differences.

Justice

Apart from emphasising the relativity of law, rural justice implies more than simple access to legal services or, as it is known in popular terms, 'the administration of justice'. While 'access to justice' is often considered to be synonymous with having the services of a professional lawyer, our understanding is wider and seeks to touch upon larger questions concerning social equality and the distribution of resources. The specific rural–urban dimensions of rural justice are considered below in our discussion of the debate on the changing nature of the countryside. At this point we concentrate on the relationship between justice and legal services in rural areas.

Whether legal services actually promote or inhibit social, or civic, justice is a question which clearly cannot be answered outside particular historical circumstances (Abel, 1979, 1985; Trubek and Trubek, 1981; Sarat, 1981). In our view, it is a question that is therefore best left open. We have already stated that our conception of law is a broad one which includes legal services covering generalist advice, information and represent-ation given by 'para-legals' to specialist legal work done by the legal professions in the private and public sectors – as well as state-financed dispute-processing services in courts and tribunals – and therefore extends beyond the formal legal system. As regards justice, our basic assumption is essentially negative: while not excluding the possibility that legal services can promote both individual and social justice, neither do we assume that they inevitably serve these goals. As with 'informal justice' (Abel, 1981, 1982; Matthews, 1988), rural justice may be a vehicle for either 'conservative' or 'creative' conflict – for social control or social change.

These possibilities have inhibited us from using the language of 'legal needs' which presupposes that legal solutions are superior to any other in the resolution of social conflict (Lewis, 1973; Paterson and Nelken, 1984). Instead, we prefer to think of the terms 'territorial justice' and 'legal contact' which focus on the distribution of legal resources – and the *opportunities* of access – rather than imputing a priori values as to their use, or non-use, by potential clients and claimants (Coates and Rawstron, 1971; Mayhew and Reiss, 1969). While we do not assume that all gaps in the provision of legal services need to be filled, we do think it important to identify geographical areas and areas of law where they exist so that informed decisions can be made about which, if any, could or should be filled.

Whereas previous studies (Abel-Smith, Zander and Brooke, 1973; Mayhew and Reiss, 1969) on the distribution and use of legal services have concentrated cither on variations based on the social class of clients or the 'social organisation' of the legal profession – hence 'law for the poor' in urban ghettos dominated the legal services literature and movements of the 1960s and 1970s – rural justice moves beyond social stratification by introducing a spatial dimension in the explanation of the mobilisation of legal services. This is not to say that questions relating to rural social structure and stratification are unimportant in explaining the work of rural courts and lawyers; rather that rural justice which is socially constructed within specific local contexts – or local legal cultures – will inevitably differ from urban justice.

Local Legal Cultures

In order to see how rural justice operates we have sought to understand the interaction between the providers of legal services in rural areas and the consumers of these services. The term 'local legal cultures' has been used to account for differences which may be found among the providers – or legal actors – who represent the legal system in particular localities, to some extent moulding it to fit in with local conditions (Boyum, 1979; Church *et al.*, 1978; Church, 1982). Others have focused on the influences the legal system has on potential users (Kritzer, 1988) or, in an opposite direction, the influences users may have on the local legal system (Engel, 1980, 1984, 1987; Landon, 1982, 1985, 1990). To these attempts linking legality and locality we introduce a specific rural dimension. Local legal culture is in essence, then, concerned with how norms originating from the state interact with norms generated by local cultures and we emphasise this gap between state legal norms, a product of the city, and indigenous norms which evolve in rural communities.

Although we concentrate on empirical investigations of this gap, 'local legal cultures' also has implications for legal theory. Cotterrell (1989: 10–11), for example, has drawn attention to the 'internal–external dichotomy' in contemporary legal theory whereby orthodox jurisprudence and the sociology of law take up opposing standpoints on law, the former presenting an 'internal' view of law, the latter an 'external' one. Traditional legal philosophy aims to clarify the *concept* of law and techniques of legal reasoning; accordingly, it examines the nature of legal rules, norms and the role of the judge as adjudicator. Sociology of law, on the other hand, has a tendency to focus on the external *behaviour* of law within society. Although recent developments in legal and social theory have sought to collapse this internal/external distinction (Nelken, 1986), 'local legal culture' in one sense preserves it by maintaining a distinction between 'insiders' and 'outsiders'. It offers a way of looking at law which incorporates more than the individual yet less than society and, at a more general level, hints at the fundamental antinomy between the universal character of law and its relativity. The notion of 'local legal cultures' reminds us that while law is all-pervasive and has an impact which transcends its institutional boundaries, it always remains subject to local customs, attitudes and circumstances.

RURAL JUSTICE AND THE DEBATE ON CHANGE IN THE COUNTRYSIDE

If the debate on legal services has for the most part been limited to finding the optimum mix of public and private legal services (the 'mixed delivery' system) in order to create and sustain an accessible network of courts and lawyers, the debate on the countryside has to a large extent been concerned with balancing conflicting values, for example reconciling environmental conservation with modern agricultural technology. Particularly over the past decade, technology and the greater emphasis placed on the role of market forces have disrupted the relative stability of lawyers and the courts, as well as many other aspects of rural life. As a result we are witnessing a breakdown of the consensus which had emerged in favour of the mixed delivery system for legal services and the special provision of services for rural areas. And yet in both of these debates we find little attention given to the role law might play in helping rural communities adjust to changing economic and social circumstances. Through examining the nature of conflict management within rural communities as well as raising questions about the allocation and distribution of resources between rural and urban areas, rural justice challenges a number of stereotyped images which dominate the way we think about law and the countryside.

Rural justice, in other words, encourages us to make social rather than purely visual judgements about the quality of rural life (Newby, 1980, 1986). Moreover, while the provision of legal services in rural areas will to some extent be determined by constraints coming from the infrastructure of rural society (primarily resources but also in-built attitudes limiting expectations) it is important to realise the potential law has as an instrument of social change (Cloke and Little, 1990). In this sense, rural justice can be seen to reflect rural society while at the same time holding the potential to transform it. In this book we concentrate on plotting the parameters of current legal practice in rural areas from the point of view of the providers and consumers of legal services. This we see as a vital step towards understanding the full potential of law and legal services in helping rural communities reconcile the competing claims of agriculture, forestry, conservation, recreation and community development. The goal of comprehensive legal coverage to which rural justice aspires is therefore important not only from the standpoint of the legitimacy of the legal system and the rule of law; it is also perhaps a precondition for the development of rural society.

By way of introduction to the empirical work we have done on legal services in the contemporary rural UK we should explain our use of 'accessibility' and 'rurality' in the context of developments in the current legal and geographical literature. These are important themes which recur in our efforts to investigate legal practice and lay the foundations for a theory of rural justice.

Accessibility

The theme of 'accessibility' has been of central importance in both the legal and geographical literature but, oddly enough, there has been no dialogue integrating this body of knowledge (Economides, Blacksell and Watkins, 1986; Blacksell, Watkins and Economides, 1986; see generally Smith and Lloyd-Bostock, 1990). As far as the legal literature is concerned, two contributions have influenced the direction our research has taken. At a general level, the important comparative study directed by Cappelletti (1978–81), the Florence Access to Justice Project, encouraged us to move away from 'formal' access towards 'the right to effective access'. The importance of this study has been to identify, as a result of comparative analysis, a series of economic, psychological and social barriers that operate to prevent, or inhibit, the citizen's access to the legal system (Cappelletti and Garth, 1978). Moreover, the Florence project also analysed a number of possible strategies and promising solutions which could inform policymaking in the field of legal services and as such provided an invaluable source for this study.

The second contribution which we found of assistance has been the body of work carried out by European legal sociologists on the distribution of legal services (Schuyt, Groenendijk and Sloot, 1976, 1977; Niemeyer, 1978; Johnsen, 1978). Although one critic has argued that 'the concept of "access" should be banished from the empirical study of the distribution of legal services because it has no empirical referrent' (Griffiths, 1977:282), the empirical work Schuyt and Niemeyer conducted in the Netherlands, and Johnsen's work in northern Norway, have refined quite considerably the concept of access. Whereas the Florence project overlooked the significance of geographic barriers to access, these researchers uncovered evidence of a 'filter-effect' correlated with distance whereby certain categories of work became progressively more difficult to obtain with distance (Schuyt, Groenendijk and Sloot 1976: 119). The importance of this 'filter-effect' varied depending on the type of legal problem, and who was involved – but it was always apparent to some degree.

As might be expected, the geographical literature attaches considerably more importance to accessibility. As Cloke and Park (1985: 303) have argued,

> It has become increasingly apparent over the past decade that *access* to rural resources, even more than the large-scale presence or absence of the resources themselves, has become the crucial challenge in rural resource management.

For most geographers distance is the key variable determining levels of access even though it is always significantly modified in practice by a range of social and economic criteria. The 'friction of distance' ensures that, all things being equal (which of course in the real world they never are), the further a consumer is located from the point of supply for any given service, the more difficulty he or she will have in gaining access to it. It is a strongly positivist concept which has been tried and tested in a large number of empirical situations with reference to many different services, over many years (Brush and Bracey, 1955; Joseph and Phillips, 1984), though notably not hitherto with reference to legal services. It has also given rise to an important body of both theoretical and empirical work aimed at defining and predicting the spatially most efficient distributions for different kinds of service (Haggett, 1965). A whole range of *location–allocation* and *market potential* models have been developed with a view to help policymakers and retailers choose the optimum location for services – optimum usually being defined as the ability to reach the maximum number of people at the minimum cost (Taylor, 1977; Massam, 1980).

The pattern of physical accessibility can only provide, however, a relatively crude backdrop against which the ability of individuals actually to avail themselves of services can be measured (Marsden and Murdoch, 1990). Aggregate population figures always incorporate important local variations and rural areas now house a number of quite distinctive groups, ranging from a shrinking agricultural labour force, to the retired, long-distance commuters, part-time farmers, self-employed businessmen and the unemployed. The local cultures and service needs – including 'legal needs' – of each group are different, but all will be forced to spend a larger than average part of their income on transportation just because they live in a rural area and are therefore remote from services of all kinds. When attempting to typify what the town or locality means for different groups, it should be remembered that the smaller an individual's gross income the greater the share that will be swallowed up by transportation costs, simply because the fixed costs of running a car or paying for public transport takes little account of a person's financial circumstances (cars do vary in price and there are some fare concessions on public transport for the young and elderly, but such things by no means wholly reflect the variations in income level).

An important development in the study of accessibility has been a shift of emphasis from *households* to *individuals*. Figures for car ownership, or even the frequency of public transport, can be rendered meaningless if individuals cannot gain access to these facilities. A number of studies have now appeared which demonstrate how isolated and deprived certain categories of people living in rural areas can be, notably housewives, the elderly and children (Moseley, 1979; Rhys and Buxton, 1974; Garden, 1978). Indeed, one is left with the distinct impression that more groups, with the exception of those actually working, are likely to experience severe difficulties in gaining access to services. As far as legal services are concerned, this is of crucial importance, since there are significant barriers to providing information and advice by post or telephone, and mobile services are still very restricted.

There have been a large number of initiatives aimed at improving the levels of accessibility in rural areas, but they have suffered from a lack of co-ordination and consistency at both local and national levels. The potential value of co-ordination by local authorities has been demonstrated by a study in the Lewes area undertaken by East Sussex County Council (Searle, 1982), but it has yet to lead to any national transport policy other than a drive to reduce the restrictions on public transport operators (Nutley, 1984). Certainly, no specific attempt to evaluate the relevance of these schemes for legal services has been made and we would argue that this omission ought to be rectified.

While the importance of physical accessibility in rural areas is clearly an issue which ought to be investigated with respect to legal services, we have also sought to incorporate the economic, social and psychological barriers in our analysis of the accessibility of rural justice. This is essential, for while rural communities may be excluded from having legal services that are easily to hand, it may also be the case that some rural clients choose not to take their dispute to a lawyer. It may be, for example, that certain types of legal service are attractive to some clients, yet repellent to others (Mayhew and Reiss, 1969). In examining rural accessibility it is therefore essential to look at the relationship between the supplier and consumer, or potential consumer, of the service under investigation.

Rurality

Although, as we have noted already, it is common to draw a distinction between the country and the city there has been no agreement as to what constitutes 'rural'. There have been various definitions put forward by geographers and planners and many 'internal and infernal discussions' (Gilg, 1985: 4; see also Hoggart, 1988; Cloke and Edwards, 1986; Champion and Watkins, 1991) about the best way to distinguish between urban and rural areas. The problem is insoluble since the exact means of making such a distinction are as varied as the criteria underlying the concepts of 'urban' and 'rural'. Nevertheless, the existing literature suggests that two main groups of criteria may be considered.

Physical criteria

The simplest, and probably most useful way of distinguishing between urban and rural areas is the relative proportion of 'countryside'. Wibberley (1972) regarded 'rural' areas as essentially 'those parts of a country which show unmistakable signs of being dominated by extensive uses of land'. This simple and common-sense definition unfortunately has inherent problems of scale. Is the small country town rural? How does one place the large housing estate associated with a military airport or the buildings of a holiday camp in this framework? Phillips and Williams (1984: 5–6) have pointed out that 'If called upon to specify the exact factors that characterise an area as "rural" the majority of people could define the gross features or extreme locations fairly easily, but would have great difficulty in distinguishing the intermediate localities.' The problem is, therefore, that although everyone can point to rural areas such as the moorland of Dartmoor, or urban areas such as the centre of the city of Plymouth, how can the exact bounds between the two be drawn?

Social criteria

The physical definitions above take no account of the rurality of the population and this is crucial, for the way in which society is organised is more important for understanding properly the prevailing legal culture, than the superficial aspect of the landscape. Traditionally it was held that there was a clear distinction between rural communities in villages (*Gemeinschaft*) and urban communities in cities (*Gesellschaft*), but this crude duality has long been rejected, even though certain attributes of rural communities, such as dependence upon agriculture as a source of income and a way of life, remained distinct until well into the middle of this century (Williams, 1963). A generation ago, however, sociologists were arguing that there was something more akin to continuum of social organisation between the country and the town (Frankenburg, 1966; Pahl, 1968) and, more recently, the impact of processes like commoditisation, whereby all products and activities are expressed in terms of their cash value (Marsden, 1989) has come to be recognised as the key to understanding the fundamental restructuring of the rural economy that is now under way (Marsden, Whatmore and Munton, 1987).

Rather than explaining rural society in terms of a single, integrated, entity, it is currently fashionable to conceptualise it as a multiplicity of coexisting social groups, the boundaries between them varying depending on socio-economic, and other, circumstances (Knorr-Cetina, 1988; ACORA, 1990). Improved and more flexible forms of private transportation, in particular more widespread car ownership, mean that a life in the country is now open to a broader spectrum of society, a fact reflected in the increase in the population of many rural areas recorded in the 1981 census of population. Areas which since the mid-nineteenth century had had moribund populations were, by the late 1960s, beginning to attract people from the urban UK, notably groups such as commuters and the retired, and the processes of repopulation and social restructuring have been gathering pace ever since.

Rather than there being any one rural locality or local culture in a given area, there are now more likely to be several superimposed one upon the other, yielding a complex hierarchy of relationships. It is a transformation widely referred to as 'counter-urbanisation' (Champion, 1989) and it has made it infinitely more difficult and complicated to define rural areas in social terms, though this is not to say that, because of their sparse, if growing, populations, they do not have special characteristics and needs.

In this book an essentially pragmatic distinction between urban and rural areas has been made. This was relatively straightforward because of the nature of the area in which we carried out our empirical investigations: four pieces of research carried out in the 1970s, including Cloke's 1979 analysis of sixteen 'rurality' variables, taken from the population census, confirm the common-sense view that Devon and Cornwall are predominantly rural (Phillips and Williams, 1984: 7). Moreover, all the districts in the two counties, apart from Exeter, Plymouth and Torbay, are classified by Cloke and Edwards as either 'extreme rural' or 'intermediate rural' in their 1981B index (Cloke and Edwards, 1986: 301 – see Fig. 1.1). It is also worth mentioning that the physical and social criteria of rurality, which differentiate between form and substance, in part correspond with the internal/external distinction which was made in the context of discussing 'local legal cultures'. Rural justice, however, moves us beyond superficial analysis of the physical attributes of legality and rurality by laying the foundation for a social ecology of law and rural society.

THE NATURE OF THE BOOK

The chapters that follow examine the operation of justice in rural areas from a number of different perspectives, both structural and regional. The main emphasis is on the situation in south-west England, but important comparisons are drawn with other parts of the UK and with the very different geographical, social and legal contexts in rural areas elsewhere in the world.

In developed, democratic, countries the main providers of legal services and, thus, the gatekeepers to justice, are the members of the legal profession. In terms of numbers, their representatives in England and Wales tend to be solicitors in private practice and Chapter 2 considers the changing national distribution of these men and women, concentrating in particular on the balance between urban and rural areas. It emerges that people living outside the major towns and cities are by no means

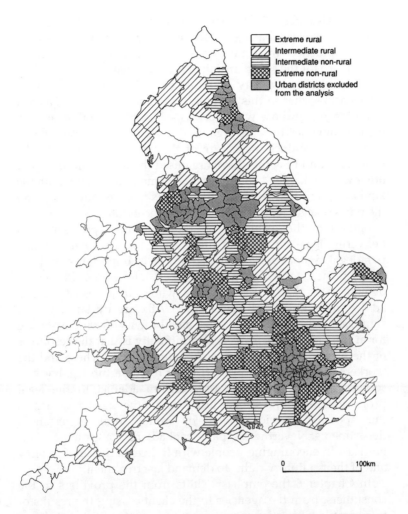

Extreme rural
Intermediate rural
Intermediate non-rural
Extreme non-rural
Urban districts excluded
from the analysis

Figure 1.1 Rural England and Wales according to Cloke and Edwards'
1981B index.

generally deprived in this respect, though remoteness does pose
problems of access for those residing in more isolated
communities.

Other forms and sources of legal advice, such as those
provided by publicly-funded law centres and CABx, are on the
other hand noticeably more urban-orientated and the network of

courts is also increasingly being rationalised and centralised. As a result, it is clear that the future of the network of solicitors in private practice in rural areas is a matter of overriding importance for the safeguarding of access to justice.

Given the multiplicity of localities and local legal cultures referred to earlier in this chapter, it is, therefore, of the greatest importance that those who work as solicitors in rural areas, and the way in which they are organised, are thoroughly understood. Chapter 3 examines the nature of the people employed in the profession and how they have organised themselves in firms and other ways. Chapter 4 continues this theme by analysing both the kinds of client that solicitors themselves believe they serve and the types of legal work on which they concentrate.

Although the primacy of the solicitors' profession in delivering legal services in rural areas is unquestionable, other, para-legal, agencies are growing slowly in importance and are being turned to by growing numbers of people. Chapter 5 demonstrates that in the UK as a whole, in terms of general advice, including legal advice, the CABx are by far the most significant with bureaux in most small towns offering a service for at least part of each week. The difficulty is that the resources of the service are severely stretched almost everywhere and the workers are not trained primarily to provide a full legal advice service. At best, therefore, they are an adjunct to the legal profession. Much the same is also true of other agencies, such as the specialist advice given by some local government departments. Nevertheless, para-legal advice is a growing force, not least in encouraging people with little experience of the law and of their statutory rights to demand just treatment.

In Chapter 6 the emphasis shifts from the providers to the consumers; from the agencies to the clients. Using the results of two detailed questionnaire surveys, an attempt is made to identify the kinds of people who use the different types of legal service and for what purposes, as well as probing to establish the levels of legal competence among those living in rural communities. This chapter also seeks to establish the kinds of perceived barriers to justice among the rural population and the ways in which they could best be overcome or ameliorated.

The focus on the UK and the south-west of England in particular is not simply a matter of convenience, it reflects the fact that in many important respects legal services and legal cultures are specific to the jurisdiction under which they operate. The legal system in England and Wales is different from that in Scotland, not to mention other parts of Europe and the rest of the world. Nevertheless, precisely because we are dealing with what happens at the periphery of the legal system, there are many common features in the problems faced by those trying to ensure that rural areas are served adequately by legal services, and Chapter 7 looks in a comparative way at how they have been approached and solved in a number of different countries. The aim is not anything approaching a comprehensive survey, but rather to provide a broader context for the detailed analysis in earlier chapters.

Finally, Chapter 8 reviews the whole question of how access to justice in rural areas might be improved, with particular reference to the reform of legal services in the UK that has been going on since the early 1980s. From the evidence presented in this book it is possible to draw at least some tentative conclusions as to whether or not special provision is required for rural areas and how the extent of any such provision might best be ascertained and planned.

2. The Geography of Solicitors and Legal Services

Access to justice for most people is heavily dependent upon the nature and extent of their access to legal services, which in turn is largely governed by who a person happens to be and where she or he happens to reside. Wealth and social status are always factors in determining individual levels of service, but proximity to the services themselves also plays a vital role. The distribution of the main kinds of legal service provides, therefore, an indispensable context for the detailed examination of the anatomy of services in rural areas, and to the study of public reactions to them, which form the main themes of this book.

The bulk of this chapter comprises an analysis of the distribution of solicitors in England and Wales, since they are overwhelmingly the most significant source of professional legal advice in the two countries, but there are also further sections dealing with publicly funded law centres and the largely para-legal CABx, both of which are locally very important. Finally, courts and the structure of the court system are considered, since it is here that many of the more serious legal disputes are finally adjudicated.

THE DISTRIBUTION OF SOLICITORS

Between 1973 and 1984 the number of solicitors with practising certificates in England and Wales rose by 72 per cent, from 26,541 to 45,732. This dramatic growth in the profession has made the only thorough, nationwide study of the distribution of solicitors obsolete and in urgent need of updating, so that the true extent of the service they provide can be clearly determined. Foster (1973) used the *Law List* of 1971 to assess the location of solicitors at that date and went on to relate the distribution of solicitors to selected socio-economic variables. It was a pioneering paper which has been widely cited. However, the growth in the profession has required a reassessment of the statistics and this has been undertaken by various researchers and includes our own work (Abel, 1988).

The growth in the number of solicitors is very much in line with the overall expansion in the service sectors of the economy, which has been gathering pace for more than a generation (Daniels, 1983). There is some argument as to whether the change is due mainly to burgeoning demand, or to a general failure among service industries to improve labour productivity at a similar rate to manufacturing industry (Damesick, 1986), but as far as solicitors are concerned, there seems very little doubt that the growth in the volume of work is the root cause. Higher levels of home-ownership and the greater complexity of people's affairs generally have made calling on legal advice almost obligatory for the well-off, while the intricacies of the welfare state and the bewilderingly wide range of state benefits now available have encouraged the poor to seek legal advice as their entitlement.

The greater demand for legal services has in turn raised new questions of access. Solicitors are overwhelmingly in private practice and, therefore, economic realities mean that certain groups, such as those living in remote rural areas, will suffer because the level of demand is too low to allow the provision of a comprehensive service (Cloke and Little, 1987). It is a problem that has affected access to other professional services, in particular primary health care (Williams *et al.*, 1980). Indeed, in the latter case there has been a tendency to rationalise poor provision in rural areas by arguing that people who live in the country are healthier and therefore have less need for medical attention (Stockford, 1978). Similar thinking may well have affected official policy on legal services in England and Wales in that publicly funded law centres, open free of charge to all, are only to be found in urban areas, because of the way that they have been funded through the Urban Aid Programme (Cooper, 1983).

In view of the importance of legal services, it is rather surprising that they have attracted little or no attention from geographers. Two early studies of service provision in the United States did include lawyers (Berry, 1967; Cole and King, 1968), but none have considered access to legal services in either the UK or the United States in any detail. There is no logical reason why this aspect of service provision should have been so neglected, but part of the problem may lie with the almost total lack of contact between lawyers and geographers, even though recent work in the UK and America is showing the value of such academic collaboration (Blacksell, Watkins and Economides, 1986; Jones, 1986; Clark, 1985; Johnston, 1984). Until recently another possible reason for the lack of geographical analysis of legal services in the UK was the absence of readily available national statistics about the legal profession (but see now Marks, 1984, 1985, 1986, 1987–88; Harwood, 1989–90; Chambers and Harwood, 1990). The majority of solicitors in private practice are self-employed, and they are not included, for example, in the census of employment. Moreover, much of the stimulus for studies of accessibility has come from research carried out by planning authorities in the production of development and structure plans, and the private professions, such as solicitors, architects and surveyors, largely fall outside the scope of these plans.

There is no obvious explanation as to why geographers should have failed to appreciate the importance of the provision of legal services generally, and the distribution of solicitors in particular. It may be that there has been a superficial assumption that difficulties of access to legal services do not exist, or that legal advice is only needed by the wealthy minority who can afford to travel long distances to obtain such services. If this is so, it is a long way from the truth for a number of trends (the increasingly complex nature of society shown, for example, by the plethora of tribunals which have been established since 1945; the rise in unemployment with the consequent dependence of many on welfare and social security benefits; the increasing 'take up' of the various forms of public legal aid, and the growing levels of home ownership) suggest that many people who would not previously have thought of taking legal advice now have little option but to consult solicitors.

Lawyers themselves, although becoming increasingly aware of the regional variations to be found in the granting and refusal of the different forms of legal aid and advice (Civil and Criminal Legal Aid and Green Form work) and court sentencing (LCD, 1986a; Tarling, 1979), have paid comparatively little attention to regional variations in the provision of legal services by the legal profession. This is surprising because *where* a solicitor practises is recognised as one of the key factors affecting the type of work a solicitor does and how much he earns. As Abel has pointed out, in relation to the profession as a whole, 'Geography affects the power, wealth and status of practitioners in both branches [of the profession], but these differences appear to generate more tension among solicitors, perhaps because the majority are located in the provinces, while professional advantages are concentrated in London' (Abel, 1986; see also Abel and Lewis, 1988(3): 120–1).

In this chapter we consider the whole range of issues raised by the distribution of solicitors in England and Wales and, using the 1985 *Solicitors' Directory*, calculate the number of persons per solicitor at regional, county and district levels, as well as their distribution in relation to a number of socio-economic variables derived from the census of England and Wales, 1981. We also bring Foster's work up-to-date and consider the changes in distribution between 1971 and 1985. Moreover, the provision of data by the publishers of the 1985 *Solicitors' Directory* and advances in computer technology have enabled us to refine and examine in greater detail than was possible previously the relationship between the number of solicitors and selected socio-economic characteristics of the population of England and Wales. Full details of the methodology used have been published elsewhere (Watkins, Blacksell and Economides, 1988).

Regional Distribution of Solicitors

The regional distribution of solicitors is shown in Table 2.1, and, in broad terms, it indicates that a third (32%) of all solicitors are found in Greater London and a further 18 per cent in the 1974–86 metropolitan counties. Just under half of all solicitors are found in the English counties and only 4 per cent are in Wales. The number of solicitors is also broken down by standard economic region and here the South-east dominates with almost a half (49%) of the total. Other regions with a relatively high proportion of solicitors are the South-west (9%), the North-west (11%) and the West Midlands (8%). Apart from Wales, the regions with the lowest proportion are East Anglia (3%) and the North (4%).

Table 2.1   The regional distribution of solicitors in England and Wales, 1985

Region	No. solicitors	%	Population	%	Location quotient
Greater London	11779	32	6608600	14	2.29
Metro Counties (1974–86)	6534	18	11156100	23	0.78
County Councils	16740	46	28007100	57	0.81
Wales	1588	4	2749600	6	0.67
South East	17912	49	16553300	34	1.44
North West	3884	11	6362900	13	0.85
South West	3371	9	4251200	9	1.00
West Midlands	2792	8	5098600	10	0.80
Yorkshire & Humberside	2564	7	4810500	10	0.70
East Midlands	1893	5	3782000	8	0.62
Wales	1588	4	2749600	6	0.67
North	1447	4	3067400	6	0.67
East Anglia	1190	3	1845200	4	0.75
England & Wales	36641	100	48521400	100	1.00

The extent to which individual regions depart from a national average may be geographically illustrated with the help of a simple location quotient (Cox, 1977; Joseph and Hall, 1985). A quotient of 1.0 means that the number of solicitors in the region in question is exactly proportional to the region's share of the population. Values of less than 1.0 indicate solicitors are under-represented, while values greater than 1.0 show that the region has a greater share of solicitors than population. The quotient for Greater London (2.29) underlines the overwhelming predominance of the capital in terms of the provision of solicitors. The concentration is further emphasised by the high value of the quotient for the South-east as a whole (1.44). None of the other areas shown in Table 2.1 has a quotient greater than 1.0, although the South-west has a value of exactly 1.0, indicating that its share of solicitors is equal to its proportion of the national population. Areas with a low quotient are the North (0.67), Wales (0.67) and the East Midlands (0.62).

Another way of comparing the provision of solicitors in different areas is to calculate the number of persons per solicitor. Table 2.2 shows this figure for each region, and again the dominance of the South-east, with only 924 persons per solicitor, is brought out. Other well-provided regions are also in southern England and include the South-west (1,261) and East Anglia (1,550). The worst-provided regions are in the Midlands and the North, the two worst-provided regions being the East Midlands (1,998) and the North (2,119), both of which have more than double the number of persons per solicitor than does the South-east.

Table 2.2 Regional variations in the number of persons per solicitor in England and Wales, 1971 and 1985

Region	1985	1971	1971–85	% decrease
South East	924	1746	822	47
South West	1261	2316	1055	46
East Anglia	1550	2985	1435	48
North West	1638	2834	1205	42
Wales	1731	2985	1251	42
West Midlands	1826	3247	1421	44
Yorkshire & Humberside	1876	3412	1535	45
East Midlands	1998	3684	1686	46
North	2119	3607	1488	41
England & Wales	1324	2418	1094	45

For comparison and to give some indication of the way the distribution has changed nationally, the number of persons per solicitor as calculated for each region by Foster is also shown. For England and Wales as a whole, there has been a 45 per cent *decrease* in the number of persons per solicitor over the fourteen-year period. This was to be expected, of course, because of the rapid increase in the number of solicitors over the period: Marks has shown that the number of solicitors with practising certificates grew by 61 per cent between 1973 and 1983 (Marks, 1984). The decrease in the number of persons per solicitor has, however, been remarkably even, varying from a maximum of 48 per cent for East Anglia, to a minimum of 41 per cent in the North. In general, the North, North-west and Wales have shown slightly less of a decrease in the number of persons per solicitor than East Anglia, the South-east, the South-west and the East Midlands. Four of the regions changed rank in terms of the number of persons per solicitor between 1971 and 1985. The substantial increase in the number of persons per solicitor in East Anglia resulted in it moving from joint fourth rank in 1971 to third in 1985, while the North ousted the East Midlands from bottom rank in 1985. A possible reason for the rather high number of persons per solicitor in the East Midlands compared to the West Midlands or the North-west is the relatively small size of its main cities of Nottingham, Leicester and Derby in comparison with the major conurbations of Birmingham, Liverpool and Manchester, which would attract lawyers simply as a result of the range of legal work that they generate.

County Maps

In order to assess the unevenness in the distribution of solicitors in greater detail the number of persons per solicitor has been mapped in sextiles at the county level (Fig. 2.1 and Table 2.3). Those counties in the top sextile in 1985 are all found in the South, the two main groups being London, Surrey and Sussex and a group of four south-western counties: Somerset, Devon, Avon and Dorset. The remaining county in the top sextile is South Glamorgan. There is in fact a broad band of well-provided counties in the top three sextiles running from Cornwall in the South-west to East Anglia. There is a further group of better-provided counties to the north including Cumbria, North Yorkshire, Lancashire and Manchester. Between these two groups lies a broad belt of relatively poorly provided counties

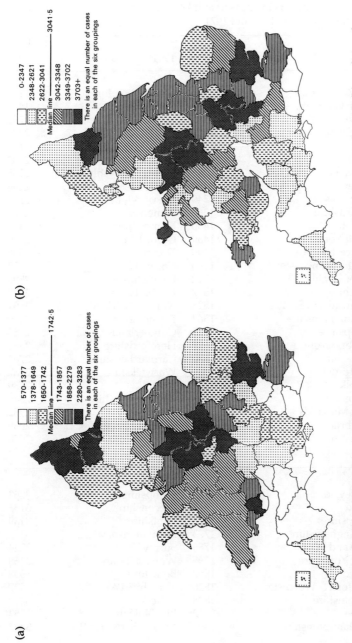

Figure 2.1 The number of persons per solicitor in England and Wales by county (a) new counties 1985, (b) traditional counties 1971

Table 2.3 Solicitors in England and Wales, the number of persons per solicitor by county, 1985 and 1971

1985		1971	
Greater London	561	Greater London	1161
South Glamorgan	963	Cardiganshire	1438
Dorset	1086	Westmorland	1732
East Sussex	1151	Devon	2075
Devon	1154	Caernarvonshire	2117
Avon	1195	Sussex	2133
Somerset	1246	Montgomeryshire	2138
Surrey	1279	Gloucestershire	2196
West Sussex	1349	Isle of Wight	2277
Oxfordshire	1360	Somerset	2418
Norfolk	1430	Hampshire	2448
North Yorkshire	1439	Oxfordshire	2489
Gloucestershire	1490	Dorset	2508
Greater Manchester	1490	Cornwall	2533
Isle of Wight	1512	Lancashire	2593
Wiltshire	1517	Denbighshire	2603
Cornwall and Scillies	1528	Northumberland	2607
Buckinghamshire	1562	Radnorshire	2609
Hampshire	1623	Cumberland	2633
Cambridgeshire	1628	Herefordshire	2662
Lancashire	1630	Carmarthenshire	2705
Hertfordshire	1631	Warwickshire	2787
Suffolk	1635	Norfolk	2789
Gwynedd	1635	Nottinghamshire	2849
West Midlands	1639	Wiltshire	2982
Cumbria	1644	Glamorganshire	2989
Berkshire	1703	Huntingdonshire	3020

median
line

Merseyside	1736	Shropshire	3063
Dyfed	1765	Breconshire	3131
Shropshire	1772	Flintshire	3189
Nottinghamshire	1773	Merionethshire	3207
Tyne and Wear	1785	Surrey	3224
West Yorkshire	1795	Worcestershire	3268
Clwyd	1802	Berkshire	3333
Hereford & Worcester	1820	Yorkshire (West R.)	3337
Lincolnshire	1828	Suffolk	3342
Powys	1832	Lincolnshire	3354
Northamptonshire	1895	Yorkshire (North R.)	3417

Table 2.3 Continued

1985		1971	
Kent	1931	Leicestershire	3474
West Glamorgan	1934	Pembrokeshire	3475
Bedfordshire	1969	Cambridgeshire	3518
Cheshire	2030	Yorkshire (East R.)	3641
Humberside	2057	Kent	3664
Gwent	2140	Hertfordshire	3689
South Yorkshire	2251	Monmouthshire	3692
Leicestershire	2252	Northamptonshire	3713
Derbyshire	2272	Buckinghamshire	3717
Essex	2291	Anglesey	3717
Staffordshire	2296	Bedfordshire	3831
Cleveland	2358	Essex	3969
Warwickshire	2373	Cheshire	4042
Mid Glamorgan	2506	Staffordshire	4117
Northumberland	2985	Derbyshire	4832
Durham	3237	Durham	5795

which takes in most of Wales and the West and East Midlands. The counties of Staffordshire, Derbyshire, Leicestershire and Warwickshire are all served particularly poorly. The remaining badly provided counties are those of Essex and Kent to the east of London and the three counties in the North-east, Northumberland, Durham and Cleveland.

Figure 2.1 and Table 2.3 also show the number of persons per solicitor in 1971, mapped in sextiles by the pre-1974 counties used by Foster, thus enabling a comparison to be made with the 1985 situation. There have, of course, been significant changes in the county boundaries between the two dates as a result of the reorganisation of local government, but even so it is possible to see some broad similarities between the two distributions. In particular it is clear that a group of counties in southern England and the South-west, together with a further group centred on the Lake District, are well provided with solicitors at both dates. It is striking that in 1971 most of the counties in the top sextile (excluding Greater London) such as Devon, Westmorland, Sussex and Cardiganshire are attractive, largely rural areas, suggesting that solicitors may be attracted to live and work in these areas, either because of the relatively large, wealthy, retired population, or because of the attractiveness of the countryside itself. The importance of the last factor is demonstrated by the results of the AJRBP survey which found that although earnings were perceived to be lower, and opportunities, in terms of range of work, fewer than in other parts of the country, the South-west remained attractive to many solicitors in terms of the quality of life (see Ch. 3).

The maps show that the number of Welsh counties in the top sextile has declined since 1971, though as Wales was particularly affected by the boundary changes this may not actually be significant. One group of poorly provided counties in 1971 was the north Midland counties of Cheshire, Derbyshire and Staffordshire. By 1985 there had been little fundamental change in this situation; Cheshire had moved from the sixth to the fifth sextile, but Derbyshire and Staffordshire remained in the bottom groups and had been joined by Warwickshire and Leicestershire. A second group of poorly provided counties in 1971 was found to the north and east of London, but here there had been some substantial changes by 1985. Although Essex remained in the bottom sextile, Northamptonshire and Bedfordshire had moved up to the fifth and Buckinghamshire had shown a dramatic rise from the bottom sextile in 1971 to the second sextile in 1985. This can be partially explained by the loss of the outer London estates of Slough to Berkshire when the counties were reorganised, and the development over the same period of the new town of Milton Keynes, which now has a population of over 200,000.

District Map

The county maps are useful for looking at broad distributions; but the counties themselves are not homogeneous, and for a more detailed assessment of the differences between urban and rural areas it is appropriate to consider the data in sextile form mapped at district level as shown in Fig. 2.2. In very general terms the pattern shown by the county maps is repeated, but the district map shows that there is considerable variation in the provision of solicitors *within* counties. At one extreme there is Somerset, which has four of its five districts in the top sextile with the remaining district in the second sextile; at the other extreme there is Leicestershire with one district, Leicester itself, in the top sextile, but six of the remaining eight districts in the bottom sextile.

The best-provided districts fall into a series of distinct categories. First, there are districts in the capital cities, such as the City of London, Westminster and Cardiff, where the high

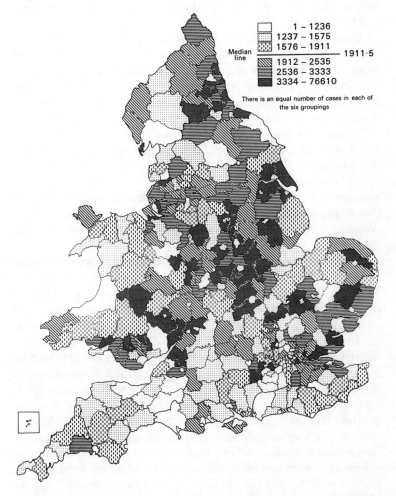

Figure 2.2 The number of persons per solicitor in England and Wales by district, 1985.

concentrations of legal expertise reflect a national, rather than a purely local, demand. Then there are the main industrial cities, Birmingham, Manchester, Liverpool and Bristol, where commercial business provides the attraction. A third category, which overlaps somewhat with the second, is the long-established county administrative centres, such as Norwich, Exeter, Lincoln, Worcester and York, where there are concentrations of ecclesiastical and local government functions which generate legal work.

These are all traditional focuses for legal expertise, but they are now being supplemented by other centres. Along the coast, especially in the south of England, there is a growing number of districts with very large populations of retired people, giving rise to a burgeoning legal trade in the areas of wills and probate. In a similar vein, there is also a group of predominantly rural districts, including Chichester, West Somerset, Ceredigion and South Lakeland which are also popular retirement areas, but which are in addition, and this may well be more significant, districts from which the urban centres have not been separated out for the purposes of local government administration. As a result, the distribution of solicitors in these districts gives a much more realistic picture of the overall level of the extent of rural provision.

The worst-provided areas, too, fall into a number of separate categories. There are a few districts, such as Radnor (in Powys) and Teesdale (in Northumberland), which may truly be described as remote rural, since they have both low population levels and low numbers of solicitors. Then there are those relatively sparsely populated rural districts adjoining urban districts that are well-established administrative centres, such as South Herefordshire, South Cambridgeshire and North Kesteven (in Lincolnshire). The people here are probably adequately served by solicitors working from those same administrative centres, but this must remain a matter for conjecture. Finally, there is a group of suburban and urban districts lying close to major urban centres where there are large concentrations of solicitors, which have failed to attract an adequate local service. Blaby (which adjoins Leicester), Gedling (which adjoins Nottingham) and Torfaen (which adjoins Newport) all fall into this category.

Clearly, the number of persons per solicitor in a district can be materially affected by the positioning of the administrative boundaries. Where a town has its own district, with closely circumscribed boundaries, it is likely to have a higher proportion of solicitors per person than where the boundaries include a peripheral sparsely populated area. Conversely, where a district has had its main administrative town excluded, then it is likely to have a relatively low number of solicitors per person. For example, we can consider the case of the districts of Cambridge and South Cambridgeshire. Cambridge itself is one of the 20 best-provided districts with 641 persons per solicitor; but the district which surrounds Cambridge, South Cambridgeshire, is one of the 20 worst provided, with 53,610 persons per solicitor. If the two districts are combined, however, the equivalent figure is 1,409 persons per solicitor, which would fall into the second sextile. A less extreme, though similar, situation exists with Hereford (1,070) and South Herefordshire (3,852) which combined have 1,667 persons per solicitor.

It follows that those districts with a number of small administrative centres, such as the district of Yeovil, which includes several small towns like Chard, Ilminster, Crewkerne, Yeovil and Wincanton, individually all too small to form separate districts, are likely to have a high proportion of solicitors to population. On the other hand, those districts whose administrative centre is in a separate district will tend to have a low proportion of solicitors to population. The importance of these factors is shown by Fig. 2.3 and Table 2.4 which show the 20 worst- (>5,587 persons per solicitor) and 20 best- (<820 persons per solicitor) provided districts in England and Wales. The 20 worst-provided districts are concentrated in the Midlands and East Anglia, and all but four of them, such as Broadland to the north of Norwich, and Holderness to the east of Hull, adjoin administrative centres with a relatively high concentration of solicitors. The four districts which do not immediately adjoin administrative centres (Torfaen, Gwent; Rhondda, Mid-Glamorgan; Easington, Tyne and Wear, and South Staffordshire) are all on the periphery of large urban areas. A striking feature of the map is that none of these 20 districts are found in the South-west or South-east, reinforcing the point that, nationally, southern England is generally well provided with solicitors. The

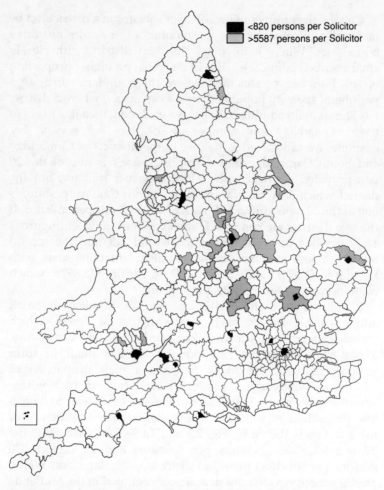

Figure 2.3 The twenty best- and the twenty worst-provided districts with solicitors per head of population in 1985.

20 best-provided districts include the two national capitals (Cardiff and four central London districts), together with 17 regional administrative centres. Apart from the anomalous Isles of Scilly, all these are small districts with very high concentrations of solicitors which reflect the commercial, financial and administrative importance of the cities concerned.

Table 2.4 The twenty districts worst and best provided with solicitors

Name	No. of persons per solicitor	Cloke's rurality index
(Twenty worst-provided districts)		
Blaby	76610	extreme non-rural
South Cambridgeshire	53659	intermediate non-rural
South Staffordshire	24046	extreme non-rural
Bolsover	23453	extreme non-rural
Gedling	20815	extreme non-rural
Holderness	15288	intermediate non-rural
North Warwickshire	9940	extreme non-rural
Easington	9138	extreme non-rural
Torfaen	8974	urban
Daventry	8191	intermediate non-rural
Broadland	8123	extreme non-rural
Cleethorpes	7592	urban
South Derbyshire	7481	intermediate non-rural
South Ribble	7479	extreme non-rural
North East Derbyshire	7415	extreme non-rural
Oadby and Wigston	7243	urban
South Northamptonshire	7112	extreme non-rural
Rushcliffe	6570	intermediate non-rural
North Kesteven	5587	intermediate rural
Rhondda	5418	urban
(Twenty best-provided districts)		
City of London	1	urban
City of Westminster	21	urban
Camden	152	urban
Islington	310	urban
Isles of Scilly	463	intermediate rural
Norwich	535	urban
Manchester	577	urban
Oxford	603	urban
Exeter	614	urban
Cambridge	641	urban
Bournemouth	655	urban
Kensington and Chelsea	677	urban
Cheltenham	715	urban
Newcastle upon Tyne	740	urban
Bath	764	urban
Cardiff	770	urban
Nottingham	793	urban
Bristol	797	urban
Watford	812	urban
York	817	urban

THE PROVISION OF SOLICITORS AND RURALITY

Previous studies of the distribution of solicitors in England and Wales have virtually ignored the rural areas, and although Foster did consider the national picture, the discussion in his paper is angled towards selected urban areas. How well provided with solicitors are the rural areas today? This is a difficult question to answer because of varied definitions of what is meant as 'rural' (Gilg, 1985; Hoggart, 1988). Reference has already been made to the standard 'index of rurality' based upon data from the 1981 census calculated by Cloke and Edwards (Ch. 1). This is based on an earlier index produced from the 1971 census which has been widely used and cited (Cloke and Edwards, 1986). The authors used a principal components analysis on selected variables which reflected rural or non-rural characteristics to produce a classification of rural areas. Urban areas, defined with reference to the proportion of built-up area in the districts concerned, were excluded from the classification. Of the total of 403 districts, 180 were defined as 'urban', leaving 223 for which an index of rurality was calculated. Cloke and Edwards used a simple quartile classification to segregate the non-urban districts into the four categories of extreme rural, intermediate rural, intermediate non-rural and extreme non-rural.

In Table 2.4 the rurality class of the 20 districts best and worst provided with solicitors is shown. Four of the 20 worst-provided districts are classed as urban. Of the remaining 16, 15 fall into the non-rural class (with 10 extreme and 5 intermediate) and only one district (North Kesteven in Lincolnshire) is classed as rural. In marked contrast, of the 20 best-provided districts, 19 are defined as urban, the single anomaly being the Isles of Scilly. Thus, only one of the worst-provided districts is rural and similarly only one of the best-provided districts is classed as rural. Moreover, none of these 40 'extreme' districts falls into the 'extreme rural' class.

The provision of solicitors in relation to rurality is demonstrated further in Table 2.5 which shows the percentage of districts for each sextile class of population per solicitor in each of the rurality classes. Taking all districts first, it can be seen that the majority of the 180 districts defined as urban are below the median in terms of persons per solicitor (56%). In contrast, the majority of the 223 non-urban districts (56%) are above the median in terms of persons per solicitor. However, if we consider the non-urban districts in greater detail, it can be seen that there are considerable variations between the rurality classes. For example, three-quarters (74%) of the districts in the extreme rural class have below the median number of persons per solicitor, while the great majority (85%) of districts in the extreme non-rural class have more than the median number of persons per solicitor. Furthermore, over half (55%) of the intermediate rural districts have below the median number of persons per solicitor.

Table 2.5 The percentage of districts (for the sextiles of population per solicitor) in the different rurality classes

Rurality class	Total % below median	Population per solicitor (sextiles) Median						Total % above median
		1	2	3	4	5	6	
Extreme rural	(74)	16	24	34	14	7	5	(26)
Intermediate rural	(55)	11	24	20	19	17	9	(45)
Intermediate non-rural	(35)	7	12	16	26	14	25	(65)
Extreme non-rural	(15)	0	8	7	17	22	46	(85)
All non-urban	(44)	8	17	20	19	15	21	(56)
Urban	(56)	27	16	13	13	19	12	(44)

Note: Using chi-square there is a significant difference at the 0.01 level between the number of persons per solicitor in the four non-urban classes. There is also a significant difference at the 0.05 level between the number of persons per solicitor in the urban and non-urban classes.

In general Table 2.5 shows that the more rural the non-urban district, the greater the chance that it will have a relatively low ratio of population to solicitors. Thus rural districts nationally in England and Wales are *not* badly provided with solicitors in terms of number. There is a parallel here with the provision of doctors in rural areas. Phillips and Williams have noted that 'Rural locations often appear to be quite adequately staffed purely in terms of the ratio of patients to health care professionals' and go on to point out that in 1976 East Anglia and the South-west contained the smallest proportion of general practitioners having list sizes of more than 2,000 persons (Phillips and Williams, 1984: 191–2). Any study of the provision of legal services in rural areas therefore needs to investigate in greater depth the range and quality of legal services available, and the difficulty that people may have in travelling to see a solicitor, rather than simply considering the ratio of persons to solicitors, all issues that are dealt with in detail in later chapters of this book.

THE DISTRIBUTION OF SOLICITORS – A PRELIMINARY EXPLANATION

To understand the variations in the distribution of solicitors across England and Wales, we must now consider in rather greater depth why they choose to practise where they do. In his pioneering study nearly two decades ago Foster showed that, on a county basis, the location of solicitors was closely correlated with the level of retail sales per head and concluded that 'towns which are good shopping centres with extensive spheres of influence are also those which attract solicitors' (Foster, 1973). Subsequently a study of solicitors in Birmingham published in 1975 noted that 'it is likely that the provision of solicitors in a particular city or town is a mark of the extent to which it acts as a regional centre, serving the interests of people or organisations in a region as a whole' (Bridges *et al.*, 1975: p.18).

These are hardly surprising conclusions and in broad terms they continue to hold true. They indicate that generally there is likely to be a significant relationship between where solicitors choose to practise and regional variations in the levels of economic activity. Using data from the 1981 census we were able, in the AJRBP, to extend Foster's work using a wider range of variables (Watkins, Blacksell and Economides, 1988). The importance of the overall level of economic activity was once again underlined by the close correlation between the numbers of solicitors in an area and the levels of employment, but other factors, notably the numbers of retired people and the extent of owner-occupation among households, also emerged as highly significant.

The correlations are not in themselves surprising and reinforce the findings from the county and district distributions of solicitors discussed previously. Buying and selling houses has long been the mainstay of the businesses of most solicitors in private practice and the elderly not only have a propensity to own their own homes, but also generate disproportionately high levels of probate work, another lucrative market for solicitors.

The importance of these findings lies rather in the new light they shed on established notions about the factors governing where solicitors practise. The Birmingham study concluded that solicitors naturally gravitated towards urban areas (Bridges *et al.*, 1975), but the AJRBP findings indicate that, while towns and cities are still attractive, there are also a number of increasingly important counter-forces, allowing more and more solicitors to choose rural locations for their businesses. Retired people are not tied to the major centres of employment in the ways that most other sections of society tend to be and, in consequence, they provide a reliable stream of work in more rural locations. At the same time more widespread individual home-ownership has affected rural as well as urban areas and has provided a steadily growing source of income for solicitors practising outside the larger commercial centres. Lastly, new developments in information technology, and the ways in which it is being applied to the delivery of legal services, strongly encourage centripetal tendencies, making it increasingly possible for solicitors to practise effectively away from the major urban centres (Clark and Economides, 1990).

As far as solicitors themselves are concerned the popularity of rural locations is clear to see. As will become apparent later, some are quite prepared to forgo the high status within the profession associated with working in the main administrative centres in order to gain prestige within a small-town community. Others prefer to work in a small country firm because they are more likely to obtain an equity partnership (which will allow considerable control over how the firm is managed) more easily early on in their career. Finally, many prefer to work in rural areas simply because of the attractiveness of the environment and the fact that it enables them to avoid unpleasant costs like long-distance commuting. Only when all these factors are taken into account does the evolving distribution begin to make sense.

The pull of the countryside is discussed in greater detail in Chapter 3, but its importance is emphasised by the style of advertising used by employment agencies. The following copy from an advertisement in *The Times* (6.6.89) which appeared under a photograph of rolling countryside illustrates this point:

> 'Have you never dreamt of leaving the crowds behind? Of moving to a place where you and your family would have more space to breathe, more scope to express your individuality and to be someone – on your own terms? Unfortunately, for many solicitors a dream is what it remains. Because they believe they are tied to London and the South East for the sake of their careers. Mistakenly as it turns out. There is a firm in Yorkshire which can offer you a similar level of professional challenge, prospects and quality of work as you would find anywhere in London.'

Clearly this is a call which many solicitors have already heeded.

THE DISTRIBUTION OF LAW CENTRES

Law centres are an almost entirely urban phenomenon, and this is clearly shown by Fig. 2.4 which maps the law centres in existence in June 1989. The reason for the urban nature of law centres lies in the history and development of the law centre movement. The first was opened in North Kensington in 1970, and was quickly followed by a second in Brent, north-west London, and a third in Cardiff (see Garth, 1980; Cooper, 1983). These centres were established in 'areas of urban decay, whose inhabitants were on low incomes, badly housed and vulnerable . . . [where activists] were motivated by the knowledge of vast areas of unmet need for legal services' (LCF, 1989). From 1973 public funds were provided for law centres in the form of Urban Aid Grants from the Department of the Environment. Between 1970 and 1978 the number of law centres grew to 24, and by 1989 this number had more than doubled to 59. From 1982 onwards,

Figure 2.4 **The distribution of law centres in the UK in 1989.**

however, there has been mounting insecurity of funding with the DoE renewing grants for existing law centres only one year at a time and deferring all applications for Urban Aid for new centres. Many are partly funded by local authorities, but this source of funding has come under pressure in recent years with the advent of rate-capping, the abolition of the metropolitan county councils, and the introduction of the community charge.

Of the 59 law centres in existence in 1989 almost half (27) are situated in London, and most of the remainder are in the larger conurbations such as Birmingham, Manchester and Newcastle. Some law centres are found in smaller towns and cities such as Gloucester and Swindon, but most settlements of this size do not have one. The distribution map shows that Wales, Scotland and Northern Ireland are effectively all but excluded from even the urban-based network of law centres, with only one in each country respectively. In addition many parts of England, such as the South-west, East Anglia and the North-west, are also devoid of law centres. Equally, although some of the law centres that do exist are in towns with a large rural hinterland, in general the vast majority of their clients come from within the immediate urban communities that they serve. Efforts have been made to establish a rural law centre but without success (EDLCSG, 1981; Economides, 1982) and the current uncertainty over the funding of law centres in general indicates that there is little likelihood of this kind of expansion while present policies continue.

The Distribution of Citizens' Advice Bureaux

Figure 2.5, which maps the location of CABx in 1989, shows how extensive the network has now become, especially in comparison with that of law centres. The first CABx were established in 1939, but during the war years the distribution was uneven with most found in the larger cities. After the war, central government funding was withdrawn, and it was left to local authorities to decide whether they would continue to pay for the CABx established in their areas. The 1950s was a period of decline, with numbers falling from 570 in 1951 to 416 in 1960. However, during the last thirty years, with support from both central government and local authority funds, the number of bureaux has grown

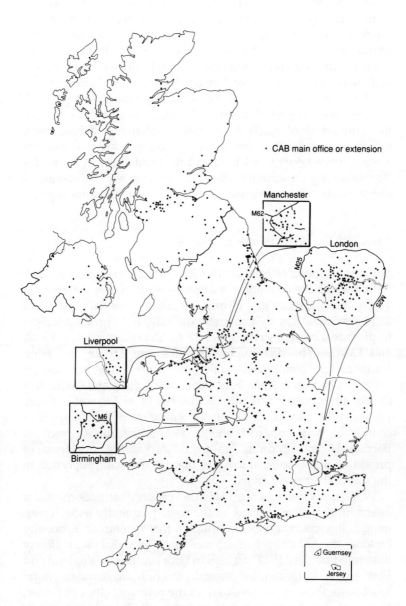

Figure 2.5 **The distribution of CABx in the UK in 1989.**

substantially and by 1987 there were 986 bureaux in the UK (Lovelock, 1984; NACAB, 1987). The map shows that, as with law centres, there are large concentrations of bureaux in London and the major conurbations, but, unlike law centres, bureaux are also found in most of the larger market towns throughout the country. In England a few areas stand out as fairly poorly provided, such as parts of Lincolnshire and Yorkshire, but in Northern Ireland, Wales and Scotland there are still large areas without easy access to bureaux. Although the network of CABx, in many parts of England at least, is relatively dense, many offices, especially those in the smaller centres, are not open for normal office hours (see Ch. 5) and the availability of advice for people living in country districts, as opposed to towns, is consequently often more restricted than may at first appear.

THE DISTRIBUTION OF COURTS

For many aspects of legal work the courts provide a framework within which the resolution of disputes is ultimately determined. To try and illustrate graphically the whole national panoply of legal services is clearly extremely difficult, but Fig. 2.6 attempts to provide a more restricted picture for the counties of Cornwall and Devon. The distribution includes: the Crown and High courts and the county and magistrates' courts, as well as various tribunals, barristers' chambers, firms of solicitors and CABx. It is clearly an extensive network and, on the face of it, courts figure prominently. Nevertheless, the concentration in the main urban centres is very apparent and some market towns, such as Barnstaple and Bodmin, have an importance in terms of providing access to legal services that is out of all proportion to the size of their populations.

What does not emerge from the crude distributions is the intermittent nature of many of the more frequently used, lower, magistrates' court services, a situation that is common nationally outside the major urban centres and one that was clearly illustrated by the AJRBP surveys in both south-west England and East Anglia. In Devon, for example, the only magistrates' courts to sit more than once a week are in the principal cities of Exeter, Plymouth and Torquay, while in Cornwall the only exceptions

Figure 2.6 Legal services in Cornwall and Devon in 1986.

are in Bodmin, Camborne and Falmouth. Most of the other market towns with populations in the range 10,000–20,000, such as Axminster and Helston, only have a magistrates' court in session between once a week and once a month. There is also a scatter of towns and villages, especially places like Callington and Probus in Cornwall, where courts sit even less frequently. Indeed in these more rural parts of the South-west the courts often only convene as and when there are sufficient cases to be heard, a situation which is mirrored in Norfolk on the opposite side of England (Slatter and Moseley, 1986a).

The significance of this lopsided provision is the way in which it subtly encourages ever greater concentration in the major

Figure 2.7 The distribution of magistrates' courts in Devon and Cornwall, 1989. (Courts for Penryn and Falmouth division meet at Falmouth and courts for Exeter and Wonford division meet at Exeter.)

centres by a process of benign neglect (Fig. 2.7). For the county and other, higher, courts such rationalisation is inevitable and desirable in terms of making the best use of the available legal skills, but magistrates' courts are an essential part of the daily fabric of even very local communities. In addition to dealing with minor crime and their domestic jurisdiction, they are also charged with such things as granting licences for most kinds of public gathering where alcohol is to be on sale and thus perform a broad social function.

RURAL LEGAL SERVICES – AN OVERVIEW

The survey of the national distribution of legal services in England and Wales contained in this chapter begins to reveal a somewhat complex situation in the rural areas. As far as solicitors, the main providers of legal services, are concerned, they appear to have gravitated away from the towns and cities in disproportionate numbers, particularly in recent years as they follow the growing army of the retired and the lucrative legal work they generate. Superficially at least, those living in the countryside are, therefore, rather well served in terms of access to legal services. It is a situation that has parallels in the medical world and, like that, needs to be interpreted with caution. Legal services cover a very wide range of skills and the presence of solicitors does not necessarily provide any guarantee that the requisite levels of expertise in a particular area of law will automatically be available locally. The more detailed analysis in Chapters 3 and 4 of the precise nature of the service that solicitors in rural areas provide is an essential adjunct for understanding the true scope of what is on offer.

As far as publicly funded law centres and CABx are concerned, the issue is much more clear-cut. In the case of the former, financial exigency has restricted the service entirely to urban areas and, as far as CABx are concerned, widespread extensions into rural areas have raised many difficult problems, some of which still defy a solution (see Ch. 5).

3. The Provincial Solicitor and his Firm

Solicitors, like clergymen, doctors and teachers, have long been an important element in the fabric of British rural society (Brooks, 1986; Miles, 1986; Partridge, 1940; Russell, 1984), but the profession of solicitor as we know it today only emerged as a distinct and recognisable category during the nineteenth century. Nevertheless, Richard Jefferies was able to write of the solicitor's office over a century ago that 'The entire round of country life comes here. The rolling hills where the shepherd watches his flock, the broad plains where the ploughman guides the share, the pleasant meadows where the roan cattle chew the cud, the extensive parks, the shady woods, sweet streams, and hedges overgrown with honeysuckle, all have their written counterpart in those japanned deed-boxes' (Jefferies, 1880: 16–17). Today the rural solicitor is still an important figure, but many of the roles he used to play, such as land agent, accountant and banker, have been taken over by other professionals. Nevertheless, as Carr-Saunders and Wilson (1933: 23) pointed out, the general practitioner of law 'is the only lawyer with whom the man in the street normally comes into contact and he is expected, not merely to extricate him from a difficulty he is already in, but also to keep him out of difficulties altogether. He thus becomes a sort of general adviser to his clients in regard to their affairs.'

Abel (1988) has described how the work solicitors carried out in the nineteenth century was grouped within two broad areas. They acted as general agents for landowners and the gentry and also developed expertise in dealing with the preliminary stages of litigation. Since the mid-nineteenth century, the role of the solicitor has narrowed considerably with regard to his work as general agent. Spring (1963) describes how property in land in the eighteenth century increasingly generated legal business, and at least one commentator has described that century as 'the great age of conveyancing'. Landowners often made their lawyers their estate agents, often termed their 'man of business'. Spring considers that the lawyer-agent was found on the majority of landed estates in the early nineteenth century. Increasingly, however, the lawyer came to be replaced by the specialised land agent (Mingay, 1963). Nevertheless, although land agency itself became less important for lawyers, they still fulfilled a wide variety of vital and lucrative roles. Official positions included clerkships to boards of guardians; navigation, turnpike and enclosure commissioners; town clerks; county court clerks and so forth.

From the late nineteenth century onwards, however, the range of these posts open to solicitors in private practice began to decline. Increasingly such positions began to be filled by full-time professionals employed by local authorities. In the present century, the development of new professionals such as accountants, taxation specialists and financial advisers, the widening of banking services into areas such as probate, and the rise of the building society, have all eaten into areas of expertise which were formerly the preserve of the solicitor. Crucially, however, until very recently the virtual monopoly over residential conveyancing, which solicitors have enjoyed since the early nineteenth century, remained in place. This monopoly was of vital importance as it provided a secure source of income, allowing cross-subsidisation and the widespread provision of less profitable general legal advice. Since 1986, however, financial and legal reforms have removed the conveyancing monopoly, thus seriously jeopardising the main source of income for solicitors in most rural firms. The changes are already having important consequences for the delivery of legal services in rural areas and the implications will be discussed in detail in Chapter 4.

The second area of work identified by Abel was development of expertise in dealing with the initial stages of litigation. This type of work has two main elements. First, the solicitor becomes the essential intermediary between his client and barristers in both civil and criminal litigation, and second, the solicitor has earned full rights of audience in the local lower courts. At present solicitors have rights of audience in all matters in magistrates' and county courts; before industrial tribunals, lands tribunals and employment appeal tribunals; planning enquiries; in chambers in High Court and in some Crown Court proceedings. As with residential conveyancing, this situation is in a state of flux because of current legal reforms, such as the Courts and Legal Services Act 1990, but any changes in this area will extend rather than diminish the amount of work undertaken by solicitors. The most important revision will be to extend rights of audience by solicitors to the High Court and the Crown Court (see ss. 27–33 Courts and Legal Services Act 1990), but, as yet, it is too early to judge what the ultimate effect of these changes will be in rural, and other, parts of the country (Chambers and Harwood, 1990: 40–44; Smallcombe, 1991).

There have been very few analyses of solicitors and their work, the main exception, of course, being Abel's (1988) major study of the whole legal profession in England and Wales. Other studies of solicitors have either been confined to the history of the profession (Kirk, 1976) or to the life-styles of solicitors and the nature of the legal services they offer in urban areas (Abel-Smith, Zander and Brooke, 1973; Podmore, 1980). This has led to rural solicitors being cast, rather uncritically, in a paternalistic role. The few books dealing with the subject tend to emphasise aspects of rural life, such as cock-fighting and poaching, which today mostly have only nostalgic overtones (Goad, 1989). Hardman, writing in the *Law Society's Gazette* in 1961, considered the country solicitor to be 'no great lawyer' but one who undertook 'tasks which require a moderate knowledge, coupled with commonsense and a kindly, courteous manner'. The country solicitor is described as doing 'an immense amount of work that carries little or no financial payment' and as being 'of great value to the community'. Moreover, he is described as acting 'for innumerable charities, bodies of trustees, church councils, and takes an interest in such varied activities as regattas and rowing clubs, youth clubs and moral welfare'. Such a description may contain a grain of truth, and it does accord somewhat with studies of rural lawyers in the United States

(Landon, 1982, 1990), but as a picture of solicitors in the rural UK, it is anecdotal and self-deprecating, playing down their all-important role as professional advisers in rural communities in favour of rather vaguely defined voluntary services to the country populace.

Given the widespread, general interest in the structure and functioning of rural society, and the important if somewhat hazy role of solicitors in the social structure, it is surprising that studies of country life have virtually ignored their role (Bracey, 1959; Newby, 1980). This is particularly curious because they have traditionally played a crucial part in the functioning of the all-important rural land and property market through their virtual monopoly over conveyancing. Nor do solicitors fare any better in the extensive research on rural service provision; studies of private professional services are conspicuous by their absence (Neate, 1981). This chapter discusses the characteristics and organisation of provincial solicitors. What kind of people are rural lawyers? How are they currently organised? How has the staffing of firms of solicitors changed in recent years? These questions are answered with reference to the results of the AJRBP survey of solicitors carried out in Devon and Cornwall in 1985 and additional survey material gathered in the course of this research project.

THE SURVEYS

The AJRBP survey of solicitors in private practice in Cornwall and Devon was undertaken during 1985, with the sampling frame provided by the 1984 *Solicitors' and Barristers' Directory*. Although there are some problems with the accuracy and completeness of the information contained in this directory (Watkins, Blacksell and Economides, 1984) it was by far the best existing basis from which to draw the sample. Full particulars of the survey methodology have been published elsewhere (Economides, Watkins and Blacksell 1985) and are summarised in Appendix 1. Briefly, however, difficulties arise because not all solicitors are in private practice. They may also be employed by government departments, local authorities, commerce and industry as well as a wide range of other organisations

(Andrews, 1989). These solicitors were not included in the survey: for the purposes of assessing the quality of the legal services available to the general public this is of no great importance, because individuals do not usually have direct access to their services for advice.

Conscious of the dangers of generalising from a limited data set drawn from only one part of the country, we also commissioned three small case studies in Norfolk (Slatter and Moseley, 1986a, b), East Ross (Paterson and Bain, 1986) and Dyfed (Thomas, 1986). These three studies broadly confirmed the results of the more systematic survey in Cornwall and Devon, and when taken together they present a national picture of the nature of the rural legal profession from which we feel it is possible to generalise with some confidence.

At the time the survey in Cornwall and Devon was conducted, there were 1,022 solicitors practising in the two counties. The total number of assistant solicitors and partners working in each firm was calculated from information in the *Directory* and the firms were then divided into three size categories (Podmore, 1980): small firms (one or two qualified solicitors); medium firms (three to five qualified solicitors); and large firms (six or more qualified solicitors). These three groups were further divided into rural and urban subgroups; urban if their office (or principal office) was based in one of the three main urban areas in the region (Exeter, Plymouth – including Plymstock and Plympton – or Torbay – Brixham, Paignton and Torquay), otherwise rural.

A 10 per cent sample of the 1,022 solicitors was selected. Only one solicitor was chosen from each firm. Ten solicitors were chosen from each of the three size categories in the urban subgroups and 24 from each in the rural subgroups. Although the potential sample contained 10 per cent of all solicitors, the proportion of *firms* sampled was much higher, with a third of the urban firms and 43 per cent of the rural firms represented in the sample. A high response rate of 83 per cent was achieved, only seven solicitors refusing to be interviewed. The main reason for non-response was that the potential respondent had left the area. Of those who were not prepared to be interviewed, solicitors from small rural firms were the largest group, probably because sole-practitioner firms in rural areas tend to have a relatively high turnover and are less likely to be willing to spare the time.

The type of information provided by the survey is of two kinds. First, there is a body of statistical information which can be used to assess such things as, for example, the characteristics of the solicitors and their firms, the relative importance of types of work undertaken and the different types of client served. Second, there is a large quantity of more subjective material in the form of personal comments and observations by the solicitors interviewed. At the time of the interview pains were taken to note down the detailed comments which the respondents made either in response to specific questions or generally over the course of the interview. They provide a rich vein of contextual material within which the more factual data can be analysed. Further information is also provided by the three regional studies referred to above and, where appropriate, the results of these have also been incorporated into the analysis.

THE RURAL SOLICITOR

Who is he?

Our survey revealed that the overwhelming majority of rural solicitors were men and their numbers had clearly grown rapidly in recent years. The reasons for the dramatic increase in the number of solicitors during the 1970s and 1980s were outlined in Chapter 2. One of the most immediate consequences of this rapid growth is the youthfulness of the profession. For the whole sample 17 per cent of the respondents were between 51 and 60; 22 per cent were between 41 and 50, but almost half (48%) were aged between 31 and 40. It might be expected that the younger solicitors would be attracted to the urban centres in the region where, as will be shown later in Chapter 4, they have more opportunities to develop specialist legal work, but the survey showed that there was little difference between the rural and urban areas in the age of respondents: 47 per cent of the rural solicitors were in their thirties while 50 per cent of urban solicitors fell into this age-group.

One minor, yet interesting, difference, between rural and urban firms was that five of the rural respondents had decided to carry on working beyond retirement age. One solicitor claimed to be the oldest practising solicitor in the country. Another, who was 85 at the time of interview, had retired to the area in 1974. He noted that it had always been a pipedream of his to retire to a small Devon town, and that he had carried on practising because he enjoyed the work and needed the income.

If the date when articles were taken, rather than age, is considered, a slightly different and more informative picture emerges. Over 70 per cent of the solicitors qualified after 1960, but there are interesting differences in the proportions in this group between the two counties. Cornwall, where 55 per cent qualified after 1960, has substantially fewer new entrants than either the rural (78%) or the urban (77%) areas of Devon. Indeed, some Cornish solicitors said they had experienced some difficulty in attracting new, young, articled clerks or assistant solicitors because the range of work and financial rewards were smaller than elsewhere in the South-west, let alone other parts of the country.

The predominantly middle-class background of solicitors in private practice is confirmed by the fact that 54 per cent of the respondents went to independent schools, a result which confirms the bias towards a private education background found by Podmore (1980) in his survey of solicitors in the West Midlands in the late 1970s. A further 39 per cent of the Cornwall and Devon sample went to grammar schools and only 6 per cent went to a technical college, or a secondary modern or comprehensive school. Just over half of the respondents took a degree at university, and 18 per cent went to either Oxford or Cambridge, a significantly lower proportion than the number of Oxbridge graduates working in the principal City firms (Abel, 1988: 428). A substantial minority of the respondents (40%) had entered the profession with no degree at all.

Professional Mobility

The stability of the profession can be considered by examining where the sample solicitors was born, where articles were taken, the number and location of the other firms worked for and the length of time that the solicitor had worked for his current firm. If birthplace is considered, then there is a strong current of local continuity. Thus taking the whole sample, half (51%) were born in the South-west, over a third had been born in the same county and as many as 16 per cent in the same town in which they currently practised. One solicitor commented that he practised in Exeter firstly because he was born there, and secondly because he was able to live at home while taking articles. This continuity of residence is particularly strong in the urban areas of Devon and in Cornwall where 65 and 62 per cent of solicitors respectively were born in the South-west. The strength of local connections is especially strong in Cornwall: just under half (48%) of the respondents were Cornish, and almost a third (31%) were born in the town in which they now practise. One of these solicitors commented, 'it is the family firm, my grandfather founded it in 1875, and I have always lived here'.

The attraction of the local region also emerges clearly when the extent to which solicitors continue to work where they are articled is considered. Over half (54%) of the solicitors continue to work in the same region in which they were articled, and almost a quarter (24%) work at the same firm. There is strong regional variation in the places outside the South-west where solicitors were articled. Most (25%) were articled at firms in the South-east, and only 18 per cent were articled in the Midlands or North. Although a considerable number of solicitors have local connections, few have family connections with their firms. The idea that many solicitors are part of a family firm with partnerships being handed down from one generation to another is not substantiated by the survey. Indeed, only 15 per cent of those interviewed had any kind of family connection with their firm.

The solicitors in the rural firms tended to change firms less frequently than their urban counterparts. Of those practising in Cornwall and rural Devon, 79 per cent have been with their present firm for five years or more compared with 64 per cent in the urban areas. Cornwall again stands out as the most stable region, with well over a third of the respondents being at their current firm for more than 20 years. This is considerably higher than the equivalent proportion for either rural Devon (13%) or the urban areas (14%). Although there was a strong element of stability in the careers of many solicitors, this was not by any means true for all, and over a quarter of the solicitors had worked with three or more firms in their careers. There was little difference between urban and rural solicitors in this respect. Moreover, nearly 60 per cent of the solicitors interviewed had experience of working with a firm outside the two counties at some time in their career. Many had moved to the South-west after previously gaining experience in London or one of the major cities.

The career choices of some solicitors exemplified some of the attractions of working in a predominantly rural area. One noted that he had made a positive decision to come to the West Country to practise and that he had had enough of commuting to London. Another pointed out that he liked to be a big fish in a small pond and that quality of life was important to him. He also considered that he made as much money in his current practice as he would do in London. Many of the reasons for moving were based on a subjective attraction to the countryside and coastline, rather than hard-headed assessment of business opportunities. One solicitor had 'fallen in love with' the coastal resort he now practised in when he first visited the area in the 1930s at the age of 14. He subsequently had his honeymoon there, and finally decided to set up a practice 30 years later. Others had moved to their current towns partly because of their enthusiasm for yachting or for croquet.

The solicitors' profession in Cornwall and Devon is therefore characterised by a stable core of members who were born in the South-west and who either continued to work in the region for their whole career, or have moved back after gaining experience elsewhere. This core is supplemented by a large number of individuals who have specifically chosen to move to the area because of the desire to work in pleasant surroundings. These findings provide a detailed local context for the results of our study of the national geographical distribution of solicitors discussed in Chapter 2, which showed that in general there are more solicitors in rural areas than would be expected from the size of the local population. Nevertheless, despite the attractions in terms of quality of life, some firms, especially in the remoter rural areas, do have difficulty recruiting solicitors.

The case studies undertaken elsewhere in the UK mirror the

findings in Cornwall and Devon. In the small Welsh market town of Haverfordwest in Dyfed six of the seven solicitors interviewed were male and all were in their thirties. Three had joined the family firm, one was born in Dyfed and the other three had come to that part of the county first because it was in a rural area. In the town of North Walsham in Norfolk on the opposite side of the UK, all the solicitors were once again men in their thirties, though in this instance the local connections were much less important. Ross and Cromarty which forms a continuous band stretching from the east to west coasts across northern Scotland is a much more remote area, but once again the solicitors were mainly younger people, though there was a markedly higher proportion of women as compared with any of the study areas further south in England and Wales. There are too few data to be able to form any firm conclusions about the reasons for this, but more than one of those interviewed commented that women solicitors were important to firms, because of the growing volume of family work.

Non-legal Work and Positions of Authority

For most solicitors the legal profession is their life. Very few of them have ever worked at other jobs or professions, and very few carry out additional, non-legal, work. In our sample, there were only seven who had had previous full-time employment outside the legal profession. There was also fairly limited movement between the different branches of the profession: only 12 had formerly been legal executives or barristers. There was little evidence of current non-legal work among those interviewed: six held company directorships; three had farming interests and two had some involvement in the hotel trade. These findings do not substantiate the nineteenth-century, or even the current popular, image of the solicitor as a key figure in the business and legal life of small-town communities.

Neither is the portrayal of the solicitor as an important figure in local administration supported by the results of our survey. Less than 10 per cent of those interviewed acted on public bodies in their capacity as solicitors. Four solicitors acted as clerks to the Tax Commissioners; two sat on social security appeals tribunals and one as a coroner. At one level, this reflects the lack of time and interest of individual solicitors in this type of work. One noted that until recently he had been part-time chairman of an industrial tribunal and also deputy registrar, but had resigned because he was too busy with his private practice. At another level, it reflects the professionalisation of many posts throughout this century. Solicitors in private practice no longer, for example, act as clerks to magistrates' courts or as town clerks. The decline in these posts has reduced the link between solicitors and the public life of communities and consequently resulted in their assuming a more specialist and restricted role.

There is one area, however, where solicitors have strengthened their links with local communities. This is in their dealings with para-legal agencies, in particular the CABx, a finding which was confirmed by all the case studies elsewhere in the UK. Almost two-thirds of those interviewed had some link, either on an individual basis or as representatives of their firms. Most of these links were as members of a rota which provided free advice, but others were members of management committees or acted as honorary legal advisers. Solicitors in rural areas, especially Devon, were more likely to be members of management committees than in those in urban areas. The relatively smaller number and size of CABx in Cornwall is reflected in a considerably lower number of Cornish solicitors being on the CABx rota as compared to Devon. The views of solicitors about the role and benefits of the CABx varied dramatically, and these issues are discussed fully in Chapter 5.

THE RURAL FIRM

Age

Many firms of solicitors in Cornwall and Devon are of considerable age. As many as 14 firms included in the sample were originally established in the eighteenth century or earlier. Overall, just under a half of all the firms had been established before 1900 and only a third since the end of the Second World War. Over a half of the rural firms had been established before 1900, while in urban areas only just over a quarter of the firms were this old. These figures indicate that there is probably a greater degree of continuity, and a lower rate of change, in the rural areas. Many of the solicitors were proud of the great age of their establishments which was often reflected in fine old Georgian buildings, spacious offices and good quality, antique, furnishings. One firm had a 'family tree' showing the development of the firm over three centuries prominently displayed in the waiting room. However, while a degree of continuity naturally derives from the age of firms, many of these old-established firms no longer had any members of the founding solicitors' families as partners; and there had frequently been extensive changes in staff in the very recent past. To some extent, the venerable appearance of some firms was a façade which was maintained because it was felt that this was an image which was attractive to clients and, therefore, good for business.

During the first half of the present century, there was a steady increase in the number of firms. Most of the new ones were located in the urban areas, in line with the growing urban orientation of society, even in a predominantly rural region like south-west England. From the mid 1950s until around 1975, there was something of a slow-down in the rate of new formations and most of the new additions were in rural areas, but in the late 1970s and throughout the 1980s, there has been an unprecedented increase in the number of firms. Over a fifth of the total number date from after 1975, with urban areas attracting rather more than rural areas. The city of Truro has shown especially strong growth in the number of new firms, this being associated additionally with its development as the county town of Cornwall and the move there of the Crown Court from Bodmin. On the one hand, this expansion reflects the tremendous expansion of the total number of solicitors over the same period (see Ch. 2), but the growth in the formation of new firms also reflects the relatively low level of capital needed in order to establish a new practice. Our data only include firms that were extant at the time of the survey, and it could be argued that at any given time there is a group of firms of recent origin which is destined only to survive briefly. There is, however, no evidence to support this interpretation, and the large number of new firms does appear to be a direct outcome of the growth in the profession.

Organisation

Once a firm has become established, there are a number of ways of expanding the income and number of staff. One is simply to employ more fee earners at the same site. This may eventually mean moving to bigger premises. Another way of expanding is to open branch offices. If the town is large, these could be situated in a new district of the same town, but in the South-west and the three other case study areas in Dyfed, Norfolk and Ross and Cromarty, it is more likely that the new branch would be established in a different town or village. These branches may be formed *de novo* or may result from the take-over of an already established firm. The borderline between branches and firms is not always clear. Where a merger has taken place, sometimes two offices in the same town are kept open. In one town, two firms had been merged for 20 years, but to an outsider they still appeared to be totally separate from each other, with different names and distinctive notepaper. When two Exeter firms merged in the late 1970s, they kept separate offices for a number of years. On the other hand, in the case of at least one firm, the two branches were to all intents and purposes entirely separate firms, with the partners at the two 'branches' acting completely independently of each other, maintaining different accounts, although they did use the same auditors. It would appear on the basis of rather flimsy evidence from the case studies that branch offices are a sign of vigour. While they were not universal anywhere, they were fewest in Haverfordwest, of all the towns we studied the one where the organisation of the private legal profession was most conservative.

How are the firms in Cornwall and Devon organised? Overall the 83 firms included on the survey had 167 separate offices, a ratio of almost exactly 1 : 2. However, half of the firms had only a single office. At the other extreme only four firms had more than five offices, and all of these had their head office in a rural area. There is little evidence, however, that multi-office firms are a particularly rural phenomenon. In rural Devon the ratio of firms to offices was 1 : 2.2; in Cornwall 1 : 1.9 and in the urban areas 1 : 1.9. Of the firms which have no branch offices, half have never seriously considered opening them, and of the other half who have entertained the idea, only three were actively considering it.

The reasons for not opening branch offices were many and varied, the most frequent being that firms had enough work to do already, and did not want to expand, and that the opening and control of branch offices were too much trouble. It is clear that with some firms there is simply no desire to increase the turnover. One solicitor commented that the firm had as much work as it could cope with and that 'I've never wanted to expand; I want to continue to know all the clients'. Another noted that his senior partner did not want to bother to expand, and that branches might be considered when he retired in three years' time. Others were put off from opening branches because they were concerned about diluting their appeal to clients, or generally worried about incurring capital expenditure, at a time when there was uncertainty about the future of the profession.

Sometimes geographical factors inhibited the development of branch offices. In one case a pair of offices had split up because although they were only 10 miles (16 km) apart, it often took a day to make a return journey because of the three-hour wait for a ferry to cross the intervening river in the holiday season. In another, a firm which already did a considerable amount of business on the Scilly Isles had considered opening a branch on the islands but had been dissuaded by the high cost of the air fare, the office costs and the short working day brought about by travel difficulties. Five of the respondents considered that branch offices were uneconomic and four had had previous experience of branches which showed them to be unsatisfactory. One noted that he and his partners had tried expansion in the past. Their original premises had not been large enough so they looked for alternatives and opened a branch in a small north Devon town. They also thought of opening one in the regional centre, Barnstaple. However, disillusion quickly set in because of the greatly increased administrative cost, and they changed their minds; the branch was closed after four years, and they now consider it preferable to be under one roof. As the partner we interviewed put it: 'This is better than going to serve them in their back gardens. The public are mobile enough.' Another firm opened a branch office in a small town following the death of one of the principals of a competing firm. It was thought that there was a gap in the market, and the town served a large hinterland. The branch lasted for two years, 'It was a two days a week office, and it became an increasing burden on me. I was lumbered with it and took an interest. I spent a lot of time travelling and it did not pay.'

Most of the firms that did have branch offices saw few problems with their organisation and some were looking for ways of expanding into sparsely populated, remote rural areas of the region such as West Penwith in the far south of Cornwall, and mid Devon, by establishing peripatetic legal surgeries. One firm had chosen two villages by looking for gaps in the provision of legal services. The first village was to the south of Exeter, where one of the partners happened to live, and the other was in mid Devon. The solicitor noted that 'Mid Devon is an enormous area which is getting very isolated, basically because of the breakdown of bus services, so we thought we ought to go out and get work, rather than wait for it to come to us.' This particular solicitor pointed out that branch offices are expensive to run, and that surgeries were a relatively cheap way of providing a service. For example, one of the surgeries was being held in an estate agent's offices after office hours.

The main difficulties encountered by firms with branch offices are the problems of time and cost of travel and supervision of staff. Other objections included the conflict of interest between branches, and the difficulty of maintaining unitary control. Various instances of staff running off with funds, branches splitting away from head offices and so forth were quoted to us. One solicitor thought that it was better 'to concentrate our efforts in one place rather than to spread our resources thinly. The firm is rather like a spinning top – you don't want chunks to break off'.

Advantages are that firms with branches transfer work between them and in some cases the different branches specialised in different types of work. Most commonly, work is transferred from the branches to the head office, or to a partner working at another branch if the client requests it. One Cornish solicitor pointed out that the head office acted as the administrative centre of his firm, and that it generated most of the overheads. The branch offices, on the other hand, had low overheads and made most of the profits. Sometimes branches were seen as a means of reaching potentially remunerative new markets. Residential conveyancing is the prime example, and as one solicitor put it, 'many branch offices have opened on the back of conveyancing in suburban areas where new building has taken place'. One urban firm had opened an office in a working-class district because they wanted to expand their litigation work. The solicitor noted that the firm was also 'hoping to go into another grotty area' and commented that in addition more and more council house tenants were buying their houses and more were becoming conscious of solicitors.

It was frequently stated that success of the branches depended on the ability to staff the branches with good-quality staff. One partner noted that there was some difficulty in finding 'the quality of person who would be doing what *you* would be doing if you were there' and that getting competent people was difficult, because they were attracted by London firms. The opening hours of branches varied considerably; some were simply service branches open on market days and at other times by appointment. The general consensus seemed to be, however, that to be successful, branches needed to be open for normal office hours.

In the past ten years there has been a proliferation in the number of branch offices in Cornwall and Devon, but, even so the general attitude towards multi-office firms is one of considerable caution. Only 10 firms were even contemplating opening further branch offices at the time of the survey, and 27 had definitely decided not to open further offices in the near future.

The Location of New Offices and Branches

The importance of residential conveyancing in locational decisions is indicated by the fact that this new generation of solicitors' offices corresponds with a move away from the imposing Georgian or Victorian buildings of the older 'professional' parts of town centres, towards suburban, shopping-centre sites, often with 'open-shop' frontages. New offices tended to be established in areas where house-building was taking place or where a particularly wealthy residential area would guarantee a steady income from conveyancing. The following comments illustrate the types of locational calculations made: 'The office was sited to tap the resource of wealthy clients at [a new suburban development near Exeter]'; 'We saw a conveyancing market in Torquay's "champagne belt"'; 'We went for visible on-street premises, also close to the shopping centre, bank, insurance brokers and estate agents'; 'I am very much in favour of the shop front image. We are selling a product – law – and we have got to have a shop to do this.' These kinds of attitude have led the more go-ahead firms to seek out new markets and, in the South-west, this has led them to concentrate on the wealthy coastal development areas.

Fifteen of the 83 offices visited during the course of the survey were in modern ground-floor shop-front-style premises. Of these fifteen, three were adjacent to the office of a building society or estate agent, and four were sharing the same accommodation with a building society in such a way that the two functions were, from first impressions, indistinguishable. They were, in effect, one-stop property-shops. In addition, four more respondents reported that their firms were planning to move into new shop-front offices in the near future. Only very few respondents suggested that their firms were specifically opening offices in town centres. One Cornish firm was considering opening a branch to be near the new court at Truro, and another, whose firm had little conveyancing work, had chosen a new city-centre, first-floor, office because they needed a central site and wanted a small unit. They wanted to be close to the court and insurance offices and specifically did not want 'shop-front' trade (Harris, 1991).

The firms in the sample had minimal links with firms outside the South-west. Only one firm had any office outside Cornwall and Devon and this was a firm with a head office outside the region that had a branch in Exeter. Within the two counties five distinct, subregional spheres of influence are apparent: south Cornwall, Plymouth, including east Cornwall; Torbay, including the Kingsbridge–Salcombe area; Exeter, including Tiverton and east Devon, and north Devon. It is not surprising that such concentrations existed, but that all should be almost entirely self-contained was unexpected (Fig. 3.1). Only one firm had branches outside its own subregion: a Cornish firm with two branches in Devon. The structure that emerges is small scale and local, especially when compared with other types of professional small

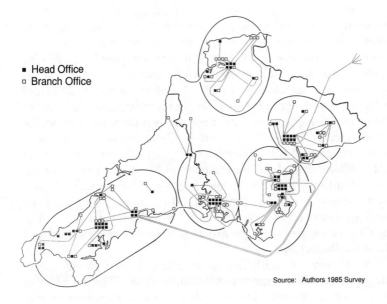

■ Head Office
□ Branch Office

Source: Authors 1985 Survey

Figure 3.1 The branch office system of solicitors' firms in Cornwall and Devon (Source: Authors' 1985 survey).

business, such as accountants, where amalgamations and take-overs have become commonplace both nationally and regionally. The situation is beginning to change, however, and over the last two or three years the number of amalgamations of solicitors' firms has been increasing. One of the firms in our sample has now become a member of the Norton Rose M5 Group which in April 1990 had a total of 261 partners and 2,470 staff (*The Times*, 7. 4. 90), a degree of formal co-operation that would have been unthinkable in the South-west until very recently.

Staffing

The evidence from our surveys and case studies throughout the UK is clear that for the most part most firms are relatively small, though the size of firms in Cornwall and Devon varies considerably. If the number of partners is used as a measure, 39 per cent of firms have one or two partners, 39 per cent have between three and five and 22 per cent have six or more partners. Thus over three-quarters of the firms in our survey had five partners or less. As far as other staff are concerned, 71 per cent employ assistant solicitors, though usually in very small numbers, and articled clerks (27%) and consultants (23%) are both employed, again in small numbers, by around a quarter of the firms. Conversely, many firms employ quite large numbers of legal executives, and three-quarters (74%) employ six or more secretarial staff. It is illuminating to consider the average number of the different kinds of staff to be found in the 83 firms. For the two counties, there were on average 14.4 secretarial and administrative staff per firm, and 4.0 partners. There were 2.9 legal executives per practice, and 1.8 assistant solicitors. The smallest categories were the articled clerks (0.5 per practice) and the consultants (0.4).

The survey also gathered information on staff changes over the period 1975–85 for the 83 sample firms. The number of partners had increased in over half (58%) and decreased in only 13 per cent. Similarly, over half (53%) of the firms had increased the number of secretarial staff over the ten-year period, and only 7 per cent had seen a reduction. More firms showed an increase in the number of assistant solicitors and legal executives than had suffered a decrease. The declining number of firms taking on articled clerks is emphasised by the fact that only 6 per cent of the firms had increased their number over the period, yet almost a third (31%) had reduced their number. Cornwall stands out as the region with the lowest increase in numbers of staff over the ten-year period.

The solicitors' profession in Cornwall and Devon is dominated by men, but in solicitors' firms as a whole women outnumber men by almost two to one. Table 3.1 shows the number of men and women working in the 83 offices where the survey interviews took place. The vast majority of fee earners were men. Astonishingly, 96 per cent of all full-time partners at these offices were male. Moreover, 80 per cent of the assistant solicitors and three-quarters of the legal executives were also male. The only grouping showing a balance between men and women was, interestingly enough, the articled clerks, and this small group, which predominantly includes the more recent entrants to the profession, may be an indication of a greater equality between the sexes in the future (Abel, 1988). The divide between male 'fee earners' and female 'other staff' is emphasised by the startling statistic that exactly the same proportion (96%) of 'other staff' were female as partners were male.

Table 3.1 The gender of staff in solicitors' firms

Category	Male		Female		Total	
	n	%	n	%	n	%
Partners (f-t)	209	96	9	4	218	100
Partners (p-t)	4	100	0	0	4	100
Assistants (f-t)	68	80	17	20	85	100
Assistants (p-t)	1	20	4	80	5	100
Consultants	16	100	0	0	16	100
Articled clerks	10	53	9	47	19	100
Legal executives (f-t)	115	75	39	25	154	100
Legal executives (p-t)	6	54	5	46	11	100
Other staff (f-t)	29	4	652	96	681	100
Other staff (p-t)	6	7	83	93	89	100
Total staff	464	36	818	64	1,282	100

f-t = full time; p-t = part time

The respondents were asked to list any advantages or disadvantages that might or might not stem from having a female solicitor in the firm. The answers given confirm that many solicitors view men and women as having different aptitudes for legal work. Almost half (49%) of the respondents considered that there were advantages associated with employing female solicitors and 39 per cent thought there were disadvantages. The main advantages given were that women solicitors were good at family law (24%); that some clients like women solicitors (11%) and that they broadened the appeal of the firm (10%). The main disadvantages given were that some clients dislike women (13%); family commitments (11%); women were difficult to work with (5%) and they were poor at certain kinds of work (4%). It is notable that most, if not all, of these characteristics were equally applicable to men, but this fact seemed totally lost on many of our respondents.

Although more solicitors listed advantages of female solicitors than disadvantages, the substantial minority who listed disadvantages does indicate a significant degree of prejudice against the employment of female solicitors in Cornwall and Devon. Some respondents emphasised the fact that certain clients did not like to deal with women. One noted that in country districts female solicitors do not carry the same weight – 'they tend to be muddled up with your secretary'. Another noted that 'in a small office in a stuffy area, I don't think most of our clients would take to a female solicitor . . . the older type of client does not take kindly to being interviewed by a woman – but things are changing rapidly'. Another solicitor stated that he had no preference for male or female solicitors but that 'in a rural area you have to be wary to a certain degree (especially with older clients) of customer reluctance to consult females. This will die out in about 30 years' time'.

Some of the respondents considered that the employment of female solicitors helped the internal relations of the firm. One noted that the presence of fee-earning females reduced the divisions between the fee earners and the other staff in the firm. Another pointed out that the advantages of female solicitors included the fact that they were good at dealing with secretarial staff and 'probably command a lower salary as well!'

One of the key problems for some firms was how to accommodate female solicitors who need time off to raise a family. One respondent commented that there are no disadvantages with female *solicitors* but that the female *partner* was a problem. He noted, 'It's a great problem if they have a baby etc. . . . it's the presence of the partner at the office that is important. Also it's hell to unravel the capital commitment.' This was more likely to be seen as a problem in the small firms which predominate in rural areas: 'the disadvantage is that females get married, have kids and then you've got to take on their workload. Small firms can't carry this workload during maternity leave'. In some cases, although women were considered to be better at certain aspects of work, this did not necessarily mean that more female solicitors were employed. Thus one respondent pointed out that women were better at dealing with certain personal problems and went on to say 'we do use one of the girls on seeing people – although she is not qualified, she is virtually a legal executive'. Another noted that female matrimonial clients 'sometimes feel it is easier to talk to female solicitors, especially if there are sexual problems. We had a lady legal executive who was helpful in that sort of case'.

A number of solicitors were at pains to point out that the situation was changing fast. One noted that in the past clients preferred to see male solicitors, but that this was no longer the case. He went on to say he would always prefer to employ females than males. Another noted that 'some older members of the profession can be patronising. There are so many women coming in now that this sort of thing won't go on much longer'. However, the following comments clearly indicate that prejudice towards women is alive and well in the legal profession: 'There are no disadvantages, except that they do put male solicitors' backs up. Other things being equal, I would prefer a good man to a good woman. [Women solicitors] tend to get ruffled a bit easier. They are easily insulted and disruptive in the firm – but I have no real experience'; 'The main disadvantages, whether real or imagined, are . . . a lack of dispassionate appraisal and with conveyancing I have found women solicitors can be incredibly pedantic'; 'Anybody who is in the position of considering this, if they have equally qualified male and female solicitors, will tend to choose the man.'

Looking to the future, recent developments in information technology may well exert the most powerful influence on future staffing levels, especially among clerical staff which form by far the largest group of employees in solicitors' firms. At the time of the survey well over two-thirds of the firms, mainly, but by no means exclusively, in the urban areas, had invested in word processors and other computer equipment. Word processors were by far the most common innovation (62%), followed by computerised accounting (32%) and computer-assisted time-costing (22%). Firms that had invested in new technology were almost always pleased with the new equipment, citing in particular the generally improved efficiency and saving of staff time. A point noted by some solicitors, however, was that the more accurate picture of the value of time, and the financial state of the firm, could lead to problems in solicitor/client relations. In particular, some solicitors felt that the new technology could depersonalise the relationship between solicitors and clients, and that this might actually discourage potential clients from consulting a solicitor at all.

Links with the Bar, other Professionals and Businesses

The great majority (90%) of solicitors stated that they would make use of the barristers at the local Bar if the appropriate specialisation were available, but some respondents had several reservations and 8 per cent never used the local Bar at all. It is significant that only one respondent was spontaneously enthusiastic about the advantages of the local Bar. The main reasons for not using the local barristers were that they did not have suitable expertise: one solicitor commented that the local Bar did not have enough competition and did not have enough senior QCs. He also thought that they tended to lose independence because they often faced the same judges. Another stated that the 'calibre of advice is much higher in London' while a third said that he never went to the local Bar: 'in my own field I have got more specialist knowledge than the local Bar. It's about time the whole system is brought to an end – it's a creaking, antique, system. . . . Generally they are not men of greater intelligence than solicitors, and there are some duffers!' Some solicitors noted that they sent specialised work to London, while the more mundane work went to the local Bar.

Solicitors were asked if they had close links with providers of professional services, for example accountants, to which just over two-thirds (68%) replied that they did. Respondents interpreted the term 'close' widely, with a range of meanings, from the simplest professional contact, to inclusion on the panel of a building society, and even more exclusive relationships. The comments made by solicitors when answering this question made reference to building societies 12 times, and estate agents 12 times. Banks were mentioned four times, and other professions mentioned less often included insurance companies, surveyors, architects, engineers and valuers. The relative importance of building societies and estate agents indicated by this somewhat circumstantial evidence is, of course, not surprising considering the importance of residential conveyancing for the work of the solicitors' profession.

More detailed aspects of the links between solicitors and other professions can be drawn from the comments made by those solicitors we interviewed. Some were extremely enthusiastic, attributing to such links the security and survival of solicitors in the future. One noted that they had very close connections with banks, building societies and estate agents and that he thought the firm would survive because it provided them with a service. He went on to comment that the managers of older-established firms of solicitors tended to play golf with building society managers, so that his more recently established firm emphasised personal contact with the lower end of management in building societies, through such things as sports, sailing and membership of the Round Table. Another solicitor commented that his firm had good relationships with building societies, surveyors and other professions 'to the extent that they approve us'. He also pointed out that this worked the other way, and his clients asked him to recommend builders, doctors and so forth.

However, some of the respondents were rather more cautious in their attitude to such professional relationships. One stated that his firm would usually send people who wanted loans to their bank and accountants but that 'we don't want to get too close. . . . I don't accept invitations to lunch etc. with, for example, building society managers. You have to be careful'. A minority of the respondents stated categorically that they did not make use of such contacts for either business or ethical reasons: 'We tend to stand apart – we get on well but have no right to live in their pockets and don't generally socialise with them. I don't like the idea of gifts to these people – they are nothing more than bribes.' There is little evidence as to whether business was affected either positively or negatively by any of the positions held on the desirability of close relationships with other professions. It is clear, however, that these relationships are not simple to interpret: on the one hand, closer collaboration with other businesses, such as the 'package' deals now permitted by the Law Society, can allow solicitors to compete more successfully for work; on the other, this type of collaboration is itself a symptom of a more competitive environment.

SOME CONCLUSIONS

The overriding impression of the rural legal profession, as revealed in the results of our surveys in south-west England and the case studies elsewhere in the UK, is one of flux. The demand for legal advice is clearly buoyant as a result of the growth in home ownership and the out-migration from the major cities which is gathering increasing momentum. As a result, existing firms have taken on new, young, staff and many new firms have been created, mostly again by younger people. They have brought a great deal of dynamism into the profession and have sought out markets in new locations. At the other end of the spectrum, however, there is a deeply ingrained conservatism which has also led to a marked resistance to certain types of change. Firms tend to be fiercely independent, both of each other and of other professions: there is little overt sign of formal links with accountants, estate agents and the like, although more recent anecdotal evidence from the South-west indicates that this may be beginning to break down. It may well be that the luxury of high principles and the option of standing slightly aloof from the more insidious commercial pressures, is a reflection of the high demand for legal services, which has allowed solicitors, even in rural areas, to dictate how their profession is organised in a way that has not been open to other groups.

4. The Provincial Solicitor: Clients and Work

Prior to the AJRBP study, there had been relatively little detailed research on the range of services offered by rural solicitors. The Report of the Royal Commission on Legal Services (RCLS, 1979) did not set out to identify the particular problems facing solicitors in rural areas. However, that it appreciated that such problems existed is indicated by the Commission's suggestion that one of the best ways to preserve, or extend, legal services in rural areas might be to provide interest-free or low-interest loans to solicitors working in those parts of the country where only limited work was available. The separate Royal Commission on the future of legal services in Scotland showed greater overt awareness of the problems facing people in remote rural areas, and argued that special measures were necessary to bring legal advice services, as well as lawyers, to isolated communities.

Nevertheless, there was concern about the quality of legal advice available in those remoter areas of the rural UK, even if much of it was based on anecdotal evidence and rather limited case studies. A detailed though very local study of rural legal services in Cornwall and Devon was conducted by Roberts (1978). He concluded that although few people experienced difficulty in contacting a solicitor, the service offered was a very restricted one, dealing with a few highly lucrative types of work. The bulk of solicitors' work related to conveyancing and probate and there was little expertise in aspects of welfare and consumer law. However, the very limited scope of the survey makes it difficult to generalise, even to the rest of Cornwall and Devon.

In this chapter use is made of material gathered during the

AJRBP survey to assess solicitors' views of their clients, of the legal services they and their firms provide, on the effects of the loss of the conveyancing monopoly on the viability of their businesses, and of the future of the profession. The views of the solicitors themselves are crucially important for understanding the nature of the legal services provided by them in rural areas. Although the profession has to be responsive to demand, to some extent out of sheer economic necessity, there is still considerable leeway for solicitors to choose in which areas of legal advice they wish to specialise and which they decide to promote among their clients.

CONTACT WITH CLIENTS

The success of solicitors' firms, as with any business, depends to a large extent on their ability in contacting and keeping clients. When respondents, all working in the predominantly rural environment of Cornwall and Devon, were asked to rank the relative importance of a list of potential means through which initial contact with the firm might be made, a very clear and consistent pattern emerged. Word-of-mouth recommendations from current clients and their family and friends were of overwhelming importance. Professional contacts such as estate agents and to a lesser extent building societies were also significant, though relatively, considerably less important (Jenkins, Skordaki and Willis, 1989).

At the other end of the scale, organisations such as unions and social services departments were of little importance in providing clients for solicitors in private practice. Unions, of course, tend to generate a relatively narrow range of work associated with employment, a category of work which did not figure even once as a category of importance to solicitors in Cornwall and rural Devon. Similarly, the social services would tend to generate work of little interest to most solicitors. The police, CABx, street signs and Yellow Pages were all seen as being relatively unimportant as a means of gaining new clients (Economides, Blacksell and Blacksell, 1991). This underlines the general lack of enthusiasm for criminal and welfare work, and the absence of any sense of urgency as far as advertising is concerned (Paterson *et al.*, 1988; Seron, 1990).

Outside the confines of the three main urban areas in the South-west, estate agents and building societies emerged as being rather less important as a means of gaining new clients than in the cities themselves. Similarly, Yellow Pages was considered most important as a source of clients in Exeter, Plymouth and Torbay. On the other hand, employers, banks and the police were relatively more important in the country districts, pointing to a rather less competitive environment in rural areas, with solicitors playing a somewhat wider and more generalist advice-giving role. However, these indications must be placed in the average context of a pattern of work throughout the region dominated by residential conveyancing, wills and trusts and family work.

The main way in which clients overcome difficulties of travel is of course the telephone. Nearly all the solicitors said that they were regularly called at home in the evenings and at weekends and one went out of his way to stress that he could not afford to discourage this type of contact. Another noted that the most extreme example of domestic disturbance was when a client rang up one Christmas Day as he was carving the turkey! Many solicitors further encourage out of hours contact by living close to their offices and taking an active part in local affairs:

> I like to be identified with the town I work in. . . . I also like to live in the community to get an idea of how people live, work and behave. If they are going to trust you, I sometimes think they like to know a little about you.

However, this is a matter of personal choice, and some solicitors specifically chose to live outside the community in which they work, so as to minimise out of hours contacts.

The great majority (82%) of respondents considered that the provision of legal services in rural areas was adequate. One pointed out that although country people may be inhibited from going to see a solicitor by the remoteness of their homes, they are not prevented from so doing. Most solicitors make some arrangements to make their services available to those clients who cannot easily get to the firm's office during opening hours. The most common method is for the solicitor to visit the client at home, and this is especially frequent with the elderly and the infirm. Surprisingly little use is made of flexible opening hours or any type of peripatetic service, despite a number of comments from the solicitors interviewed that these were good ideas.

THE IMPORTANCE OF DIFFERENT TYPES OF WORK

The relative importance of the types of work undertaken by both firms and individual solicitors in Cornwall and Devon follows a clear-cut and consistent pattern. For the purposes of analysis, work was subdivided into the 20 categories adopted by the Law Society. Respondents were asked to rank the five foremost categories of work for themselves, and for their firms. By counting the frequency with which each category was mentioned, as a percentage of the total number of rankings given to all types of work, an index was established showing the importance of the different types of work.

The most striking result is the overwhelming importance of residential conveyancing; it emerges at the head of the list no matter which permutation of the data is used and dominates all the other categories of work. Overall, for all the firms in the sample, residential conveyancing is 37 per cent ahead of the next most important category in terms of income. Even in rural Devon, where the dominance is least marked, it is 24 per cent ahead (Table 4.1). If time, rather than income, is considered, the dominance is rather less, emphasising the fact that residential conveyancing was very profitable in comparison with other types of work.

As far as individual solicitors are concerned, all types of fee-earning staff derived more income and spent more time on conveyancing than on any other category of work. It seems that conveyancing was a significant part of the total work-load even for those who did not record it as the most important type of work, since very few solicitors listed it among the areas of work which they personally did not deal with. Only five solicitors said they did not usually deal with residential conveyancing; this contrasts with the 23 respondents who did not deal with litigation. Conveyancing was described as the 'bread and butter' or the 'backbone' of general practices and the 'bedrock of small provincial firms'. Respondents also commented that, in comparison, other types of work such as family and county court work could be stressful and uneconomic.

Some way behind residential conveyancing in order of importance are three other categories of work: wills and trusts; family and general litigation. For the firms there is little to choose between wills and trusts and family in terms of either income derived, or time spent. Family work, however, appears to be rather less profitable, especially in urban areas. This is corroborated by the data for individual solicitors which show that family lags well behind wills and trusts. Under these circumstances, it is not surprising that there is a general impatience with family work and one solicitor said rather grandly that he was 'trying to reduce matrimonial work'.

The data on general litigation are rather inconsistent and difficult to interpret. A number of respondents thought it was increasing in importance and one considered that the balance had moved in favour of litigation over the years: 'Until say fifteen years ago, one turned one's nose up at litigation, now it is important.' Another stated bluntly that 'litigation is not very profitable, but it is a client getter'. Certainly, there has been a marked increase in the amount of general litigation undertaken by most types of solicitor included in the sample.

The middle-ranking group of categories includes agricultural property, general crime, commercial property, business affairs and accident and personal injury litigation. As might be expected, agricultural property is both profitable and especially important in rural Devon and Cornwall. General crime, on the other hand, is unimportant in rural Devon, and everywhere apparently unprofitable. Commercial property is most prominent in the urban areas, and seems to be particularly profitable. The same is true, to a lesser extent, of business affairs. At the lower end of the scale, there are a number of categories of work which hardly figure at all among the most important for firms. Most prominent among these are child care, with only one mention in rural Devon; juvenile crime, with one mention in Cornwall; employment, with one mention in urban areas; and welfare, with one mention in Devon. Planning and bankruptcy are only mentioned twice. Housing, taxation, consumer problems and commercial litigation are cited sporadically in all three sub-regions, but are widespread in none.

Table 4.1 Solicitors' estimates* of the relative importance of different categories of working (using the standard Law Society definitions†) in terms of *income* and *time*

(a) All firms in Cornwall and Devon

Income		Time	
Residential conveyancing	100.0	Residential conveyancing	100.0
Wills and trusts	62.6	Family	76.5
Family	61.2	Wills and trusts	73.5
Litigation – general	46.1	Litigation – general	59.7
Crime general	35.2	Crime – general	47.4
Commercial property	28.8	Litigation – accident	34.7
Litigation – accident	28.8	Commercial property	32.1
Agricultural property	20.1	Agricultural property	19.4
Business affairs	12.3	Business affairs	13.8

All other categories (housing, commercial litigation, taxation, consumer problems, bankruptcy, planning, other z, child care, juvenile crime, employment, welfare) are less than 10 in terms of both income and time.

(b) Rural Devon

Residential conveyancing	100.0	Residential conveyancing	100.0
Wills and trusts	76.4	Family	75.3
Family	66.5	Wills and trusts	75.3
Litigation – general	60.1	Litigation – general	64.2
Commercial property	33.5	Commercial property	35.8
Agricultural property	30.0	Litigation – accident	35.8
Crime – general	26.6	Crime – general	32.1
Litigation – accident	23.2	Agricultural property	28.4
		Business affairs	10.5
		Housing	10.5

All other categories are less than 10 in terms of either income, or time, or both.

(c) Cornwall

Residential conveyancing	100.0	Residential conveyancing	100.0
Family	64.5	Family	76.3
Wills and trusts	61.5	Wills and trusts	76.3
Litigation – general	60.1	Litigation – general	64.1
Crime – general	42.0	Crime – general	60.1
Litigation – accident	32.5	Litigation – accident	35.9
Commercial property	33.5	Commercial property	35.8
Agricultural property	19.5	Agricultural property	20.2
Commercial property	16.0	Commercial property	20.2
		Business affairs	12.1
		Commercial litigation	12.1

All other categories are less than 10 in terms of either income, or time, or both.

Table 4.1 continued

(d) Urban Devon (Exeter, Plymouth, Torbay)

Income		Time	
Residential conveyancing	100.0	Residential conveyancing	100.0
Wills and trusts	63.3	Family	79.2
Family	47.2	Wills and trusts	68.3
Litigation – general	47.2	Crime – general	52.2
Commercial property	41.9	Litigation – general	47.5
Crime – general	36.7	Commercial property	42.1
Litigation – accident	31.4	Litigation – accident	31.7
Business affairs	21.0	Business affairs	21.3
Consumer problems	10.5	Taxation	10.4

All other categories are less than 10 in terms of either income, or time, or both.

*Data derived from the AJRBP survey of solicitors in Cornwall and Devon.
†For the full list of the Law Society's categories of work, see Appendix 2.

Over three-quarters (78%) of the firms included in the sample undertook work which they knew to be unprofitable. In most cases, this related to one or two categories, but for a few rural firms the number was as high as four or five. The making of wills was by far the most common type of uneconomic work, followed by crime in Cornwall and family in rural Devon. The remainder was a mixture of counselling clients; social welfare; court and Legal Aid work. Some of this work was only unprofitable in the short term, and was part of a long-term strategy to bring more profitable work to the firm. One solicitor noted that if his firm had a long established client such as a farmer, 'we take the rough with the smooth. We might make a lot out of a farm conveyance and therefore need not charge for minor work'. Another solicitor commented that 'you have to lay down wills like wine, they are an important way of keeping clients'.

Nearly all the firms surveyed offered both a free diagnostic interview or a fixed fee interview scheme for new clients. From solicitors' comments it is clear that there is some unease that these facilities mean that some clients are getting something for nothing. Most solicitors, however, see both schemes as a means of identifying legal problems and therefore as a source of business. Many of these enquiries come from people who are eligible for financial help under the Green Form Scheme and most solicitors have no hesitation in advising enquirers of this and enrolling them.

The great majority of the firms dealt with Legal Aid and for most solicitors it was standard practice to establish whether or not clients were eligible for Legal Aid. Nevertheless, despite the routine way in which the Legal Aid Scheme was viewed, the survey showed some interesting variations in its importance in the different parts of Cornwall and Devon. A much higher proportion of clients enquired about the possibility of receiving Legal Aid in both Cornwall and rural Devon than in the urban areas, a possible reflection of the pervasive rural poverty in the region. Almost a fifth (19%) of rural Devon solicitors, and 10 per cent of Cornish solicitors estimated that over 40 per cent of their clients enquired about Legal Aid. In the urban areas, the equivalent figure was 4.5 per cent. Moreover, while Legal Aid is perceived as important as a source of income for most firms, providing between 10 and 40 per cent for two-thirds of the firms, it is of greatest importance in the rural areas. In rural Devon, over a third (38%) of firms derived 30 per cent or more of their income from Legal Aid work; in Cornwall over a quarter (28%) of the firms derived 30 per cent or more of their income in this way. In urban areas, however, the corresponding figure was 9 per cent.

Most of the solicitors considered that the Green Form Scheme could be made more easily available and 80 per cent thought that it should be available on postal application. In some cases, the solicitors' comments indicated that firms already did this, and one or two respondents even thought this was already standard practice. These views are similar to those of the Lord Chancellor's Legal Aid Advisory Committee, which noted in its 1985 Annual Report that personal applications should no longer be necessary (LCD, 1986a). Much more caution was shown, however, by the respondents when they were asked about the possibility of providing legal advice by post. A fairly typical response was that 'You can only advise someone properly if you get down all the details. Most people are poor at setting out a case on paper, especially what is important in law. You *have* to see them to get a detailed history from them – after that you can write to them.' A general point raised by some solicitors was how many rural people were inarticulate, both in speaking and in writing. It was thought that postal advice could bring problems for these people. At the opposite extreme, a solicitor considered that postal advice was 'a damn good idea' because he had many clients with simple problems who lived outside the town.

Within most firms there is some degree of specialisation. Only a small number actually refused to undertake certain categories of work because they lacked suitable expertise or felt it would be unprofitable. However, individual solicitors frequently stated they did not undertake certain types of work. The types of work most likely to be avoided included litigation of all sorts; and to a lesser extent, crime, taxation and family. It follows that requests for expertise in these areas are referred elsewhere in the firm. In most firms (68%) this happens without question, and in a significant minority, work is transferred to other partners after consultation with the client. The way that referrals are organised within the firm varies dramatically from firm to firm. One solicitor noted that 'it's all rather haphazard really' while at the opposite extreme another noted that 'we are wholly compartmentalised; the computer would stop us if we tried to work outside our areas'.

CHANGES IN CONVEYANCING

The solicitors surveyed made estimates of any tendency for categories of work to increase or decrease in importance over the decade 1975–85. As well as showing the general expansion over the decade, the responses indicated that there was a slight tendency for income from residential conveyancing to decline over the period. Respondents were more willing to group conveyancing into the static or declining categories in terms of income, than other areas of work such as family or crime. In terms of time, however, conveyancing showed a slightly greater increase over the decade. This reduction of profitability reflects the beginning of competition and cost-cutting in this important area of work in the firms even as early as 1985.

The general picture that emerges is that of a broad-based dependence on residential conveyancing, backed up by wills and trusts, family and general litigation. There is little evidence of specialisation by either firms or individuals in other areas. There are a few pointers to subregional expertise, with agricultural property being most evident in the rural areas and commercial litigation and business affairs in the urban areas. Finally there are those categories of work where expressed demand is low and local expertise lacking. On the one hand, they include highly specialised areas such as bankruptcy and taxation which are technically complex; on the other, they include areas such as welfare, housing, planning, juvenile crime, child care and consumer problems, which often have a large social welfare element and tend to be unprofitable.

In view of the heavy dependence on residential conveyancing, it was somewhat surprising to find that solicitors were fairly confident about any possible effects of the loss of the conveyancing monopoly on their firms in 1985. Just over half (51%) of the respondents considered that the loss would have relatively little effect on their firm. A large minority of the respondents (42%) did consider that the loss of the monopoly would affect their firms adversely, and over a quarter (28%) thought that the impact could, potentially, be drastic, leading to the closure and amalgamation of firms and offices. Only one solicitor thought the change would be beneficial and make existing firms more efficient.

The reasons for confidence over the loss of the monopoly varied from client loyalty to the fact that conveyancing fees had already fallen due to competition within the profession. One respondent considered that the loss would begin to hurt his firm in the medium to long term: 'What is happening in the Midlands will creep down and affect us . . . solicitors cutting their own throats by reducing conveyancing charges.' Others, however, felt that conveyancing charges had been reduced to a minimum and doubted that competitors, whether solicitors or licensed conveyancers, could do it any cheaper.

Beyond this fairly general level of information about competition deeper anxieties were expressed, and seemed to indicate the onset of intensified price wars in the urban areas (Exeter, Torbay and Plymouth) and also Truro. Eight of the sixteen respondents who brought up the subject of competition were from within or close to these areas. One solicitor whose office was eight miles (13km) from Exeter noted that he was not now getting recommendations from estate agents and that the work seemed to be going to Exeter where there were generally cheaper prices because of fierce competition. A Truro solicitor said that there had already been a price war in the town and that other towns might also be affected. He knew of two firms that had laid off staff and two that had closed branch offices.

The relative lack of competition faced by solicitors in rural areas as compared with urban firms was illustrated by attitudes towards advertising. Throughout the region, the large majority of firms (83%) did not intend to exercise their newly established right to advertise their services, especially if local competitors did not break ranks. Among the minority of firms that did intend to advertise, the urban firms stood out, indicating the greater apprehensiveness about the threat of competition in the urban areas (Paterson *et al.*, 1988; Seron, 1990).

Overall there was clearly a reluctance to advertise, but at the same time a growing realisation that it might in the longer term become a necessity. In some districts, solicitors had actually gone as far as having an informal agreement not to advertise. In north Devon, for example, lawyers had 'decided not to advertise: if everyone advertised piecemeal, only the advertising agencies would benefit'. One common reason for not wishing to advertise was that solicitors did not consider it to be professionally correct. One considered it to be 'making the profession into a retail trade' and another considered it to be a 'desperately unseemly business'.

One of the main threats posed by estate agents was that they would direct clients towards the more competitive price-cutting firms or towards property shops. A respondent noted that 'whether you get conveyancing or not depends on the estate agents, who can make or break you'. There was some nervousness at the prospect of competition from licensed conveyancers, especially if they were employed by estate agents. Nevertheless, for a variety of reasons, the threat from licensed conveyancers was not seen as too serious. Respondents felt that they could do a better job, and that licensed conveyancers could not do the work any cheaper. Some rural practitioners noted that their firms would be the only agency available to undertake conveyancing locally and that licensed conveyancers would not be geared to undertake work in areas where title remained unregistered.

Deep anxiety was expressed, however, about the possibility of building societies and financial houses moving into conveyancing. It was felt that if this happened 'building societies could corner the market' and 'there would be a drastic impact'. One solicitor thought that the effect in rural areas would be catastrophic, with many firms having to close down as a result. Another thought that two out of three firms would have to close. The concern about the effects of in-house conveyancing centred around what was seen as the inability of solicitors to compete with practices which amounted to 'unfair competition'. During the 1989 debates on the Lord Chancellor's Green Papers which paved the way for the Courts and Legal Services Act 1990 this concern became known as the 'level playing field' argument. It was felt that the costs of conveyancing could be concealed by small increases in mortgage interest rates. In addition there was the issue of potential conflict of interest.

There was also a general feeling that if building societies and banks were able to undertake conveyancing then there would be a decline in the quality of professional services provided by solicitors. They would no longer be able to spare the time to get to know their clients well and give them a personal service. The changes were seen by some as a symptom of deep-seated change within the legal profession: 'The traditional values of the profession are going out of the window – it's a full frontal government attack. The government is trying to make us commercial and we shouldn't be.'

The group which was most frequently considered to be 'at risk' from the loss of residential conveyancing was the traditional rural family practice, a finding which was of particular interest for the AJRBP study. It was an opinion which came from respondents in both rural and urban firms, although with a variety of permutations which bore some relationship to the location of the respondent. The critical view from urban solicitors was that country firms were of 'low calibre', that they 'don't keep up with the law' and were generally not sufficiently competitive or specialised, relying heavily on residential conveyancing, wills and trust and family work. A somewhat more sympathetic view was that rural firms operated under considerable handicaps and that their loss would be a disaster for the provision of legal services in the country: 'Once these firms have gone, they won't be replaced by anyone.'

Rural solicitors tended, not surprisingly, to emphasise the difficulties and drawbacks of rural practice and their inability to compete with specialised urban firms. However, there was at the same time a body of opinion among rural lawyers which considered that, for a variety of reasons, the rural firm would survive the loss of conveyancing. It is worth looking at this point of view first, before examining the counter-argument that liberalisation of the market for conveyancing would result in the wholesale decimation of rural legal services.

The basic strength of the rural firm was seen as its broadly based general practice. Rural respondents argued that this general level of service provided by rival firms was the basis of their good relations with the general public. Respondents noted that they were 'more personal' and 'very much general practitioners'. One pointed out that 'We are family oriented here – there is a greater loyalty between solicitor and client.' Clients' families were often known over several generations and had long-term loyalty to one firm of solicitors for all types of legal work. The links between solicitors and other professions were also seen by some respondents to be closer in rural areas: 'We have a closer liaison with our counterparts in other professions, and our competitors. I think this gives the client a better deal.'

The close-knit nature of the professional community in country towns was expected by some to act as a brake on the progress of competition. Change was expected to happen only slowly and it was felt that good friends would not attempt to undercut each other by breaking ranks over advertising or opening property shops. The type of work done by rural practices was also seen as offering some degree of security. Additionally, respondents from central and north Devon and western parts of Cornwall considered that they would be protected in the immediate future from cut-price competition by the fact that land registration had not reached these areas.

Solicitors who emphasised the vulnerability of rural firms – and this was a majority of comments on the situation of rural firms – saw them as threatened by the in-built inefficiency of family practice and also the limited range of alternative work which could replace the fees earned from conveyancing. The time spent with clients is a major source of inefficiency:

> In an urban firm there is less visiting of clients. Also here, people will sit and wait for hours to see you. Generally there is an expectation that a rural solicitor will be available at all times. Also they expect you to know more about the family – clients tend to be more old fashioned and naïve. If you go out to see a client you may have to stay for tea or lunch – there is generally a more leisurely approach. This sort of thing is difficult to bill.

> It's very difficult to charge the 'good talkers' as much as you could. Farmers are the worst – you couldn't charge them the full amount – you would never see them again. In the country you can't afford to be tight on costings – it's a matter of throwing bread on the waters.

Some firms had started to cut back their costs by charging for many more items of work, but often this was as far as rationalisation or innovation went and there was concern that this might destroy the special relationship with clients enjoyed by rural firms:

> People are accustomed to popping in for all sorts of odds and ends. We don't charge . . . but this is already stopping . . . we are increasingly looking at doing everything on an economic basis, from necessity rather than choice.

The type of broadly based general practice found in rural areas may be 'inefficient' in economic terms simply because of the lack of specialisation: 'We have a tradition of providing a service. We don't refuse anything on economic grounds and we have little specialisation. This is why we are not a rich firm'; 'We do uneconomic work as a service to the community. Around here we have got a lot of poor people.'

The family firm was seen as a 'dying breed' by some rural respondents, since factors such as population mobility were breaking down the tradition associated with a family solicitor. One solicitor saw the family client as an 'endangered species' and considered that clients, especially businessmen, used different firms for different purposes rather than relying on a single firm of solicitors. Another noted that:

> There is a different type of client now who treats lawyers as an unfortunate necessity. The old-established country client works on a different principle. I often don't charge the 'old' type of client for small things because of his loyalty.

The retired population of Devon and Cornwall could, it seemed, be relied upon still to use solicitors, while the younger suburbanite or poorer rural resident was becoming more cost conscious:

> At Sidmouth there are many old people who are used to dealing with solicitors who they know and trust. At Ottery there's a generally younger population, not so affluent, who have not been accustomed to using a solicitor.

> Clients down here are those who retire and will pay for professional services. There are a surprising number of cash purchasers through retirement, etc. This may be abnormal compared to the rest of the country.

Increasingly, however, respondents saw that improved personal mobility and information meant that the influence of competition would be felt in rural areas:

> When I first started, clients were loyal. Solicitors were considered the family adviser. They were respected. Now you have people 'phoning around to get cheap advice.

> Specialisation is increasing. The public is beginning to realise that general practice is out of date. They expect referral.

There was general agreement that rural areas had lost some former areas of work and saw few alternatives for profitable alternative specialisations which might be developed if conveyancing was lost. A few commented that their firms no longer had the resources to act as land agents for individuals or large estates as they had done in the past. The private mortgage business, once quite common in rural areas when building societies would not lend on agricultural or other country property, had almost disappeared. One respondent also commented that mid-Cornwall was 'not a terribly criminal area' and so his firm did not have much court work. Some rural respondents suggested that expansion into new, more profitable, areas of work was unlikely to come their way and that, for the most part, they were counting on legal aid work to sustain them. They were also, in some cases, hoping to reduce costs, the most frequent suggestion being, as already described, cutting back on time given to cases, although this did also carry the accompanying risk of loss of client loyalty. Cutting back on uneconomic areas of work was another possibility with the additional dimension of staff reductions.

REACTIONS TO THE FUTURE

Some insight into solicitors' views of the future was provided by the question in the survey which asked what the consequences might be for their firms of the possible loss of the so-called conveyancing monopoly. In this section a fourfold typology of firms derived from an assessment of responses to broader factors at the level of both the individual and the firm is introduced, the categories being loosely described as 'pessimists', 'entre-preneurs', 'specialists' and 'fatalists' (Economides, Blacksell and Blacksell, 1991; see also Paterson *et al.*, 1988).

While 50 per cent of respondents considered that the loss of the conveyancing monopoly would have little effect on their firms, 42 per cent were of the opinion that there would be noticeable consequences. These consequences covered a wide range of possibilities, from a probably drastic effect which could not be overcome to the necessity or, indeed, opportunity for the firm to become more competitive. It is interesting to examine some of the reactions at the extreme 'positive' and 'negative' ends of this spectrum with a view to suggesting some of the individual or firm characteristics which might have generated these particular responses.

Fourteen respondents (17% of the whole sample) represented the most pessimistic viewpoint, seeing changing circumstances as likely to mean at worst a drastic effect on the profession as a whole or at best a marked decline in income for their firms. By contrast, 14 respondents emphasised most positively the steps towards greater efficiency or diversification taken by their firms. For some of these respondents, the general feeling was of some anxiety for the future, while others were less concerned because they felt that changes had already taken place which had been successfully negotiated. However, they represent a fairly coherent group of responses which represents the opposite extreme from the most pessimistic group.

A third group was one in which respondents were fairly unconcerned because their firms did little residential conveyancing. They did, however, offer some interesting comments on the future. The largest group of all, those who were relatively unconcerned even though their firms did a considerable amount of conveyancing, was very amorphous. The range of reasons for their comparative lack of concern was very diverse. In consequence, it is less easy to categorise this group, although some broad conclusions will be considered in the final part of this section.

These four groups cannot be described as a comprehensive continuum of attitudes to change, since only the two more 'extreme' positions are what could be clearly defined as distinct attitude-types. Nevertheless, they do illustrate some marked contrasts, both in terms of the nature of the firms and individual 'style'. We have characterised them as 'pessimists' and 'entrepreneurs'. The 'pessimists' can be characterised broadly as older solicitors in remote rural locations who had few ideas for adjustment, and a desire for life to continue much as it always had done. The 'entrepreneurs' were not by any means all optimistic about the future, but were inclined to think through the long-term implications of expected changes and to belong to firms which were adjusting strategically to new circumstances. They tended to be in urban locations and to be younger individuals. Some were 'one-man bands' who had, so far, managed to expand rapidly by specialising in conveyancing. They were hoping to keep their competitive 'edge'. Others were in larger urban firms which were able to diversify and also not be burdened with a sprawl of branch offices which might have to be pruned in the near future.

We have characterised two further groups as 'specialists' and 'fatalists'. The 'specialists' were a very small group for whom residential conveyancing was almost completely unimportant as a component of their firm's work-load, and so their attitude to the possible loss of this type of work was fairly neutral. The largest group, the 'fatalists', cannot really be seen as focused around a single view of the future. However, we have called them the 'fatalists' because they showed lower levels of concern for the future than the 'pessimists' and a less active approach to improving efficiency or diversification than the 'entrepreneurs'. While this may not be a very accurate description of all respondents in this group, it does give some indication of the different views of the future held by the majority of respondents in the 1985 survey.

The Pessimists

Twelve (86%) of the 14 respondents in this group were in rural firms and only 2 (14%) urban, representing a much greater rural bias than in the sample as a whole. Moreover, these respondents tended to be from the more inaccessible parts of the two counties as compared to what might be seen as more suburban locations fairly close to the major urban areas. Four were located in mid Cornwall or further west and another four were in coastal towns at the northern and southern extremities of Devon. Another was located close to the Dorset border. Therefore, nine (64%) of respondents in this group could be said to represent remote rural communities. This would suggest that the vulnerability of rural firms was an important factor in the insecurity expressed by these respondents.

The firms represented in this group were relatively more decentralised than the sample as a whole. Six had three or more offices (43% compared to 28% of the complete sample) and 11 had two or more offices (79% compared to 51% of the sample). Four of the respondents were in sub-branches rather than head offices. All four solicitors had been with the same firm since starting work and had no other experience of work. In the group as a whole, five had been articled for over 24 years (four for over 30) and seven had been in the same firm for all of their working lives. At the other end of the age range, two respondents were only very newly qualified. It would seem, therefore, that both firm structures and individual characteristics are factors which contribute to vulnerability to possible branch closures or staff redundancies.

It is possible, of course, that the older average age of this group is the reason for expressions of concern and adverse comments on the way the profession is going, simply because those nearer retirement age feel they have nothing to lose in expressing such views. Respondents in this group did not seem inclined or able to make adjustments to new circumstances. For thirteen of the fourteen firms, and for nine of the respondents personally, residential conveyancing was the most important in terms of both income and time. However, the main adjustment to the possibility of the loss of conveyancing seemed to be cutting back on unremunerative work. None mentioned that their firm might pursue an active policy of advertising or adopt new technology to cut costs. Their comments suggested that they could see few possible alternatives to conveyancing or strategies which might be adopted. One, for example, did not want to be concerned with matrimonial or general litigation and stated that he did not 'want the problems or the people it brings'.

Mergers, closures and staff reductions were seen as a possibility for their firms by eight of these fourteen respondents, and a further two considered that the effect of the loss of conveyancing could be 'devastating' or 'catastrophic' for the profession. One said, 'the whole thing is in the melting pot. Computer conveyancing etc. – it's very worrying personally and for the firm. I think it will mean a further reduction in fees. It may mean a reduction in staff'.

The majority of the group also felt threatened by other aspects of current changes such as the narrowing scope of legal aid, the change in the prosecution system, the centralisation of specialist work into urban areas, fiercer competition for referrals from estate agents, national advertising by solicitors' firms outside the South-west, and the erosion of professional standards. This group seems, therefore, to be a combination of somewhat inflexible individuals in firms which were more than usually vulnerable to mergers, closures or staff reductions as a result of the loss of conveyancing.

The Entrepreneurs

Fourteen respondents took a view of the future which, while in some cases showing considerable anxiety about anticipated changes, was at the same time involved in strategies to enable adjustment and was far less pessimistic than the attitudes of the previous group. Ten (71%) of this group were from urban or suburban areas. Although two respondents had been articled for 26 years, this group was younger than the pessimists with an average age of 39 and an average of 15 years since taking articles. They were also more flexible individuals, only three having remained with the same firm all their working life. Among the group of fourteen, there were four sole principals and one senior partner who had set up their present firms. Two of these firms had only two fee earners and the other two fewer than six. In total, seven firms (50%) had fewer than six fee earners and, unlike the firms in the previous groups, these firms had fewer branch offices than the sample as a whole. Ten of the 14 (71%) had one or two offices and 8 had only a single office.

It is possible that the more entrepreneurial views expressed by respondents in this group could have been to some extent a public relations exercise – and perhaps, in some cases, not entirely correlated to the actual circumstances of the firms. However, indications of considerable dynamism came from expansions recently completed or about to be undertaken by these firms. Four had expanded in the previous three years (by take-over, branch opening or employing new staff), two more had expansion plans definitely under way (one was opening a new branch, and another employing extra fee-earning staff) and two others were actively considering expansion.

Residential conveyancing was most important in terms of income and time for 11 of the 14 firms in this group, but seven of the respondents did not, themselves, specialise in it. A combination of criminal litigation and family work were the most important areas of work for five of the respondents, while another specialised in business affairs and another in mining and mineral law. The prevailing attitudes were principally concerned with ways of improving levels of efficiency and competitiveness and diversifying activities in order to survive increased levels of competition and the possible loss of the conveyancing monopoly.

All but one of the 14 firms had begun the process of investment in new technology by installing word processors and eight used computers for time-costing and accounting. Several respondents commented that this had allowed the firms to streamline their operations, cost time effectively, reduce overheads and become more competitive. Routine conveyancing work, especially in those urban areas with extensive housing estates, could now be done by secretarial staff. Several firms had been able to reduce their secretarial staff, or could now do more work with the same number of staff.

While several respondents talked of making clients more aware of the services they provided, advertising among this group was at a surprisingly low level – although compared with the whole survey sample, the degree of interest in advertising was relatively high. Whereas among the survey sample 48 per cent (40 respondents) said their firms were not at all interested in advertising, among this group of 14 only 4 (29%) showed no interest. Seven were undecided and were waiting to see what other firms did, which might mean group advertising or producing their own occasional brochures. Two of the group had actually started advertising, although one had only placed advertisements in local papers when the firm had changed its name. The other was the single case in the whole survey sample of a firm advertising regularly – and, moreover, using relatively sophisticated techniques to aim its advertising at particular target groups. One more was considering advertising – but only for new areas of work such as business affairs and taxation which the firm intended to develop.

A process of diversification into new types of work was being actively pursued by seven of the firms. Four of them, all in Exeter, Torquay and its environs, were expanding into commercial areas – company work, commercial property, taxation and bankruptcy. One firm had been set up in Totnes, close to Torbay, deliberately to attract commercial work, and its success supports the comments made by rural respondents who felt that it was only in more urban locations that specialisation in such expanding and profitable work was possible. Four respondents mentioned the possibility of going into estate agency or joining homebuyers' groups. Others, for the most part the smaller firms, intended to streamline their conveyancing operation in order to undercut all possible competition. One was opening a new branch to catch the now burgeoning council house sales, but had also opened a branch in Devonport, Plymouth to expand the litigation side of the business. Two other firms had taken on fee-earning staff in order to do more litigation and one respondent thought that 'If we go through a bad time we can survive doing litigation.'

The Specialists

There were seven respondents in the survey who viewed the possible loss of the conveyancing monopoly with little concern because their firms did not rely on residential conveyancing to any great extent, or did none at all. As might be expected of firms which were relatively specialised, the majority were urban firms. Three were located in Exeter, one in Plymouth and a fifth was located only five miles (8km) from Exeter and could, therefore, be considered suburban.

Five of these firms were concerned with a combination of litigation and family work, business affairs and commercial property. One one-man firm specialised entirely in business affairs, combined with management consultancy, and another firm specialised in litigation for several unions. Generally their view of the loss of the conveyancing monopoly was detached, one commenting that residential conveyancing would be left only for the competitive firms and that some would collapse. However, two respondents in this group considered that there could be a knock-on effect, since other firms, who at present relied on residential conveyancing, would come after their litigation work.

The Fatalists

The majority (58%) of respondents are grouped into this category but they, nevertheless, expressed a wide range of opinions about how the future would affect their firms – and why. Generally, these were individuals in firms which had seen plenty of work and steady expansion. They also tended to take the view that while prospects might not seem too good for the profession as a whole, their own firms would survive – for a wide variety of reasons. Some respondents in rural areas considered that factors such as client loyalty, land registration and the difficulties of conveying rural properties and agricultural land would protect them, at least temporarily. This was, however, a minority opinion compared to those who considered that rural firms were likely to be worst affected. Urban firms were considered more able to make adjustments to new specialisations. The small urban one-man band dependent on conveyancing was seen as vulnerable by some, although others said it was best placed, with low overheads, to undercut other firms. Large firms were seen by some as unable to achieve a flexible response, while their position was defended by those who saw them as sufficiently broadly based to survive the loss of some areas of work.

The period of expansion of the profession had left many respondents with confidence that profitability might be reduced but no more. Indeed, many were currently so busy that they had no time to plan alternative strategies for the future. The chief adjustments mentioned by respondents in this group were to charge less for conveyancing and more for other types of work, to work longer hours or cut back on time spent with clients and to make some moves towards litigation, although this was mostly at that time an idea rather than anything which had been put into practice in these firms. There was an air of caution in that taking on new staff or opening new branches had been put off because of uncertainty about the future, even though this sometimes meant that the work-load for present fee earners and staff was very heavy. It was generally felt that these measures had already made firms more competitive and that they should be able to survive further increases in competition. The chief uncertainty was, however, the threat of competition from banks and building societies which was the major concern of the respondents in the survey.

SOLICITORS AND RURAL LEGAL SERVICES – A SUMMARY

The detailed analysis of solicitors in the rural UK and the service they offer, contained in this chapter and in Chapter 3, provides some important lessons for the administration of, and access to, justice, as well as pointing to the significance of local variations in the prevailing legal culture. Everywhere the profession has burgeoned in recent times and, in rural and urban areas alike, there are now many more lawyers practising than there were a generation ago. Even though, in terms of numbers, it is the urban areas that have benefited most, in proportion to the size of the local populations, rural areas have actually fared better.

Presence or absence is, however, only a part of the story; it is the work that solicitors do that is of real significance when it comes to judging the efficacy of the service they offer. Here the universal, and overwhelming, concentration on residential conveyancing must be highlighted, because of the way in which it overshadows all other areas of legal work. For the most part, and certainly in rural areas, firms which fail to specialise in this area of work will almost inevitably fail financially, if only because of the element of cross-subsidy that this lucrative source of income makes possible. It is a situation that has changed little in the past thirty years and, despite the threat of change with the ending of the solicitors' guaranteed monopoly over the conveyancing market in 1986, there is as yet no real evidence of any fundamental shift in the balance of work having occurred, though the prospect is at least now being actively debated.

It is the types of work that they do that so clearly differentiates solicitors in private practice from the providers of legal services in the public and voluntary sectors. As will be seen in Chapter 5, organisations like the CABx and law centres concentrate on those areas of law, such as consumer problems, child care, welfare and debt, which are traditionally of least importance to solicitors. In one sense it is a sensible division of the available expertise, but in another it serves to categorise a poor person's law for those who happen not to own property. The distinction has serious implications for the future training of solicitors and for clients living in rural areas where public and voluntary services are only thinly represented, if at all, causing potential problems of access to legal services for the most vulnerable groups in society.

As far as the future is concerned, our surveys showed that solicitors practising in rural areas, particularly those in the more remote locations, are much more pessimistic about the future of their businesses than those in the cities. For many rural solicitors traditional types of work, especially residential conveyancing, are on the wane and other avenues are not obviously emerging to replace them. In contrast, those in the major urban areas recognise the threat to the monopoly they have enjoyed in the residential conveyancing market, but see new opportunities as well in areas such as litigation.

However, it would be wrong to conclude that the profession generally in rural or urban areas feels seriously threatened. Although there is a widespread acceptance that competition will inevitably be fiercer in the future, there is no sense of a service or a way of life under real siege. Most solicitors see themselves as the main providers of legal services in rural, as in other, areas for the foreseeable future and as long as their confidence is not misplaced, they will continue to set the tone of the legal services on offer to the public.

5. Para-legal Agencies

There are many agencies and individuals other than professional lawyers who deliver legal services to the general public. They are commonly loosely described as para-legal services and are drawn from a wide range of very disparate public and private bodies (Johnstone and Flood, 1982; Blacksell *et al*, 1990). In most cases, providing legal advice only forms a part of their work, but frequently it is a major part and overall they make an important contribution to the fabric of legal service provision in the UK. The agencies involved range from local authority departments, such as social services, housing and trading standards, to grant-aided bodies like the Citizens' Advice Bureaux (CABx) and Shelter, to self-help groups, which emerge spontaneously in response to a specific local need (Baldwin, 1988). In most instances the advice they give relates to a fairly limited range of legal matters arising directly from their primary area of interest; for example, Shelter is mainly concerned with housing matters and the Child Poverty Action Group with questions of welfare benefits. Indeed, probably only the CABx on their own would claim to provide anything approaching a comprehensive service, although there are often strong informal, and sometimes formal, inter-agency links.

As with any service, one of the recurrent issues in the debate about the effectiveness of para-legal agencies is how accessible they are to the public they are supposed to serve. Since most suffer from chronic underfunding, there is a tendency for outlets to be concentrated where they are likely to reach the maximum number of clients, which in turn dictates that most are located in urban areas (see Fig. 2.6). The urban concentration is further reinforced by the fact that in many instances the grant-aided agencies have received the bulk of their funding from monies specifically allocated for urban redevelopment, such as the Urban Programme, which since the mid-1970s has sought to revitalise the services available in rundown inner-city areas. Outside the main towns and cities, therefore, provision is patchily and thinly spread and many people living in remote rural areas are, in practice, denied access to help and advice from important para-legal sources. Nevertheless, para-legal agencies have made an important contribution to ensuring that rural legal services are put on the national social policy agenda, despite their own limited presence in rural communities as compared with solicitors (see Ch. 2).

In the past decade there have been fundamental changes in the way in which many of the services in rural areas are delivered, with a general shift from public to private provision (Bell and Cloke, 1989). In this chapter we examine the emerging role of the main para-legal agencies and the ways in which they co-ordinate their activities with each other and with solicitors and other sources of formal legal advice and guidance in order to provide a comprehensive service.

CITIZENS' ADVICE BUREAUX: THE DEVELOPMENT OF A SOCIAL SERVICE

Since it was founded as a wartime measure in 1939 the CAB service has come to play an increasingly important part in the delivery of legal services in the UK. Originally, the service acted as a free source of general advice for the public and, more particularly, as a means of disseminating information from government and other sources. All the bureaux were set up as a result of local initiatives and were staffed entirely by volunteers. As the wartime emergency receded during the 1950s the CAB service went into something of a decline, though the example of a voluntary advice service was widely admired and even copied outside the UK, for example in the then colony of Southern Rhodesia, present-day Zimbabwe (Brasnett, 1964).

Since the late 1960s the whole concept of the service has been revived and re-established on a much more ambitious footing, with a growing emphasis on permanent professional staff working in tandem with volunteers. The aim is to provide not only advice, but also to mediate on behalf of individual citizens, who are in dispute with state or private agencies. The CAB service now performs a key role in ensuring, for example, that people receive the welfare benefits to which they are entitled, that they obtain their legal rights with respect to housing and employment, that consumer rights are properly enforced, and that debt repayments are scheduled fairly. In all these areas, the issues are in part legal and, in many instances, they are only finally resolved by arguing a case before a tribunal, such as a social security or employment tribunal, with CAB workers actually representing the plaintiff.

The value of the CAB service has been repeatedly endorsed in recent years. In 1979, the Final Report of the Royal Commission on Legal Services, chaired by Lord Benson, recommended that the service should form the basis of the primary level of advice-giving throughout the country. More recently an official government review of the National Association of Citizens' Advice Bureaux (NACAB) undertaken by Lord Lovelock in 1984 ringingly endorsed the movement as 'an invaluable national asset . . . . the dedication and competence of which have earned widespread respect'. Even within the legal profession the value of the service is clearly recognised. A report jointly commissioned by the Bar Council, representing barristers, and the Law Society, representing solicitors, recommended with specific reference to CABx that: 'a strong, independent and publicly-funded advice service sector is necessary to support the work of the two branches of the legal profession; advice agencies should be seen as complementing the services available to those in need of legal help rather than being a substitute for the advice of solicitors' (Marre, 1988).

The structure of the CAB service reflects its national role. In 1988 it had a total of 1,243 bureaux throughout the UK of which 992 were main offices and the rest extensions (Fig. 2.6). Some 25,000 people worked in these bureaux, 90 per cent of them volunteers, and they handled 7.69 million enquiries. In England, Wales and Northern Ireland the service is supported centrally by NACAB, which has a central office in London and 22 area offices covering the whole of the three countries; 19 in England, two in

Wales and one for the whole of Northern Ireland. In Scotland Citizens' Advice Scotland, formerly known as the Scottish Association of Citizens' Advice Bureaux (SACAB), performs a similar function, though without the network of area offices.

Each bureau has a manager, who is responsible for the day-to-day management, and a management committee. The committee is responsible for: overseeing the operation of the bureau and making sure that it complies with the requirements of the NACAB membership rules; determining local policies; recruiting staff; and ensuring that the bureau has sufficient resources and adequate premises. The members of the management committee are drawn from representatives of the local community and from bureau staff, but there is considerable local discretion in determining the actual size and composition. Every committee nominates one member to sit on the local area committee and the area committees in turn nominate one representative each to sit on the council of NACAB. The council is the main policymaking body of NACAB, so that the area committees act as the formal channel of communication between the individual bureaux and the council, advising it on the formulation of policy and relaying policy decisions back to the local management committees.

NACAB is primarily funded by an annual grant from the Department of Trade and Industry, which in 1987/88 amounted to £8.17m. Most of this money is used to finance the infrastructure of the central and area offices, but £1.8m. is passed directly to the individual bureaux to help them with their running costs. The bulk of the bureaux's finance, however, is generated locally, mainly from local authorities which in 1987/88 contributed over £10m. The information department of NACAB's central office also provides every bureau with a copy of the NACAB information system which is regularly updated. The aim of this service is to ensure that all bureaux are in a position to provide as high a quality and as uniform an advice service as possible. There is also a telephone consultancy service available at central office, which enables workers in the individual bureaux to raise any queries they may have about the information system, or to ask about matters not included in the published materials. These generalist sources of information are supplemented by specialist units, such as the Tribunal

Representation Unit based in Wolverhampton, which assists bureau workers in advising clients who have problems involving employment or social security law.

The flow of information is not only one way; another important function of NACAB is the collection and feedback of information from the bureaux. This information is used internally to monitor performance and externally to influence public policy at both national and local levels.

Of crucial importance for the success of the service is the quality of the training offered to bureaux workers. Everyone who works as an adviser in a bureau, either in a paid or voluntary capacity, must undergo training, which is co-ordinated by NACAB central office, but carried out locally under the supervision of the area offices.

The area offices and their staffs are the main point of contact with NACAB for bureaux. They are required: to give assistance to managers and management committees; to provide a local consultancy service; and to help bureaux with the recruitment of new staff. In short, area offices are responsible for ensuring that all the bureaux within their region meet the standards required for NACAB membership.

DELIVERING THE CAB SERVICE IN RURAL AREAS: AN EMERGING ISSUE

When they were first established during the Second World War, CABx were essentially devoted to providing advice and information to those living in urban areas. Many of the early commentators seem implicitly to have assumed that bureaux would only ever be located in towns and cities, because of the difficulties inherent in serving small and scattered communities (Bourdillon, 1945; Brasnett, 1964). Gradually, however, attitudes started to change and it came to be accepted that ways and means would have to be found to overcome the problems of gaining access to remoter areas, so that the service could become a truly national one, serving both town and country (Citron, 1989; Brooke, 1972). Even so progress was very slow and had to contend with much entrenched scepticism from both inside and outside the service as to whether CABx could ever make a significant contribution to rural legal services (Roberts, 1978). As recently as the early 1970s there were very few bureaux in small market towns, let alone the countryside proper, and it is only in the past decade that the picture has begun to change in any material way. However, throughout the past decade there has been mounting pressure for the need of those living in rural areas for advice of all kinds, and legal advice in particular, to be taken more seriously. The problem has been demonstrated empirically by the service itself in rural areas such as Northumbria (Elliott, 1984) and national organisations, like the National Council of Voluntary Organisations in England and Wales (RAIC, 1984) and the Scottish Consumer Council (SCC, 1982), have campaigned effectively for solutions.

CABx in Cornwall and Devon, 1986

Evidence from Cornwall and Devon underlines that, for the most part, the CAB service in rural areas is a relatively recent phenomenon. Only three of the 24 main bureaux operating in the two counties date back to the wartime origins of the service and they are all in the main Devon cities of Exeter, Plymouth and Torbay. Two-thirds (16) of the present bureaux were founded in the flush of growth that occurred nationally during the 1970s, while two date from the 1950s and three were founded in the 1980s. To a degree, the relatively small number of main bureaux masks the true extent of the service, for there are 10 extension offices in Cornwall and Devon, all serving small rural communities (Fig. 5.1). Moreover, one bureau provides a peripatetic service in five small towns in east Devon, the first such service of its kind in the country and a specific attempt to solve the problems of bringing the service to a rural area (NCC/NCSS, 1978; Kempson, 1981). Nevertheless, there are still substantial areas, notably in parts of Cornwall and north-west Devon, where there is no local bureau.

Naturally, the fact that there is a bureau at any particular location does not mean that the service there is always open and available. Only three of the main bureaux in Cornwall and Devon are open for more than 30 hours per week, while one is open for under 10 hours. Even so, all offer some period of service on at least four days a week.

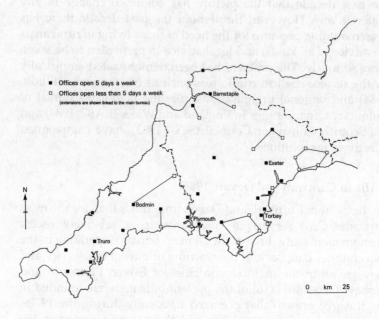

Figure 5.1 Citizens' Advice Bureaux: main offices and extensions in Cornwall and Devon.

The opening hours of extensions, most of which serve locally important market towns, such as Launceston, Torrington and South Molton, are even more limited, in most cases under 10 hours per week. In Ottery St Mary, in east Devon, the office is only open for two hours per week, that in Launceston, in north Cornwall, for two and a half hours, and those in Seaton and Sidmouth, in east Devon, for four hours. None of these towns can be said to be adequately served by their bureaux in that they are unable to respond to the immediate needs of clients for a substantial part of the week. This is not to say that the service on offer is not useful or professionally competent, simply that it is unavailable for most of the time and, therefore, inherently inaccessible if a potential client is unable to get in contact when the bureau is open, or if the problem requires urgent attention.

The fundamental importance of local bureaux is underlined by the analysis of where enquiries come from, even in the present age of advanced telecommunications. The majority of clients throughout the two counties are local, with only a small proportion of enquiries emanating more than five miles (8 km) away from the bureau (Fig. 5.2). In some cases, such as Falmouth, Helston and Kingsbridge, the number of enquiries from more than 10 miles (16 km) distant is negligible. However, for some of the remoter bureaux in the north and west of the region, such as Bodmin, Bideford and Tavistock, callers from more than 10 miles (16 km) away make up a more significant proportion, though it is still a small minority of the total.

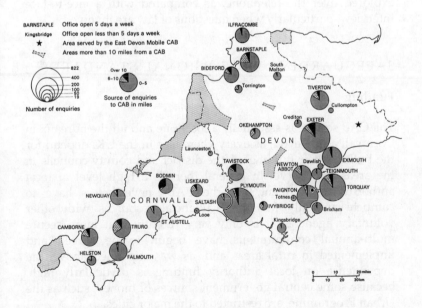

Figure 5.2 The number and source of enquiries to CABx in Cornwall and Devon.

The general reliance on a local service, accessible in person, emphasises the relative deprivation suffered by those parts of Cornwall and Devon that are more than 10 miles (16 km) from a CAB. The telephone, while perfectly adequate for routine inquiries for advice and information, has severe drawbacks for more complex matters and that includes most types of legal advice. There are still many households without private telephones and a lack of privacy in the home may be a major obstacle to using them, even when one is installed. For any length of call, cost is also an issue which deters people, though a Freefone service may offer a way out of this particular difficulty in some circumstances. In north-west Scotland and the outer isles the Freefone Adviceline Scheme has proved invaluable in bringing an advice service to the scattered rural communities in that part of the UK and a similar experiment has been funded by the Rural Development Commission in East Anglia since 1986 (Paterson and Bain, 1986). However, such schemes do not overcome the limits to the depth to which an issue can be explored over the telephone, as compared with a face-to-face interview, particularly when questions of law are involved.

SAFEGUARDING PROFESSIONAL STANDARDS

Funding

The CAB service is essentially a local one and all the bureaux in Cornwall and Devon, as everywhere else in the UK, depend for the bulk of their funding on the district and county councils in the areas they serve. In general there is a high level of local authority commitment, but the CABx nevertheless have to compete annually for scarce financial resources with other voluntary agencies. It is only very recently that more secure multi-annual commitments have begun to be agreed and implemented in rural areas and, as was explained above, the dependence on local authority funding is particularly high, because some central government sources of money, such as the Urban Programme, are restricted to the major cities.

For many bureaux managers in Cornwall and Devon (40% of those interviewed in the survey) the insecurity of funding is seen as the most serious problem they have to face, both because of the uncertainty it creates about the future and because of the way it distracts them from their primary function of advising the public. The following comment was a typical reaction:

> I hate the insecurity, ranging from my salary to the paying of bills and the premises. It is hand to mouth and awful. . . . We have to go cap in hand to different bodies. . . . we draw the line at jumble sales.

The chronic uncertainty hinders attempts at long-term planning and development for the service and even impedes good practice towards employees, such as the adoption of pension schemes for salaried staff.

When they are negotiating with their paymasters, CAB managers have always traditionally had to compete for funds with a whole range of other claims on local authority resources and there is always the nagging fear that the CABx case might go by default. CABx are usually lumped with requests from small charitable organisations, which only require relatively small amounts of money, such as, for example, sports and social clubs. There is a clear resentment among some voluntary bodies at the size of CAB budgets and the amounts of money that bureaux receive, especially now that the numbers of salaried staff they employ have begun to increase sharply. Coping with such pressures is always difficult, but when budgets are only agreed a year at a time, they can seriously undermine the quality and efficacy of the service.

One solution that has been widely instituted in Cornwall and Devon, as well as other parts of the country, is partnership schemes, whereby the local district and county councils, together with NACAB, guarantee the funding of a bureau for a number of years (in Cornwall and Devon between three and five years). The schemes are based on a gradually escalating commitment by the local authorities, and by the bureaux themselves through raising funds from other sources, while the NACAB contribution is gradually phased out.

At the time the interviews were carried out, the partnership agreements in Cornwall and Devon had mostly only just started, or were still in the process of being negotiated, but the hopes of the managers were high that they marked the advent of a new era of greater financial certainty. Nevertheless, there were those who expressed reservations. In a small minority of cases, the complexity of the schemes, which involve concerted action by at least two councils, as well as NACAB, was a cause for concern and there was a hankering among some managers for all funding to be channelled directly from central government, despite the loss of direct local involvement that would inevitably ensue.

In practice the partnership agreements have so far functioned well and have gone a long way to providing the stability bureaux have sought. The local authorities have not reneged on their agreements and have accepted individually that, if the annual budget of the bureau is agreed by one council, then it must automatically be accepted by them all. The only problems have stemmed from the inflexibility of the original agreements and the difficulties for the bureaux themselves as they have to raise a share of their budget from other sources in the later years of the agreement. The inflexibility arises because the agreements normally do not allow for any growth in the scope of the services offered by the bureaux. Changes, such as more paid workers and improved support services, have to be negotiated outside the framework of the original agreement and cannot rely for funding of the same sharing of the costs. It has meant that the more innovative and dynamic bureaux have had to face the double jeopardy of trying to manage a more varied service, as well as funding arrangements that are increasingly complex. Significantly, it is NACAB, rather than the local authorities that has usually resisted renegotiation of the original partnership agreements. The funds allocated to NACAB by central government have been insufficient to allow it to expand its commitments to individual bureaux, especially those enjoying the relative financial security of partnership agreements.

Partnership agreements do not of themselves, of course, ensure that budgets are large enough to provide the level of service demanded by the clients, or desired by the workers and management committees. The problems caused by inadequate budgets are legion and can be especially acute in rural areas. Nearly half the managers in Cornwall and Devon who were interviewed would have liked to be able to open rural extension bureaux in their areas, but were unable to do so due to a shortage of funds. It is not just the costs of the physical facilities which raise problems; recruiting and keeping workers are both more expensive and difficult in rural areas. In one case where the manager was responsible for both a main bureau and an extension on a total budget of £5,000, more than half the money had to be devoted to travelling expenses. These were essential, because of the 14 volunteer workers at the bureau, 10 lived outside the two towns concerned, a situation all too common in rural areas, where workers (and clients) are often dubious about providing a sensitive advice service within the confines of the small community where they live. They therefore volunteer to work elsewhere in a neighbouring bureau and inevitably incur greater costs.

The higher costs of delivering a rural service manifest themselves in many different ways. The sheer distances that many potential clients have to travel, the inadequacy of public transport and, for many people, the lack of access to private transport, mean that alternative modes of delivery have to be devised, most of which are expensive. Peripatetic services have been tried in a number of instances, such as the east Devon experiment described above, and one Cornish manager interviewed went so far as to say that if money could not be found for a mobile facility in his area, then it would be impossible to deliver an effective service.

Another consequence of the chronic underfunding that afflicts most bureaux and one which is a serious concern for managers is the generally unsatisfactory nature of the premises they occupy. The small size of many rural bureaux means that, although the problem is by no means exclusive to them, the problems are often particularly acute in these areas. Short leases are the norm and more than half the managers in Cornwall and Devon (54%) complained that their offices were too small and restricted to enable a satisfactory service to be provided. The kinds of limitation they cited were: a lack of interview rooms, first-floor locations that are inaccessible to the old and the disabled, and inadequate parking space and access to public transport. Any one of these can tip the balance when a person is attempting to make the difficult decision as to whether or not to ask for help.

Independence

One of the fundamental tenets of the CAB service is that it is completely independent and free from all outside interference. Independence is, however, something that is easier to assert than to achieve and constant vigilance is required if this article of faith is not to be compromised. The almost total reliance of bureaux on public funding, the need for close co-operation with the legal profession and other advice agencies, and the frequent, often routine, contacts with central and local government services can all pose threats to the independence of the service. In rural areas, the problem is thrown into particularly sharp relief, because the numbers of CABx and the variety of agencies with which they co-operate are relatively smaller than in urban areas, so that the danger of cosy understandings developing is all the greater.

For the majority of bureau managers in Cornwall and Devon (83%) the issue of CAB independence is, however, not a worry that is uppermost in their minds. The most obvious scope for conflict is with the county and district councils who are their chief paymasters, but there is no real evidence of bureau workers ever having been seriously constrained in dealing with complaints by clients about local authority services. Indeed one manager pointed out that councillors on the management committee, rather than sitting in judgement on the CAB, use their position to gain a feel for the shortcomings of their local authority administration and services, rather than using it to interfere with the work of the bureau. Nevertheless, in a minority of cases, doubts were expressed by those interviewed and there is some evidence that councillors will be pressurised to prevent CABx giving advice on specific issues, such as, for example, help for gay people. The following situation is fairly typical of the experience of a number of CABx:

> We put up a Gay Switchboard poster. Someone came into the bureau and complained saying 'we don't want that filth' and 'people like that should be thrown in the river'. He threatened to complain to a local councillor he knew and get them to stop funds to the bureau.

Only one of the managers interviewed felt strongly that a real threat to bureau independence did exist because of the nature of the funding arrangements and that the situation had to be carefully monitored. Significantly, her bureau is not located in local authority premises, a fact she welcomes, as she does not want clients to feel that there is even an implied connection between the CAB and the local authority, because of the large number of complaints which involve them.

The other major conflicts that can arise in bureaux stem from their relationships with the management committee and NACAB. The structure is intended to make bureaux as independent as possible, yet responsive to local needs and conforming to national norms. In Cornwall and Devon, however, there is a belief among some managers that certain of the local authorities abuse their position and try to exert undue control over the bureau, for example by trying to insist that a member of the council is always chosen as chair of the management committee and the views of the local authority are thus fed directly into the policy-making process. For the most part, such undue influence is little in evidence and managers have mixed feelings about the levels of involvement by members of management committees; some resent the interference of the more active councillors, others regret the lack of interest shown by the more passive members.

In rural areas there is often an extra dimension to the question of independence, because a single management committee may be responsible for several bureaux and may have to make difficult choices between them when it comes to allocating resources or deciding on policy priorities. Of the 24 CABx in Cornwall and Devon, 12 are presently controlled by separate management committees, while the other 12 share one. However, the management committees of a further two bureaux are actively considering merging with others, so that in the future it is likely that only in the larger urban areas will there be a separate management committee for each bureau.

The relationship between individual bureaux and NACAB can also give rise to conflict. In order that they may use the CAB logo, bureaux must conform to NACAB membership rules and this can inevitably limit the scope for developing their own policies and forms of practice. When asked what they thought of the supportive role of NACAB in developing the services they offered, most of the managers in the survey (63%) were complimentary, but a substantial minority (27%) found at least some cause for complaint. Indeed, more than any other question asked, it roused strong feelings and polarised opinion. The supporters of NACAB tended to mention the quality and usefulness of the services provided, in particular the monthly information pack. Those who were critical dwelt on the remoteness of the national body and its bureaucracy, in much the same way as solicitors, especially those in Cornwall, viewed the national Law Society in London. There is also a feeling that NACAB is too dominated by urban values and does not appreciate how bureaux in rural areas work. Managers are especially critical of what they see as the constant harping on issues such as equal opportunities and racism, which are not central to their local, rural, needs and in some respects positively detrimental to what the bureaux are trying to achieve. One manager described particularly graphically how at some post offices and pubs she had been refused permission to display a new NACAB poster which included black people, on the grounds that it was not relevant to the local community. Her solution was to try to persuade the person to change their mind, but, if this proved impossible, then she offered them instead a previous poster, which did not explicitly include a reference to the NACAB anti-racism policy.

Professionalism and the Safeguarding of Standards in Rural Areas

The root of much of the uncertainty about the competence of CABx to provide a legal advice service lies in the whole question of the professionalism of bureau staff. To what extent is the spread of full-time paid workers necessarily linked to higher professional standards of advice-giving? It is an issue that has taxed the CAB service just as much as outside critics and has led, additionally, to a widespread and rapid change in the nature of the service. The number of full-time paid workers has grown steadily and training requirements, both for them and for volunteers, have become increasingly rigorous and demanding. In parts of London, the process has progressed so far that the service is now staffed almost entirely by paid workers, transforming the original CAB voluntary ethos.

In rural areas such a radical change is generally neither feasible, nor desired. There is no prospect of sufficient resources being widely available for staff to run anything other than a volunteer service and, in any case, there is a widespread belief that the basic strength of CABx still lies in their tradition of volunteering. As one manager commented: 'I wouldn't want to see the voluntary aspects go as in London.'

Despite this divergence of view about the future direction of the service, the evidence from Cornwall and Devon demonstrates clearly that fundamental changes are occurring in rural areas as well, but that they are not necessarily the same as in the major urban centres. The most striking difference is in the nature of many of the more senior CAB workers themselves. The stereotype of a manager has traditionally been that of a middle-class, middle-aged, woman doing voluntary work in her spare time, much of which still rang true in rural areas until very recently: of the 24 managers in the survey, 21 were women, only four were under 40, and 17 were employed part-time. Significantly, however, 19 were in salaried posts and there was strong support expressed by those interviewed for the greater use of paid staff in the CAB service, though not at the expense of a core of volunteer workers. Since the survey was completed the process of professionalisation in Cornwall and Devon has continued and now all the bureaux in the two counties have salaried managers.

Closer analysis reveals quite clearly that the dominant arrangement in rural bureaux is for there to be a group of volunteers, supported by a small, part-time, salaried staff, usually comprising no more than one or two people. In the survey, there were only five managers working full-time in paid positions; three in the cities of Exeter, Plymouth and Torbay; one in Tiverton, a small town with an unusually large industrial base; and one in the East Devon Mobile CAB, which started as a nationally funded experiment to bring advice services to a scattered rural population. In Cornwall the general shortage of specialist skills in rural areas has also been to some extent recognised and the Rural Development Commission has provided funding for the Cornwall Money Advice and Welfare Information Project (COMAWIP), based in Camborne. Since 1988, this has enabled two full-time workers to give central support and advice to all the CABx in the county in matters relating to debt and welfare benefits.

The significance of the greater reliance that rural bureaux place upon part-time workers and volunteers lies less in the intrinsic quality of the service provided, than in the attitudes of the staff. Almost by definition, the CAB is unlikely to provide their main source of income, so that it will only attract certain groups in society with independent means and time to spare, rather than those wanting to make a full-time career out of advice work. There are no formal requirements or set procedures for becoming a CAB manager and 16 of those in Cornwall and Devon had never worked in any other bureau and only one had worked at a bureau outside the two counties. All the volunteers, and some of the salaried managers, claimed that they had joined the service out of a desire to help and to do something useful in the community, but several were retired, and others were women whose children had grown up and left home. As one of the managers interviewed explained:

> I gathered that [the local CAB] was having difficulty in keeping going. I knew virtually nothing, but made enquiries. I thought it was worth giving some time to this and it has been confirmed.

The preponderance of women among both the volunteers and the paid workers is also frequently cited as a cause for concern, because there is a belief that it may deter men from using the service. The degree of concern about this is somewhat ironic in view of chronic difficulties that women have had to face in all walks of the male-dominated society in the UK, but, of the 24 managers interviewed, 22 mentioned that there was a problem of balance, or 'spread' between the sexes and one noted very succinctly:

> You have to have a mix. We don't have enough men in the bureau, there is a good case for having a 50/50 basis and sometimes we lose a client because of this.

It is undoubtedly the case that, so long as the service in rural areas depends on volunteers and part-time workers, it will only be feasible for it to reflect the views and attitudes of those groups that are able to take part.

Such limitations are exacerbated by the generally high turnover of volunteer staff, many of whom remain less than a year at a bureau, even after having taken six months of initial training. Not only is such a rapid turnover wasteful in itself, it makes it difficult for volunteers, most of whom work for only two half-day sessions per week, to enter fully into the ethos of a bureau and to contribute with maximum effect to its work. It also means that managers have to spend a disproportionate amount of their time recruiting and training new volunteer staff, rather than devoting themselves to other areas of staff support. In rural areas problems of volunteer staff recruitment will always be even more difficult, because of the smaller numbers of people available and their more scattered distribution. This in turn heightens other more general issues, such as the gender imbalance among volunteers, the lack of people in work who are able to volunteer, and a tendency for volunteers to be drawn from the better-off sections of the community. When these characteristics are combined with the high turnover of staff, it raises a legitimate concern about the capacity of the service in some rural areas to serve the needs of all sections of the community.

The professionalisation of the CAB service nationally has profoundly altered the entirely voluntary, and somewhat paternalistic, ethos which prevailed when it was founded more than half a century ago. In rural areas the changes have been much slower than in the towns and cities and for most country people CABx are likely to provide the only readily available advice service and one that is, for the most part, still voluntary. In most of the major urban areas, on the other hand, there is a range of agencies with professional or semi-professional staffs, supported by voluntary and charitable contributions and government grant-aid which provide alternative sources of advice on legal issues, but these are almost entirely absent from rural areas. In Cornwall and Devon, for example, the only such agency which attempts to cover the two counties as a whole is Shelter. It provides free and impartial advice on housing matters, but operates from an office in the city of Plymouth with only a single roving staff member, who has responsibility for a population of nearly one and a half million and over 10,000 sq. km. Under such circumstances, it is clear that whatever the efforts made, the service could never match the public demand. Nevertheless, in rural areas too, there are growing expectations that the CABx, and any other available agencies, will offer an increasingly professional service, and living up to the higher standards demanded places great strains on the available human and financial resources.

CENTRAL AND LOCAL GOVERNMENT STATUTORY AGENCIES

Nationally, the advice services provided by CABx and other voluntary bodies are complemented by a wide range of statutory agencies all of which provide some free generalist advice in specific areas. The most comprehensive coverage in rural areas is

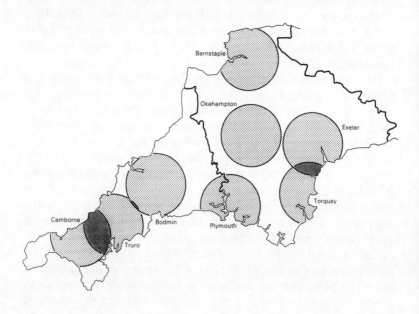

Figure 5.3 Access to county council trading standards offices in Cornwall and Devon (areas within a 10 miles (16km) radius of a Trading Standards Office).

provided by the local authority statutory services, run by the county and district councils, but for them advising the public is only part of their remit and the likelihood is that that they are as likely to be the object of a complaint as a medium for providing a solution.

All county councils have trading standards departments, charged with ensuring that the whole gamut of consumer law is rigorously adhered to and enforced. A considerable proportion of their work involves investigating complaints from the general public and where breaches of the law have occurred the officers have a duty to prosecute. Unfortunately, however, although the service is a national one, organised on a county-wide basis, the trading standards offices themselves are almost all located in the larger towns and cities. In Cornwall and Devon, for instance, there are only eight offices, three in Cornwall and five in Devon (Fig 5.3), so that people living in large parts of the two counties have to travel considerable distances, with all the associated inconvenience involved, if they wish to make a complaint or seek advice. Inevitably, this dissuades some people from using the service, especially those who, for reasons of age, infirmity or income level, are among the less mobile sections of society.

Much the same kinds of limitation also apply to all other local authority services, such as social services and the police, though in most cases their offices are more widely distributed. In Cornwall and Devon there are 38 county council social services offices, 24 of which are located outside the three major cities of Exeter, Plymouth and Torbay. Nevertheless, there are still significant areas in the north and west of the south-west peninsula where people have to travel more than 10 miles (16km) to reach a social services office (Fig. 5.4), and the same pattern is true of the vast majority of rural counties in England and Wales.

The main difficulty with these services as sources of advice, however, is not physical accessibility, but how the staff working for social services departments, the police and the like perceive their roles and how the services themselves are perceived by the public they serve. For many people, far from being seen as providing an advice service, social services staff and the police are considered to be agents of the state, enforcing the law on an unwilling and put-upon populace. The image is much resented within the services themselves, but is hard to counter. In

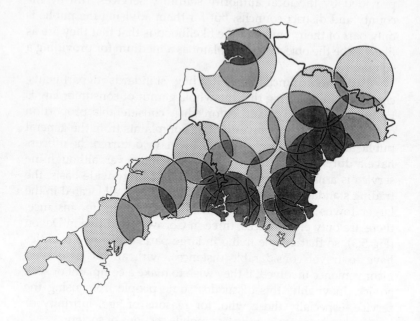

Figure 5.4 Access to county council social services offices in Cornwall and Devon (areas within a 10 miles (16km) radius of a Social Services Office).

Hartland, a remote rural community in north-west Devon, the local police constable has set up a free advice service in the village to try and promote the image of the police as providing a caring service, but in our surveys of local residents (see Ch. 6) we found little evidence that people were either aware of the service or used it. The reality is that complaints lodged with independent advice services, like the CABx, are frequently about allegedly unfair treatment by local authorities. Indeed, to view such services as in any way providing free and independent advice is completely contrary to the perceptions and experience of many of their clients.

Exactly the same kind of scenario may be painted at district council level for housing departments, although in this case the numbers of offices are considerably greater and more widespread, so that the problems of physical accessibility are generally somewhat less. Once again, however, housing officers tend to be seen as allocators of scarce resources, rather than people whose job it is to overcome the problems of homelessness and inadequate accommodation. All too often, clients contact advice services for help in challenging their decisions, for they are seen as barriers to justice and not as a means of achieving it.

Local authorities, particularly those with responsibility for extensive rural areas, are usually acutely aware of the problems that members of the public face in obtaining legal advice. Many have also actually taken steps to help by establishing information retrieval systems in association with the library services. Since, 1984, Devon County Council has operated the Public Information in Rural Areas Technology Experiment (PIRATE), which enables people to gain access to information data bases on a wide range of subjects from computer terminals located in branch libraries. The response to this and other schemes has been encouraging, but it must be emphasised that it is an information and not an advice service, let alone a professional legal advice service.

LINKS WITH THE LEGAL PROFESSION

The respective roles of professional lawyers and para-legal agencies, whether voluntary or statutory, in the provision of legal services have never been clearly distinguished and have recently tended to become rather more blurred as bodies like the CABx have become increasingly staffed by full-time professional workers. Today, one of the most important aspects of the organisation of para-legal agencies is the links they have developed with solicitors and other professional legal services. For the statutory services such links are normally routine, because all local authorities have their own legal departments, staffed by professionally qualified personnel, who can dispense authoritative advice as required. However, it must be stressed that this is invariably not a service for the general public, but a legal advice service for officers in other departments.

As far as CABx and other voluntary advice agencies are concerned there is no automatic recourse to professional legal advice, but it is most important to emphasise that both nationally and locally the service has always cultivated close and extensive links with solicitors in private practice. The scale of the overlap between the demands made of solicitors and of CABx is considerable, especially in cases involving issues such as welfare rights and housing. Nationally, it has been estimated that about a third of all enquiries at CABx would be eligible for assistance under the Green Form Scheme, were the work to be undertaken by a solicitor (Baldwin and Hill, 1986).

An interesting example of the kind of co-operation that is possible is provided by the Larkman Advice Scheme, which was started on the Larkman estate in Norwich in 1980. Its purpose is to encourage anyone who feels the need to seek free legal advice from a rota of duty solicitors and approximately the same number of volunteers from the Norwich CAB, the Social Services Department and the lay public. Everyone is seen by the duty solicitor, while the volunteers take the names and addresses and other particulars from callers on arrival and give preliminary advice if requested.

The scheme, which operates for one evening a week for two hours, is in some respects very traditional, in that it adopts a strictly hierarchical view of legal services with the para-legal workers confined to supporting the professionals as represented by the solicitors. Nevertheless, the service has clearly uncovered a demand, particularly from people with matrimonial and debt problems. To the surprise of the organisers it has also proved to be much more than just a local service, for it draws many of its clients from well beyond the Larkman estate and the city of Norwich. In the first two years of its operation 38 per cent of callers came from elsewhere in Norfolk and 16 per cent had travelled in excess of 10 km. Since Norfolk is a sparsely populated and very rural county, this gives some indication of the scale of the latent demand that exists for legal services outside the confines of urban areas.

In Cornwall and Devon there is a variety of ways in which CABx maintain contact with solicitors and make professional services available to clients. All bureaux routinely refer clients to solicitors and all but one are able to telephone a solicitor at any time to obtain free advice about a problem. Indeed, all but two of the bureaux surveyed had at least one honorary legal adviser (HLA), who had agreed to give advice on legal matters to the bureau. Most bureaux have gone even further, arranging legal advice sessions, where solicitors come to the bureau and give free advice, and more than half offer free interviews in solicitors' offices, over and above any arrangements for advice or representation under the Legal Aid Scheme.

The difficulty with all such schemes is that none is completely satisfactory from the point of view of either the client, or the CAB, or the solicitor. Periodic legal advice sessions on a rota basis in the bureau, however often they are organised, can lead to clients having to wait quite a long time before seeing a solicitor. Equally, where the arrangement is with a firm, rather than an individual solicitor, there can be uncertainty as to who will actually be in attendance, resulting in an inevitable lack of continuity. The survey generated a number of interesting comments on the difficulties of liaising with solicitors, especially with reference to the legal rota. One manager described the solicitors' attitude to it in the following terms:

> It's hard to judge. Sometimes they think it is a bit of a chore and send down the junior partner. Sometimes I'm pretty disappointed because I have to give them guidance. It is rather blurred as to what they should do when they come in. [The legal advice scheme] is supposed to be a diagnostic interview, but we use it as an introduction to people who find it difficult to speak to solicitors.

The alternative of free interviews in the solicitor's office is also potentially problematic, because even though these are only diagnostic interviews, they cut across the normal business practice which a firm operates. Solicitors are not offering free advice on demand, as are CABx; they expect that their services will be paid for, either directly by the client, or from public funds.

It would be wrong to overdramatise this conflict, but the nature of the two services is different and not necessarily complementary. It is often assumed that solicitors view their contacts with CABx as a source of business, but there is little evidence that this is the case. Many referrals involve work that is inherently unattractive to them in financial terms. Indeed, there is a tendency rather for some solicitors to refer certain categories of work to the CABx, either because they believe the service to be better able to deal with it, or because it is not financially attractive to them, or both!

One of the manifestations of the tension between solicitors and CABx is the dissatisfaction with generalist legal advice. As CABx have become more expert themselves, they have increasingly wished to pick and choose the solicitors to whom they refer clients. Many solicitors, on the other hand, resent such external and, as they see it, ill-informed evaluations of their professional competence. Thus there have been moves by CABx to draw up lists of specialist legal advisers for particular areas of work, but such developments have usually been resisted by local law societies.

The relationship between CABx and solicitors in private practice is a delicate one, but the more serious problems usually tend to occur in urban areas. Here both services routinely offer specialist services and CAB workers now feel confident enough to undertake work that has traditionally been the preserve of solicitors and only refer clients selectively. In rural areas, both solicitors and CABx offer a generalist service, and although there is a danger of overlap in theory, the relatively small number of bureaux ensures that conflicts of interest rarely surface.

FUTURE DEVELOPMENTS

The future for para-legal services in rural areas in general terms is more secure than it has ever been, in that over the past decade they have gradually established a footing in most parts of the UK, albeit at a level which is still patently inadequate to satisfy the demands of the rural populace. The precise form that these services will take in the future is, however, much more open to question. On the one hand, the rapid advances in communications technology are revolutionising the way in which people can gain access to advice and information. On the other, the government is making a thoroughgoing reassessment of how it should finance and support access to legal services for the community as a whole, which could have important and far-reaching implications for their delivery.

As far as communications are concerned, developments such as microfiche systems have enabled large and unwieldy amounts of information to be packaged in a form which makes them easily transportable and, as a result, ensured that peripatetic services have become a realistic possibility, if not a reality, in most parts of the country. The East Devon Mobile CAB, which serves a group of six small communities in the county is a pioneering example of the kinds of change in the method of delivery that are now possible. Equally, the increasingly widespread availability of telephones, especially in people's homes, together with the introduction of services that are cheap to use, has resulted in a number of telephone advice and information services, such as the Adviceline scheme in northern Scotland, being introduced. Undoubtedly in the future innovations of this kind are going to be used much more widely, though it remains doubtful whether it will ever be possible, or desirable, to give complex legal advice over the telephone. In this context it is interesting to note that solicitors are still not allowed to give advice under the Green Form Scheme by telephone and the government has given no indication that it intends to alter this situation in the foreseeable future, even if it opens up some types of legal work under the scheme to para-legal agencies.

Other developments resulting from the advances in computer technology are somewhat less certain. Undoubtedly, many office procedures will become more streamlined and efficient as a result of the introduction of technologies like word processing, making it financially possible to support legal advice outlets in locations that were previously excluded on grounds of cost. This clearly has important implications for rural areas with their small and scattered populations, but there is no indication as yet that the introduction of such technologies is going to lead to an explosive growth in, for example, the numbers of CABx. The future impact of other innovations, like interactive access via computers to remote data bases and to programs which enable routine queries to be answered by machines, is very much more uncertain. The prospects are exciting and the potential considerable, but, for the most part, the technologies are not as yet sufficiently well developed for them to have had much practical effect on the delivery of legal services (Clark and Economides, 1989, 1991).

It is much more certain that important changes are going to occur as a result of the government reassessing its role in the delivery of legal services, particularly through the Legal Aid Scheme which it finances directly from the exchequer. It has long been concerned at the spiralling costs of the scheme, by which the poorer members of society are able to receive assistance from the public purse for all or part of their legal costs, including solicitors' fees. In 1989–90 the net cost was nearly £600m. and this figure is projected to rise to over £750m. by the end of the century, so that any ways of slowing down the growth of, or even reducing, the annual bill are being studied in detail. The most obvious solution is to reduce the overall eligibility (and hence accessibility) for legal aid, by limiting further the kinds of legal work for which it is available and by lowering the income thresholds below which people may use the scheme (Murphy, 1989). Both strategies are being tried, but it seems unlikely that they will produce sufficient savings to reduce the costs significantly. An alternative strategy is, therefore, also being tested, whereby it is proposed that certain categories of Legal Aid such as Green Form be opened up to para-legal agencies in the voluntary sector, provided they meet quality criteria necessary to obtain a legal aid franchise (Orchard and Blake, 1989).

The initial focus of this franchising experiment has been a specific part of the Legal Aid Scheme, known as Green Form, which provides for verbal and written advice, assistance with interpreting and drafting documents, negotiations, letter writing, and any other kind of diagnostic help that does not involve actual representation. It is the area of solicitors' work where the overlap with advice agencies is greatest, although the prospect of any saving is remote. In 1987 the net cost of Green Form advice to the taxpayer was £67.3m., so that the attraction for the government of concentrating resources on efficient firms and CABx, even at the expense of having to monitor the quality of the service and provide some extra resources, is considerable.

Pressure for a re-examination of who does what in the field of legal advice has been mounting from a number of different sources for some time and for reasons other than cost. The Royal Commission on Legal Services in its final report published in 1979 noted the overlap between the services provided by solicitors and CABx and pointed out that no one was doing anything to see how the public monies involved might most effectively be deployed. At the same time there was a growing concern at the apparently arbitrary division between courts and tribunals (lands tribunal, employment appeal tribunals and mental health review tribunals), where clients eligible for legal aid could be represented by lawyers at public expense, and the growing array of other tribunals (industrial tribunals, social security appeal tribunals, immigration appeal tribunals, etc.) where they could not. There is ample evidence that, no matter what court or tribunal is involved, people who are represented are likely to fare better than those who conduct their own cases, so that the arguments for extending Legal Aid to a much wider range of tribunals and representatives, to ensure that litigants who are unable to afford to be represented get a fair deal, carry considerable weight. The Lord Chancellor's Legal Aid Advisory Committee, in its 1982–83 report, added its voice to those advocating that Legal Aid should be more widely available for representation at tribunals, with a clear implication that the matter should be urgently reviewed (LCD, 1983).

Eventually, early in 1986, an inter-departmental review team, the Legal Aid Efficiency Scrutiny Team, was set up by the government to consider the whole scope and working of the Legal Aid Scheme (LCD, 1986b). It reported within six months and made a number of recommendations, which involved the voluntary sector taking a much more prominent role. As far as representation at tribunals was concerned, it argued that in most instances lay representatives would be just as effective as solicitors and that, where this was not the case, tribunal procedures should be simplified to make it easier for lay persons to act. Much more controversially, however, the report also recommended scrapping the Green Form element of the Legal Aid Scheme and, instead, requiring that those eligible for legal aid should take their problem to an advice agency, in most cases a CAB, which would only refer them to a solicitor if the matter could not be dealt with by the agency itself.

The recommendations of the Scrutiny Team were hastily compiled and in many important respects poorly thought out, but this did not prevent their giving rise to a widespread debate. NACAB, acting on behalf of all the CABx, was put in a very difficult position. On the one hand, it was pleased at the confidence demonstrated in the CAB service and eager to take advantage of it. On the other, it was clear that it could only undertake such new and vastly bigger responsibilities, if it also received much more substantial government financial aid. Since one of the prime objectives, if not *the* prime objective, of the Scrutiny Team's review was to rein in the cost of the Legal Aid Scheme, it was not part of their proposal that public money, presently being spent by solicitors in private practice, should simply be reallocated to the CAB service.

However, NACAB's objections were not merely financial, in company with the Lord Chancellor's Legal Aid Advisory Committee, it also rejected the reallocation of primary legal advice to advice agencies on structural grounds. Throughout the UK, there are no more than 1,600 advice agencies, including all the CABx, as compared with at least 9,749 private practice firms located in 15,327 offices in England and Wales alone, so that any transfer of primary legal advice away from solicitors would, in effect, result in a dramatic reduction in client choice. The problems would be particularly severe in rural areas, because of the small number of advice agencies located there and, in many instances, the proposals would have meant that those living in the country would be effectively denied access to legal advice. There would be gaps in the geographical provision of legal services, as well as a reduction in their quality and scope. A further objection was that the proposals would create a two-tier service, with those dependent on Legal Aid having to go to an advice agency for primary legal assistance, while everyone else could go direct to a solicitor.

In the Legal Aid Act 1988 the government took note of these objections and did not abolish the Green Form element of the Legal Aid Scheme as such, but it did transfer the administration of Legal Aid to the newly created Legal Aid Board. The Board, which is chaired by an industrialist and has 12 members, equally divided between those with legal and advice work backgrounds and those with industrial backgrounds, has the power to open up some legal services to agencies other than solicitors if it so wishes, and this it is currently doing through the evolution of its 'franchising concept'. It seems probable that voluntary advice agencies will be able to play a more prominent formal part in dispensing primary legal advice under the Green Form Scheme, the desirability of which has been recognised by the legal professions themselves (Marre, 1988). Nevertheless, achieving such a transfer, especially in rural areas, will be difficult for the structural reasons outlined above and, unless there is a significant increase in resources, it will remain a pipedream for the foreseeable future (Economides, 1991).

6. Rural Clients

If the efficacy of legal service provision is to be understood properly, it is essential that there is a clear appreciation of how, and under what circumstances, potential clients avail themselves of services. Information about the distribution of sources of legal advice provides only a partial picture, if it is not also supported by evidence of those factors which constrain access to legal services among the people they are supposed to serve. One of the key arguments in this book is that there are identifiable local legal cultures, which result in significant variations in the experience of, and demand for, legal services among different social groups, resulting in contrasting patterns of use. There are many complex factors which give rise to such variety, but of central importance are: the nature of the available services; the needs and legal competence of the populations they serve; and the levels of physical accessibility to the services among potential clients.

Rural areas clearly offer a sharp contrast in terms of living conditions to towns and cities and, as part of the AJRBP study in Cornwall and Devon, a series of surveys was conducted to investigate in detail the expectations and use of legal services in three parishes, all of which, in a British context, were remote from urban areas. It is the evidence collected from these surveys that forms the core of the following analysis of rural client behaviour (see Appendix 1).

The chapter is divided into four sections. In the first there is a review of the whole process of advice-seeking and an attempt to explain how it may be modified specifically in a rural context. In particular, the issues of the levels of legal competence among different segments of the rural population and the effects of the various barriers to communication and travel are examined in detail. This is followed, in the second section by an analysis of the actual use made of, and perceptions of, solicitors and CABx by the populations of the three parishes, as well as a review of those issues which emerged from the surveys as having a clear legal dimension, but where formal legal advice had not been sought. In the third section brief consideration is given to the degrees of satisfaction with the available legal services and to ways in which those actually living in rural areas believe the provision of legal services might be improved. Finally, in section four, consideration is given to various barriers in the structure of rural society which inhibit access to legal services.

THE ADVICE-SEEKING PROCESS

A Theoretical Perspective

In many respects the problems facing anyone trying to get advice are the same in rural areas as anywhere else and, before examining in detail the rural situation, the whole process of advice-seeking may usefully be put into a broader context. In general terms, the process may logically be viewed as a continuum, consisting of a number of overlapping, and interacting, stages. As can be seen in Fig. 6.1, it may be divided broadly into two: internal discussions, which initially 'frame' the point at issue, and formal advice-seeking and help, involving some sort of external agency, which aids the search for an acceptable solution. However, when using this model, the following must always be borne in mind: the issue in question does not necessarily have to progress through the full range of options before it is resolved, and the actual consultations may well lead to the original issue being reassessed and redefined in very different terms. For example, a person might initially seek advice about a family matter and end up by being given legal assistance to help deal with financial matters, which are the root cause of the family matter for which advice was first requested.

The first stage (A) is the period during which the issue emerges as a bone of contention. Initially, its true significance for

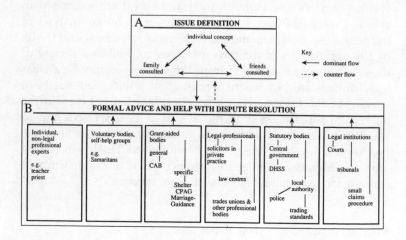

Figure 6.1 A theoretical model of the advice-seeking process, the process of framing individual issues.

the person concerned may not be fully apparent, but it will gradually become clearer, as a result of discussions with other members of the family or close friends, who may or may not have legal expertise. In our own study we were unable to analyse closely the complex interactions within families and groups of friends, other than noting when other individuals were party to the discussions and helped to decide what further action should be taken.

The second stage (B) encompasses a wide range of options for obtaining more or less formal advice and help in resolving disputes. It is important to stress that the various categories are in no way mutually exclusive, although in practice they do form a loose hierarchy, with individual, legally qualified, experts at one end and legal institutions at the other (Fig. 6.1). However, this is a very crude characterisation and, as indicated in Figure 6.1, counter-flows can be very important, as well as cross-referencing within each subsection. Statutory bodies sometimes refer clients to solicitors, or even to CABx, and solicitors may feel that some of the grant-aided bodies are better able than themselves to advise on certain areas, such as consumer, housing and welfare law. Equally among legal professionals there are also frequent referrals between law centres and solicitors in private practice where the two exist in the same area.

Turning to the hierarchy, the least formalised avenue is simply seeking advice from someone in the community who is recognised as knowledgeable and authoritative. Teachers, clergy, as well as other professional people, are often cited in this context and it might be assumed that in remote rural areas, where advice services generally may not be easily accessible, such advice would be of added importance.

Where there is a more widespread and general demand for help, spontaneous action has often been taken, leading to the formation of self-help groups, some of which have eventually become more formalised as national voluntary bodies. The Samaritans, for instance, now have a network right across the country, offering not just a sympathetic ear to anyone needing someone to talk to, but an avenue to professional advice. Other organisations are primarily a source of mutual support and a forum for sharing experiences. Whatever their origins, these bodies offer a crucial safety net, but one which is difficult to extend to areas of low overall demand, which is usually the case in sparsely populated rural areas.

Over the years, many voluntary organisations have steadily gained in status and developed their own professional expertise. This has eventually led to public recognition, as seen in the 1988 Legal Aid Act which has created the possibility of franchising generalist advice agencies to do Green Form work under the Legal Aid Scheme, work previously carried out almost exclusively by the private legal profession. Prime examples of such evolution are the CABx, most of which now have professional staff members to guide the volunteers and are almost entirely dependent on finance from public and charitable sources. One of the most important aspects of this change is that such bodies begin to offer a service for which they are held professionally responsible, rather than only directing clients to where they may find help. CABx are particularly interesting in this regard, because of the broad scope of the service they offer, but there are many other agencies, offering advice in more specific fields of expertise, such as Shelter in the area of housing and the Child Poverty Action Group in the area of welfare rights, though they have only limited representation in rural areas of the UK, where it seems unlikely that they will ever have the financial resources to enable them to provide a comprehensive service (see Ch. 5).

Solicitors as professional legal advisers have long been recognised as the main source of legal advice open to members of the public trying to resolve a dispute. For most people contact is through solicitors in private practice, most of whom still offer a generalist service, despite a growing trend towards individual specialisation in particular areas of law. Even though they are in private practice, many of these solicitors provide a service partially subsidised from the public purse through the Legal Aid Scheme, but the terms of the scheme mean that the subsidy is only available to a minority of the population. In some of the main urban areas barristers and solicitors may also be consulted by anyone, free of charge, in publicly funded law centres, but this is not an option that is widely available and, at present, is almost irrelevant to the rural population. The only other significant avenue for obtaining advice from a solicitor is through the legal departments of trade unions or professional bodies, but, by definition, such help is limited to particular groups and certain categories of issue.

Central and local government have themselves established many statutory bodies to watch over and protect citizens and regulate their behaviour. These agencies cover a very broad spectrum of social and economic affairs, and include the police service, social workers in local authority social services departments, and trading standards officers, among many others. There is much dispute as to the true function of these agencies within the apparatus of the state, but all purport to act, at least in part, for individuals in their dealings with public and private agencies.

Finally, there are the formal and informal legal institutions, such as courts and tribunals, which are empowered to settle disputes, either through arbitration or adjudication. In practice, though not in principle, access to these is more often than not filtered through one or more of the other agencies described above.

Advice-Seeking in Practice

The results of our survey revealed clearly how these various potential avenues for obtaining advice were actually used in practice and illustrated some of the realities of gaining access to law for those living in remote rural areas. As far as the first stage (A) of the process of resolving issues is concerned, our own survey demonstrated that the vast majority of people, when faced with a difficult issue, invariably first of all discuss what they might do with their family or close friends, so that the actual decision about what action should be taken is often a group, rather than an individual, one. Everyone we interviewed who had consulted a solicitor had first discussed the matter with someone else and only two of those consulting a CAB had acted entirely on their own. Those who were married mostly confided in their spouse, the young living at home in their parents, and others in a variety of close friends.

The fact that such discussions take place may, on the face of it, seem unremarkable, but it in fact runs counter to some other published evidence. A survey in Scotland, for instance, found that 20 per cent of people referred to no one before taking legal advice (Hughes, 1980). Indeed, many of the respondents in our survey also initially claimed to have acted entirely on their own in consulting a solicitor or a CAB, but when pressed admitted that they had discussed it with their spouse, other members of their family, or friends. However, none of the respondents saw these discussions as having played a significant role in determining the action that they eventually took.

Actually, it is clear that friends who have experienced similar problems can be of considerable help, offering emotional support as well as practical guidance. One woman, whose friend also looked after her children when she went to visit the solicitor, described this help as follows:

> We compared notes, you have to have someone to talk to, you can't talk to everyone. . . people don't always really want to know. . . if you've got a friend who has been through it, it's a real relief.

That the decision about what action to take is actually made within this wider context of the group is of considerable importance, for it means that it is the legal knowledge and expertise of the household and immediate circle of friends, rather than of the individual, that is the critical limit on the range of options actually open to people. Similar conclusions have also been reached by other studies, and research into accident claims indicates that the main influence on the decision about seeking legal help is having contact with someone knowledgeable about rights and sources of help (Harris and Genn, 1984).

In terms of access to legal expertise, the value of such group decisions is questionable. Only just over 20 per cent of those interviewed in our second, follow-up, survey had any formal legal knowledge and even this was very rudimentary, a by-product of their job or hobby, although a few respondents had family and close friends who were qualified as solicitors or barristers, or had relatives working in a solicitor's office. None of the legally qualified people had actually acted directly for the respondents, but in some cases they had given their opinion on the appropriateness of seeking legal advice and had been referred to subsequently in assessing the quality of the service given. There were also a number of respondents with relatives, or even friends or friends' relatives, who had worked as volunteers in a CAB and had been asked for advice.

As well as providing information, the family and wider group can also be a source of support for the decision to risk taking legal action. One person we interviewed felt that he and his wife might have let their issue drop, had they not been encouraged to continue by his parents. The issue was a serious one involving the family business and the possible consequences of taking action were complex and momentous. The outcome was also difficult to predict, so that, as is often the case, the support was of great importance. In other typical cases, a respondent's married daughter had contacted the CAB on her behalf about a consumer problem, and a mother who worked as a CAB volunteer had checked some information for her son at the bureau.

Nevertheless, discussion of many types of issue, certainly outside the confines of their immediate family, is not for everyone living in a close-knit rural community. Some people took great care not to divulge their problems. One person, talking about an issue affecting his business, remarked that he definitely did not talk to neighbours or local people about it, because it would only lead to harmful gossip. Others were also cautious, though only to the extent of being selective to whom they confided:

> In a small village you can't (discuss things). . . . There's friendliness in a village, and also there's an awful lot of gossip.

Put slightly differently, a common reason advanced for not taking legal advice and action was the fear of invoking the displeasure of the local community. One woman, in dispute with her neighbour, felt strongly that there was pressure in the village not to cause trouble. The husband of a friend had advised her:

> Don't go to law, it makes for bad feelings and is never forgotten.

Even so, on reflection her reaction was:

> I wish we hadn't listened to him. . . but you can't make a fuss can you? That's the attitude down here. . . and the thing is that you're not on good terms with them anyway are you?

Another man put it more succinctly:

> In rural life you have to be a little more forbearing; everybody knows everybody else.

However, the benefits of such forbearance may often be questionable. A sidelight on such a cautious attitude is that in three of the cases from our follow-up survey where the respondent had decided not to proceed, there was still, or had been, a high level of bad feeling between the parties involved, even though no action had been taken.

On the other hand, there were some people who would have liked to have had more opportunity to talk to someone, but could find no one to whom they could turn. One woman we interviewed felt that there was no one locally whom she could trust and, in her case, the CAB worker became a confidant as well as an informed advice giver. Another was a newcomer to the area, who had consulted the CAB in the first instance about local facilities, because she did not feel she knew anyone sufficiently well to obtain the information she really needed.

With respect to formal advice (B), our own data are derived mainly from two sources, CABx and solicitors. This was quite intentional as we were primarily interested in the availability of these options in rural areas. Even so, we also gained a number of illuminating insights into other aspects of the provision of formal advice and, because of the relevance of this information to the general model (Fig. 6.1), it is incorporated in the discussion that follows.

Individual, non-legally qualified, professionals

Non-legally qualified professionals in the local community emerged as relatively unimportant as advisers, which runs counter to popular myth but is in line with the findings from other studies elsewhere in the UK (Elliott, 1984). The most common immediate reactions of those needing more formal advice were, either to go to the local post office and see what leaflets were available, or to consult the local parish councillor. No one we interviewed had approached their local priest or schoolmaster for help with the issue under discussion, though one woman had asked her vicar for help in the past, but he had not been able to provide much assistance. Nevertheless, a number of respondents did cite the local vicar as someone who could be approached, if they were in difficulty. Many people mentioned their doctor as the person whom they would naturally consult over a medical problem, but no one indicated that they would refer to their doctor about non-medical issues. On the other hand, some professional people certainly see themselves as performing an essential generalist advice-giving role in rural areas, though on the evidence from the survey they probably overestimate the importance of their role in this regard. A doctor who was interviewed maintained that not only was he frequently asked for advice, he saw it as part of his duty as a professional man to provide it.

There are, however, certain categories of dispute, usually internal to a community, where people do take a conscious decision not to seek legal advice and in such cases the resources of the community itself can be important (Adamsdown Community Trust, 1978). Seven such issues emerged in our follow-up survey, six of which could loosely be classified as neighbour disputes and the other debt. In each case the person concerned decided, after consultation within the community, that it was not worth proceeding, their explanations falling into three distinct categories. One person decided that it was not worth the bother to continue. Two would have liked to continue, but were fearful of the costs of using a solicitor and taking legal action. The other four were all dissuaded from proceeding by the threat of being ostracised by the close-knit, rural community in which they lived.

The whole question of client attitudes to the cost of legal advice is discussed in more detail later in this chapter with reference to solicitors, but it is interesting to note that this fear of the unknown actually prevented some people from even trying to pursue a legal remedy. In one such case, the issue was a serious one where legal advice was much needed, but as the person involved rather bleakly put it:

> If I go to a solicitor, it's going to cost me money which I can ill afford. It's a case of if you have money you can fight it, if not, you can't.

Voluntary bodies

Voluntary bodies, such as Gingerbread and Cruse, were used by some respondents as an initial source of help in their search for legal advice and sometimes played a crucial role in allaying fears about the cost of consulting a solicitor and how best to choose one. In practice, as explained above, voluntary bodies often have difficulty in reaching out into rural areas, but, in the areas that they do cover, they serve an important function in signposting clients to where they may find professional help.

Grant-aided bodies

Of the grant-aided bodies CABx are the only ones offering anything more than a token service in rural areas, and, as they provide a generalist advice service, they cover a very wide range of issues. The service is also free and access is only limited by the capacity of bureaux to deal with enquiries. The results of our surveys showed that the details of the issues taken to CABx

varied widely, but that clients had firm views about their reasons
for turning to the service for help:

> Because they (the CAB) know you know; well they know quite
> a lot about everything don't they?

> I went there because of its name, the Citizens' Advice Bureau,
> the logic of the name persuaded me I suppose.

> The only people I could think of who would help.

> A bit like the Samaritans; you ring them up when you have a
> problem; you are aware they are there and they start you in
> the right direction.

The comparison with the Samaritans is an interesting one, for it is
clear that clients expect the same kind of strictly confidential
advice from the CABx, but, in addition, more concrete
suggestions about how to resolve their problems. A number of
people we interviewed were desperate for advice and
information and called into the CAB on the spur of the moment,
because they had heard about it through the media. The name
struck a chord as an organisation that could be consulted in an
emergency:

> I felt we couldn't go on. . . . I just thought I'd go in and see
> what they had to say.

Other respondents had much more specific questions in mind by
the time they consulted the CAB. They were already in dispute,
usually with a central or local government agency, like the DHSS
or the housing or social services departments, and wanted advice
about the best way of pursuing their case. They needed guidance
about where to go, who to see and what to say. In most cases,
they felt let down by the statutory agencies and required
independent advice about what they saw as their rights, as well
as support for continuing the fight. In general the expectation
was that by consulting the CAB, they would be better equipped
to stand up for themselves. It was not assumed initially that the
CAB would, or could, act on their behalf. Indeed, in only one
instance had a CAB acted as a mediator, the dispute in question
being with the owner of a shop over the sale of faulty goods.

The last, clearly identifiable, group, were those who saw
calling on the CAB either as a substitute for, or a first step

towards, consulting a solicitor. These people did not expect the CAB to be anything other than a staging post and, although their reasons varied in detail, all wanted to be sure of their ground before involving themselves in unknown or unwarranted costs, or in costs which they could not possibly afford. One respondent was particularly open about this:

> I asked them (the CAB) how much they'd (a solicitor) charge for an initial consultation, which is what the CAB worker was advising. He said not more than £25 to £30 if initial letters were involved, but not to quote him. This was helpful and useful and turned out to be right. It's less embarrassing than going in and asking the solicitor directly what he is going to charge.

Although nearly everyone knows about the CAB service and what it does, many people are loath to consult it and have taken a conscious decision not to do so. Their reasons range from outright hostility to the whole concept, to a feeling that it is a service for the poor. At one extreme, a respondent from a well-paid professional background described CAB staff as interfering do-gooders, who encourage discord and belligerence. He damned the service for the poor quality of the advice it offered and its lax administration, though, significantly, it transpired that he had never actually visited a CAB himself. Then there were those who believed that you got what you paid for and that by going to a solicitor you would receive higher quality, professional, advice than you would from a CAB:

> I always feel if you pay, hopefully they may give a little better advice.

> I think I'd go straight to a solicitor and get it from the top.

Some of the people who rejected the CABx service in favour of solicitors did so out of a sense of loyalty to existing contacts of long standing. They saw themselves as being served by a family firm of solicitors and automatically consulted it, on the basis that it was better to stay with the devil you know. Finally, there were those who felt that they were sufficiently well-off to be able to afford to pay for legal advice and that they should not deprive those, less fortunate than themselves, who might have no other option than to rely on a CAB.

Legal professionals

For most people the decision to seek professional legal advice and consult a solicitor is a momentous and, sometimes, a difficult one, signifying that they are taking the issue in question seriously and, in most cases, are prepared to invest money, time and energy in getting it resolved.

> My husband and I discussed it and we decided that going to a solicitor did seem the only way out. It really was a last resort.

Half of those reinterviewed in the follow-up survey had taken this step for issues ranging from litigation, to consumer problems, family matters and employment. For the majority, the main impetus was either a desire for a professional opinion on where they stood, or a firm belief that they would add weight to their case and bring it to a speedier conclusion by calling on the services of a solicitor. It is worth noting, however, that in one case involving the drawing up of a simple contract, the latter assumption turned out to be ill founded. The respondent's conclusion was that by going to a solicitor he had involved himself in unnecessary delay and extra cost, though there was no way of knowing how the solicitor might have responded to these criticisms.

Usually the decision to go to a solicitor was taken after consultation, though the precise form that this took varied widely. For some it meant no more than talking with other members of the family or with friends; for others it was taken after initial consultation with another professional person or with an organisation such as a CAB; while for a few the matter was effectively taken out of their hands and decided for them by their trade union or insurance company. Significantly, however, in only one instance was the decision in any sense viewed as routine and the person involved not only had business and social contacts with solicitors regularly through his job, but also was covered by legal expense insurance, which probably meant that he did not have to bear the direct cost of any consultations.

In general, people seem to choose a solicitor very much on the basis of a previous contact or personal recommendation, relying on limited and *ad hoc* information, with little evidence of the weighing up of possible alternatives. Those who already had dealings with a solicitor in the past, usually for quite different purposes, tended to use the same person. Typical comments were:

> He knows who I am, and I know him.

> There was no choice as such. It was a person I had used before and I used him again.

Others relied on the recommendations of friends, or, less commonly, on advice from voluntary bodies, a CAB, or another professional person, such as an accountant. There were a few who had had nothing to do with the solicitor chosen in his professional capacity, but had met him under quite different circumstances. He might have been known to them as a customer or client of their own and they simply decided to reciprocate the contact. Sometimes even the most chance and ephemeral of contacts were seized upon in a moment of stress:

> I needed to know where I stood and I was a bit uncertain what I should do. I didn't feel like just picking up the 'phone and ringing one up from the Yellow Pages. I'd met this solicitor at a friend's party so I rang him up; I was emotional, I didn't know quite what to say, it was a nice way to do it, I knew his name.

All those interviewed in the follow-up survey who had used a solicitor had been under stress to some degree and their main aim was to reduce this. Any suggestion that they might not have made an optimal decision tended, therefore, to be suppressed. For example, one woman chose a solicitor thinking she had used him before, but realised, after she had entered the office, that she had made a mistake and that it was a different person. She was confused and embarrassed by her mistake, but instead of simply apologising and walking out, she still continued with the consultation.

One group using solicitors that does form a rather special, and separate, category, is those people on whose behalf a solicitor is consulted through some intermediate agency. The most common occurrence of this nature is an insurance company engaging a solicitor to fight a case on behalf of one of their clients. Clearly it is for just such a contingency that insurance is taken out in the first place and there are a number of clear-cut advantages in matters being arranged in this way, the most important being that the insurance company will know of those solicitors with the appropriate expertise. From the point of view of the client, however, there is sometimes a danger of disenchantment setting in, because he or she is not directly involved with the litigation.

The other main example of a solicitor being engaged on behalf of a client is when a trade union or professional association becomes involved with an issue and calls on the services of their own legal department. In rural areas the National Farmers' Union is very important in this regard and our survey revealed clearly that farmers value greatly the high quality of the legal advice it provides. In this situation there is less danger of the client coming to feel manipulated, as he or she will have originated the action, even though it is being pursued through an intermediate agency.

Statutory bodies

Our survey was not specifically designed to examine the advice provided by statutory bodies, such as the police, the DHSS or local government departments. Nevertheless, many of these agencies had been involved in the issues we were studying and comments from respondents shed some interesting light on the way they are regarded.

In only two cases had respondents had any direct dealings with the police. In one, the person concerned was surprised how little help was offered in suggesting what action should be taken after a traffic accident in which he alleged he was the innocent party. In the other, a woman found the attitude of the police equivocal in relation to a neighbour dispute. An officer she approached said that there was little he could do, but suggested she contacted the local environmental health officer, while a second officer refused to get involved at all as no criminal offence had been committed.

Obviously there is no way of knowing how typical these reactions may or may not be, but since one of the 'functions' of the police is to 'befriend anyone who needs their help and to cope with emergencies, both major and minor' (Royal Commission, 1962: 22), they do indicate that some policemen interpret their role rather narrowly. It is not clear whether this attitude reflects official, police authority, policy, though it would seem to imply a move away from the kind of 'community policing' pioneered in Devon and Cornwall in the mid-1970s. With the exception of personal initiative taken by the constable at Hartland referred to earlier (see pp. 121–22), there was no evidence of the police providing an advice service, let alone a legal advice service, in the sense referred to in our survey.

Advice had been sought from various local authority departments, including, at county council level, trading standards and social services, and, at district council level, environmental health and housing. Experience naturally varied depending on the department and the circumstances, but a universal difficulty, which our survey unearthed, was how to contact the right person in the right department. Communication problems are particularly difficult in rural areas, such as the three parishes in our survey, where people are living in places remote from the offices concerned. For instance, the nearest trading standards office to someone living in St Keverne is in Truro 47 km away. For the most part, these problems of access loomed much larger for our respondents than complaints about the actual quality of advice received.

Courts and tribunals

No one we interviewed had sought advice directly from a court, or tribunal, although magistrates' clerks and other court officials are often approached by members of the public about how to obtain legal advice. The only comments about advice dispensed through the court system related to the county court small claims procedure, which enables the public to recover small debts without engaging solicitors or other formal legal assistance. Several people had explanatory leaflets about this service, though in some cases they appeared not to have always fully understood their contents. One woman respondent, for instance, thought she could not initiate proceedings because the debt exceeded £500. She was surprised, and not a little annoyed, to discover subsequently that she could have pursued the claim in the county court herself without engaging the services of a solicitor. Such a breakdown in communication serves to emphasise the widespread lack of complete and accurate information about access to legal remedies and legal services among the general public.

Legal Competence

The extent to which people are able to perceive a legal dimension and a potential legal solution to an issue depends on many factors, including: their legal qualifications, if any; their access to relatives and friends who have undergone legal training; the degree to which they have absorbed information about legal matters from their reading and from the media; and their previous contacts with the law and advice services.

None of those interviewed were professional lawyers, but more than half claimed to have some legal knowledge. The form and source of such knowledge varied greatly. Most commonly it derived from having access to family or close friends with legal expertise, or from having worked in a solicitor's office, but people had also obtained legal information through their work and hobbies. A number of people also claimed that they sought legal advice from other professionals, such as accountants, with whom they had regular dealings. It was significant that a minority of respondents believed firmly that talking informally to friends and neighbours was as good a way as any of gaining legal and most other sorts of advice. They appeared to be suspicious of the law and legal professionals, believing that they were unlikely to produce the most appropriate solutions for their personal problems.

In order to gain some measure of the legal awareness of those living in rural areas, in the follow-up survey we probed in detail about the extent to which people had tried to improve their legal expertise through books, leaflets and other published materials, as well as through television and radio. It emerged that very few people had ever used, let alone relied on, any published materials. Only one person had tried to check her legal situation in a book (an aunt's copy of *Know Your Rights*), though four people owned legal encyclopaedias, even if they had not used them to resolve their current issue. A more important source of published advice was trade journals and other magazines containing legal information. Most important of these was the Consumers' Association journal, *Which?*, read by six people regularly and by a further 11 occasionally, while the *Reader's Digest* was also quite important. Advice gained in this way was not, however, necessarily treated as conclusive. One business-man explained that he found trade journals useful, but that he would always consult a solicitor to check about any specific problem.

Greater reliance seemed to be placed on published leaflets, but several people commented on the difficulties involved in obtaining such information in villages. The post office was generally viewed as the most obvious and convenient outlet, though opinions varied as to how well subpostmasters and sub-postmistresses were presently performing their public inform-ation role. One respondent had picked up a leaflet at the post office, but it had only told her how to contact the nearest CAB or DHSS office, rather than offering any specific advice. Another person, who had no transport of her own, felt that much more effective use could be made of the post office in her village. Only a very narrow range of information leaflets was displayed and she felt the aim should be to have as many leaflets as possible available as a public service. More generally, there were several people who saw the main value of the post office as a place where information could be exchanged, since everybody used it:

> In a small place like this people in the post office are very useful. It's such a small place and they know everybody; I've heard them telling the old dears.

An alternative suggestion to the post office was that more use could be made of the mobile library to bring advice and information to people living in rural areas, though many of the same limitations would apply to this service as well.

The level of recall of television and radio programmes providing useful information on legal matters was very limited. Few respondents could remember specific programmes, let alone actual advice. The only example of either service providing direct assistance was a woman who heard an item about the CAB on local radio, which led her to call into the bureau when she was passing to discuss an issue she was very worried about and which she felt she could not discuss with anyone local.

In order to probe more deeply into people's viewing and listening habits, we decided to use prompts and ask in more detail about a selected list of nationally networked programmes, in which we were particularly interested. Of the television programmes (Table 6.1), all but four of the follow-up sample watched *That's Life* 'occasionally' and over half 'quite often'. There were eleven respondents who could immediately recall a legal item they had seen and, of these, five claimed to have found the information personally useful. However, several people had a strong aversion to *That's Life* and certainly did not consider it a useful source of advice.

Table 6.1 Check-list of TV/radio programmes and of respondents' viewing/listening habits (source: follow-up sample).

Question: How often do you watch/listen to these programmes?

	Most programmes	Quite often	Occasionally	Never
TV				
That's Life	10	9	10	4
Watchdog	3	9	10	12
For What it's Worth	2	3	10	18
Out of Court	0	4	8	20
Advice Line	1	1	4	26
Radio				
Jimmy Young Show	4	3	8	17
Countywide (Radio Devon)	4	2	5	21
You and Yours	1	5	4	22
Cornwall Daily	2	1	6	23
Law in Action	1	2	0	29
You and Me (Devon Air)	1	1	1	29

The radio emerged as being far less pervasive than television with nearly half of those interviewed claiming never to listen to any programme with a legal content. The most popular programme was the *Jimmy Young Show*, which was listened to 'quite often' or even more frequently by six people, while a further eight listened to it 'occasionally' (Table 6.1). Listeners generally judged the programme enjoyable and informative and they were quick to identify it as legal, presumably because of the comfortable family solicitor image portrayed by the 'legal eagle'. There was little difference in the number of items which respondents could remember and had found useful on radio and television, but, interestingly, recall of detail was much greater for radio programmes. For instance, when asked if they had heard of the county court small claims procedure, several people volunteered that it had been brought to their attention by the *Jimmy Young Show*. Finally, it should be noted that for a minority of people local radio was seen as an important source of information and advice.

Reference to the small claims procedure was included as a separate item to try and obtain some more specific information about levels of legal awareness. The results showed that only two people had never heard of it and the majority (26) gave a broadly accurate description of its function. Two respondents had actually used the procedure successfully, five had received information about it from either the local CAB, the trading standards office or a solicitor, and, as mentioned above, two had heard about it from the *Jimmy Young Show*.

Overall, people's knowledge of legal services may be described, at best, as patchy. For the most part they rely on chance contacts and snippets of information gleaned from almost any source that happens to be available. What is patently lacking is any evidence of systematic legal education, or of training in how to get the best from the available legal services. It is a gap which the Law Society's education programme in secondary schools may help to fill in the future.

Communication and Travel

Over a decade ago Malcolm Moseley depicted accessibility as the rural challenge (1979) and, even though that might now be considered somewhat over-simplistic and limiting, accessibility is an enduring problem. Levels of car-ownership, the scope, frequency and cost of public transport, and the availability of telephones all affect significantly the degree to which people living in rural areas are able to take advantage of services that are mostly centrally located.

Access to a car

According to the 1981 census, more than 20 per cent of households in Chulmleigh, Hartland and St Keverne had no car, which meant that a lack of mobility was a widespread problem. Our survey broadly confirmed this figure, but also revealed that for certain groups the restrictions were particularly severe. Two-thirds of all the women questioned did not have direct access to a car and were dependent on public transport or other people if they needed to travel away from the immediate confines of the village where they lived.

The women fell into two distinct groups, pensioners and married women with children. The pensioners who were married and still living with their husbands experienced very little difficulty, other than the fact that they were entirely dependent on their husbands to drive them if they could not do so themselves. However, elderly women living on their own faced serious, almost overwhelming, problems. In one case, for example, a pensioner described how she was entirely dependent, either on getting lifts with friends in the village, or on the local bus service. Neither really offered an adequate solution, particularly as she was in poor health. She explained that getting a lift was complicated and not always feasible, because many of the younger people in the village shared lifts so as to reduce their travelling expenses. As a result there was often no seat available. The women with free space in their cars tended to be older and were more often than not farmers' wives who lived outside the village itself, making it inconvenient for them to come and collect her. Using the bus service also presented her with great difficulties. Not only was the service itself infrequent, the fares into the neighbouring town were more than she could afford, except on special occasions:

> I can't go very well because I don't always have the money. I'd like to feel that it were less expensive; that I could, say once a month, have a little treat and go in, but you've got to do what you can and budget. You've got to budget haven't you? That's all there is isn't it?

The limitations facing married women with children were almost equally severe. One woman, whose husband required the family's van for work, described her plight as follows:

It's alright if you have a car, but if you rely on people driving you it's 18 miles to Barnstaple and 36 there and back. You've got to pay petrol, get someone to give you a lift, and arrange for someone to look after the children.

In another case, the husband would have had to use part of his holiday entitlement to take his wife to the nearest town during working hours. Neither felt this worth while and she had simply given up making the journey. She had last gone five or six years ago:

If I need anything I ring up or write; it's too much trouble to get there.

It was quite clear from these, and similar, comments, that anyone without ready access to a car was very limited in terms of their contacts outside the immediate locality. This imposed restrictions on all kinds of activities, including the ability to obtain expert and independent advice.

Access to a telephone

The main alternative to making a personal visit to seek advice is to telephone. Since 90 per cent of those interviewed had their own telephone, this was clearly feasible in the majority of cases, even though it is difficult to be as sensitive to individual requirements when one is not dealing with a person face-to-face. Misunderstandings can arise more easily and, in any case it is often necessary to scrutinise documents during the interview. There are sometimes also additional problems of privacy and cost, which can inhibit people from using the telephone even in their own homes. In any case, many of those people without telephones are also those without access to cars, so that they are doubly deprived. Two of the women in the follow-up survey were in this situation, both married with young children, as was a young man living with his parents. He had faced a particularly difficult situation, when trying to settle an insurance claim after a motorcycle accident. In all three cases the people concerned were dependent either on using a payphone or asking a neighbour if they could use their telephone. Neither option was very satisfactory: the payphones were frequently out of order or jammed full of coins, and there was an inevitable lack of privacy telephoning from another person's home.

Contacting a CAB or a solicitor

For most people contacting a CAB or a solicitor was a relatively straightforward matter, in that they used their own cars and in only a single instance did the journey exceed 40 minutes. In most cases in the past, they had managed to combine the visits with other errands, although for nearly all those visiting a solicitor it had been the chief purpose of the journey. No one could recall that the interview had been at a time that was inconvenient; only two people had had to make any special arrangements to keep the appointment; and only one person had actually lost income through having to take time off, though several of the self-employed men pointed out that they had lost time and that, for them, time was money.

Nevertheless, the general air of satisfaction surrounding the replies of those who had actually used a CAB or solicitor must be tempered by the serious difficulties facing many of those who had not. In the follow-up survey there were nine people who for one reason or another had not been able to make a personal visit. Four were some of the women described above, who had restricted access to a car, and three were self-employed men, who could not afford the time to travel to the nearest town during working hours. One man estimated that, even by car, a visit would have cost him the equivalent of half a day's work. In only a single case was the telephone seen as an adequate substitute and this man went out of his way to explain how invaluable it was to have a solicitor who was willing to give advice and take instructions over the telephone.

On closer investigation it emerged that access to the CABx was more of a problem than that to solicitors, the main reasons being their limited distribution and also the restricted opening hours of the bureaux, a common feature of CABx in rural areas. For most it was merely inconvenient, but for others it posed more fundamental problems. One woman we interviewed had written to the CAB instead, but two other people decided to abandon trying to seek advice. There was no consensus about what the ideal pattern of opening would be, but a significant minority felt that evening sessions would be a great help.

There was ample evidence from the survey that access is a serious problem for many people living in remote rural areas, especially women, the old, the poor and, to some extent, men in work. For most people the difficulties are not insuperable, but they are trying and costly to overcome. It is also hard for the providers of services, like the CABx, to be sufficiently flexible with resources that are already overstretched to meet adequately the needs of small disadvantaged groups found within scattered rural populations.

THE USE AND NON-USE OF LEGAL SERVICES

Solicitors

Well over half the sample of the general public selected from the parishes of Chulmleigh and Hartland in Devon and St Keverne in Cornwall had called on the services of a solicitor during the period that they had lived in these remote rural parts of south-west England, although there were considerable variations in the levels of use between different social groups (Table 6.2).

Table 6.2 The number of issues taken to a solicitor during the period that the respondent had been resident in Chulmleigh, Hartland and St Keverne, according to selected socio-economic groupings (in %). (Source: First Parish Survey, n = 355.)

	None	One	Two	Three	Four or more
Owner-occupiers	31	31	19	6	13
Non-owner-occupiers	62	21	11	3	3
Farmers	24	18	8	13	37
Employees	46	25	14	10	5
Car-owners	41	27	15	6	11
Non-car-owners	43	32	23	1	1
Men	35	29	13	8	15
Women	46	27	19	3	5

The subgroups are not mutually exclusive

Almost two-thirds of the respondents who did not own their own homes, for example, had never seen a solicitor, while the equivalent figure for owner-occupiers was less than one-third. Furthermore, owner-occupiers were much more likely to have used a solicitor more than once. The figures illustrate the importance of solicitors to those with property, a point that is underlined by heavy use that is made of solicitors by farmers, more than a third of whom had used a solicitor on over four separate occasions. In general, there is little difference between car-owners and non-car-owners, although the former are more likely to have called on the services of a solicitor on more than one occasion. Nearly half the women questioned had never consulted a solicitor, compared with only a third of the men; and employees were much less likely to have done so than employers, the self-employed or the retired.

The link between the ownership of property and money and the frequency with which solicitors are consulted is inescapable and was described in the following terms by a former tenant who had just bought his council house:

> When you are a council-tenant you have no need of a solicitor. It is only when you become a house-owner that you require one. I will need one next when I make a will.

Professional legal advice is clearly heavily weighted in this direction and would appear to be perceived as having less to offer other groups. To some extent, this simply reflects the relative ability of clients to pay for what in most civil matters is essentially a private service, but it also illustrates graphically that the kinds of problem faced by those without money tend, quite arbitrarily, not to be seen as legal problems.

For the bulk of those living in rural areas, however, consulting a solicitor is an infrequent, but not unusual, occurrence. More than two-thirds of the 209 respondents in the initial survey who had used a solicitor had done so within the previous five years and 36 per cent had done so in the previous 12 months. Most had always used the same firm, but 15 per cent had consulted several firms on different issues.

The kinds of issue about which solicitors were most frequently consulted in the three parishes in Cornwall and Devon involved a relatively narrow range of legal work. Property accounted for nearly half (46%), followed by wills (24%), business (10%), litigation (9%) and family (6%). Everything else, which included general advice, crime, consumer matters, tax and money, motoring, welfare and employment, amounted to only 5 per cent of the total. Within that overall pattern, as can be seen from Table 6.3, there were, nevertheless, some significant variations in the distribution of work among different social groups.

Table 6.3 The distribution of legal work among selected social groups (in %). (Source: First Parish Survey, n = 355.)

	Property	Wills	Business	Litigation	Family
Owner-occupiers	50	22	11	8	4
Non-owner-occupiers	13	14	3	7	7
Self-employed	50	3	25	5	6
Unemployed	–	8	–	8	8
Professional	46	15	15	31	–
Farmers	55	45	24	8	5
Employees	38	5	15	10	6
18–39-year-olds	33	5	7	12	6
40–59-year-olds	42	17	11	7	7
60-year-olds and over	27	22	5	5	2
Men	46	18	13	12	4
Women	35	21	5	4	6

The subgroups are not mutually exclusive.

The relationship between the ownership of property and the likelihood of a person having consulted a solicitor has already been noted, but those living in owner-occupied property were also more likely to consult a solicitor over their wills or on a business matter. Indeed, matrimonial and family issues were the only types of case over which non-owner-occupiers were more likely to consult a solicitor than those in owner-occupied houses. If the type of issue is broken down by the respondent's occupation considerable variations are also apparent. The groups most frequently seeking professional legal advice on property issues were farmers (55%), the self-employed (50%) and professional people (46%), but none of those who were unemployed had done so. Farmers again headed the list (45%) of those who had consulted a solicitor about their will; there appeared to be a marked reluctance among other groups to do so, with only 3 per cent of the self-employed, 15 per cent of professional people and 5 per cent of employees having taken legal advice on this crucial issue. In terms of age, those between 40 and 59 generally made much greater use of solicitors than the younger and older groups, although 18 to 39-year-olds made the largest demands in family matters, and those over 60 did the same for wills. Finally, the men interviewed in the survey were more likely to have used a solicitor than the women, although a larger proportion of the latter had sought legal advice about about both wills and family matters.

The pattern of use of solicitors revealed by the survey in these remote areas of south-west England differs little in broad outline from the national picture. There are, however, two important features that need to be highlighted. On the one hand, it is striking to note the heavy reliance that the farming community places on access to legal advice; and, on the other, the fact that almost no use seems to be made of the legal profession for advice in what may broadly be termed the area of welfare law. It follows that there are many people living in such rural areas who are cut off from legal advice in important areas of their lives, though it is less clear whether they perceive themselves as being deprived as a consequence.

When choosing which solicitor to consult, ready physical access was clearly the overriding criterion for most people. They tended to use solicitors in the market town nearest to their village, especially those living in St Keverne and Hartland, both of which are on the coast and have relatively poor road links with neighbouring towns. In Chulmleigh the picture is somewhat different. Here, there are two part-time solicitors' branch offices in the village itself and there is a choice of accessible towns. Interestingly, 40 per cent of those using a solicitor still used a firm in the nearest market town of South Molton, even though it is quite small with a population of under 10,000. Firms in the regional centre of Barnstaple, which is equally well connected to Chulmleigh by public transport and is only a few kilometres further away, were used by 25 per cent, but only 9 per cent used the firms in the village itself. Clearly convenience and the possibility of being able to fit a visit to the solicitor in with other errands are important factors governing choice, but for many people convenience does not override a reluctance to use a firm within the confines of their own small community for fear of a breach of confidentiality.

A sidelight on the whole question of access is the fact that well over half of those interviewed first got in touch with their solicitor by telephone, although in most cases a personal visit had been necessary at some stage. In other words the actual location of the office was not such a material consideration. However, telephone use varied markedly with age: 80 per cent of 18 to 39-year-olds used it to make the initial contact, compared with 65 per cent of those between 40 and 59, and only 41 per cent of those aged 60 and above. Habits in this regard would appear to be in the process of undergoing a substantial change and one which is to the benefit of those living in rural areas.

Despite the undoubted importance of ease of access, considerable inertia still surrounds the way in which people choose a solicitor. Nearly half of those questioned had relied on the recommendation of a member of their family or a friend, many using the person they regarded as the family solicitor. The advice of building societies and estate agents was also very influential. In contrast, the only evidence of direct advertising by the solicitors themselves having any effect on client choice was the 2 per cent of respondents who had found their solicitor through the Yellow Pages.

A further indication of the relatively conservative attitude to legal services was the very small proportion (5%) of respondents who had ever made use of the legal services of a trade union or professional body, even though they were aware of this option. The following comments are typical of the attitudes revealed by the survey:

> If I was in any real trouble I would go to Marks and Spencer where I used to work. When I left, they said I could use them if I got into any difficulties.

> We have not used the services of the NFU, but I am not saying

that we wouldn't use them. We know they are there and feel we can use them, but we haven't made use of them yet.

There are clearly a number of factors which combine to make people cautious, the most important of which are a general lack of familiarity with the law and lawyers and a fear of costs. Many respondents felt that they had been inhibited by a lack of information in making their choice. For instance, one woman who had required advice about how to go about collecting a bad debt had tried in vain to find a solicitor specialising in this area of work:

> That is something that really did annoy us. We wanted to find one that was used to dealing with debts and we couldn't find out that information. I 'phoned several different firms of solicitors asking if there was anyone specialising in debt and I didn't get a sensible answer from any of them. They all hedged and said 'well, we do everything'. That was not what I wanted to hear. I wanted to hear that they had got Mr. So and So who was an expert in collecting debts.

This woman, together with a number of other respondents, strongly advocated solicitors being encouraged to advertise their specialisms:

> I think if they had a little bit in a shop window or newspaper, or even the telephone directory, saying what they specialise in, I really do think that that would help an awful lot of people, for you really do have to look for a needle in a haystack don't you?

Others were more resigned to the problem, accepting that word of mouth was the only way to disseminate such information:

> I think it's very difficult. It's like any professional person, you've almost got to go on personal recommendation I think. That's what I would rely on in the final analysis.

However, a number of respondents recognised the element of luck involved:

> I didn't know anything about solicitors. I was lucky and got a good one who cared and understood. I might have been unlucky.

> Until you've used one, you don't know much about it. It's trial and error or advice from someone I suppose.

A few people, especially those who had a family solicitor, approached the firm they had always used, assuming that if their own solicitor was not competent to deal with the matter, it would be passed on to someone else in the firm who was. However, in rural areas a belief that the work would be passed to someone with the requisite competence may not necessarily be very well placed (Blacksell, Economides and Watkins, 1987).

The other major bone of contention was costs, and uncertainty about the potential liability they were incurring had deterred a number of people from actually seeking legal advice. Very few people thought that their solicitor had discussed the likely costs with them adequately at the beginning of their case, and several complained that the whole question had been deliberately avoided:

> Solicitors don't go out of their way to make it easy to discuss costs during the event.

Another important aspect of the whole air of uncertainty surrounding the question of costs was the way it inhibited people from changing a solicitor they believed to be unsatisfactory, thus reinforcing the general climate of inflexibility:

> The trouble is, once you're with a particular solicitor it costs a lot of money to say I'm not satisfied and I'm going to someone else.

Citizens' Advice Bureaux

None of the parishes in the survey had a CAB, so that anyone wanting to make use of the service had to travel at least as far as the neighbouring market town. In the case of St Keverne this was Helston (10.6 miles (17 km) away), though individuals had gone as far as Penzance (21.9 miles (35 km) away), Camborne (19.4 miles (31 km) away) and even Plymouth (66.3 miles (106 km) away); from Hartland everyone had travelled to Bideford (11.9 miles (19 km) away), with the exception of one man who had gone to Barnstaple (20 miles (32 km) away); and from Chulmleigh most people went to Barnstaple (15.6 miles (25 km) away), but a few chose South Molton (10 miles (16 km) away) and one woman Exeter (19.4 miles (31 km) away). Nevertheless, virtually everyone questioned had heard of the CAB service and had a fairly clear idea of the service it offered, although only a small minority (15%) had actually made use of it and only seven respondents (2%) had done so on more than a single occasion.

Most of the respondents who had consulted a CAB had done so in person, calling in at the bureau while they were in town for other reasons. Usually the visit was pre-planned, although a few people had simply dropped in on the spur of the moment when passing, suddenly seeing the possibility of help with an unresolved issue. There was clearly a strong preference for a personal visit, as five of the six people in the follow-up survey, who contacted the CAB by telephone or in writing, specifically said that they would have gone in person but for transportation problems or the inconvenience of the opening hours.

The types of client using the CABx were very different from those using solicitors, probably being unemployed, under 40 and not house owners. They were also seeking advice on other kinds of matter, though the results of the survey revealed quite sharp variations between the three parishes (Table 6.4).

Table 6.4 The main catagories of issue taken to CABx (%). (Source: First Parish Survey, n = 355.)

	Chumleigh	Hartland	St Keverne	Total
Tax and money	26	9	15	17
Consumer	9	15	15	13
Welfare	9	24	5	13
Business	13	9	10	10
Employment	9	9	5	8
Family	13	5	–	6
Property	4	5	10	6
Litigation £500	4	–	10	5
Accommodation	–	9	5	5
Health advice	–	5	5	3
Other	4	5	15	8
Not given	9	5	5	6

In Chulmleigh, tax and money, business and family issues dominated; in Hartland, consumer and welfare issues; while in St Keverne there was a much broader spread, with tax and money, consumer, business, property and litigation all showing as quite important issues. Overall, however, and the size of the sample makes it difficult to be too categoric about the patterns of use in the individual parishes, other than to confirm that social issues predominate, rather than those relating to property and estates as was the case with those people consulting solicitors.

In the follow-up survey, the whole question of the nature of the advice being sought from the CAB service was examined in much greater detail. Nearly half of those people consulting a CAB simply required information. For the rest, the CAB helped in one of two ways. Either the worker acted in a signposting role, advising the client where to go for suitable advice and alerting him or her to any potential pitfalls, such as the cost of a solicitor; or, in a few cases, the worker actually negotiated with a third party on a client's behalf. In one case this involved contacting a government department, in the other bringing a consumer complaint to a successful conclusion. All the bureaux used a legal rota of local solicitors, rather than operating a system of specialist HLAs for particular areas of law. However, the developing liaison between CABx and solicitors in private practice was illustrated by the CAB worker who actually recommended a specific solicitor to one of the respondents, because the solicitor in question was known to specialise in employment law.

The reasons most frequently cited for choosing to go to a CAB was that the respondent already knew about it (39%), or had been recommended to go by a friend (21%), but, in contrast to solicitors, advertising and the Yellow Pages (25%) were also important sources of information. Nevertheless, there was also considerable confusion on the part of a minority of those questioned about what the service had to offer or where to find the nearest office.

Attitudes towards the two sources of legal advice were also sharply at odds with one another. People felt very much easier about simply calling in at a CAB than at a solicitor's office; over two-thirds (67%) of those who had used CABx had made their initial contact in person, rather than by telephone. For the most part clients were very pleased with the service they had received from the CABx, valuing the high quality of the advice and certainly not considering it a second-rate service. When they were asked to itemise the good and bad points of the CAB service most of the respondents were full of praise. Descriptions like 'helpful', 'effective', 'efficient', 'sympathetic' and 'good listeners' were legion, as were comments about the fact that the service was free. One man summarised his reaction as follows:

> Free advice, good advice, and someone to talk to.

Another respondent summed up the role of the CAB as

> a particular middleman kind of function. They have never actually been able to offer the absolute advice one wants but they have been a springboard from where you can go on.

Over a third of the respondents could not think of even a single bad point, but those criticisms that were voiced could be grouped into three broad categories:

1. The poor quality of the accommodation, though this was often excused, because the respondent appreciated that CABx are grant-aided bodies:

    > They could do with better premises, but that's not their fault.

    In some instances the difficulties posed by the premises were serious, as when stairs impeded access for the elderly and infirm, and a lack of privacy impeded free discussion. One woman, who had been discussing a very sensitive issue, complained that:

    > People kept diving through the interview room as I was talking.

2. Several respondents mentioned how difficult they found it to remember irregular, part-time, opening hours and the fact that it was not easy to see the same worker again quickly, since most only did one or two three-hour sessions a week. This all made planning visits difficult if anything other than a routine enquiry were involved and was particularly irksome for anyone who had to travel some distance to the bureau.

3. There were a few complaints about the actual quality of the advice given, though none were very vehement. As mentioned above, two women objected to the CAB workers

reformulating issues in terms that were different from their own perceptions of them. Others felt that more advice could have been given on the spot, rather than their being referred elsewhere:

> I might have expected more from them; they only seem to have as much knowledge as I have in some areas. Do they have any training?

Even so this particular respondent was generally complimentary, appreciating how receptive the CAB workers were to information from their clients:

> They're interested in learning the answer if they don't know – interested and helpful.

Rejection of a Legal Remedy

One of the most difficult issues surrounding the whole question of the need for legal services is the extent to which there is a latent demand for legal advice. Everyone at some time or another has to cope with issues where legal advice could be sought, but where, for one reason or another, such a course is not followed.

To try and assess the extent of the latent demand for professional legal services, the respondents in our survey were asked if they had ever been faced with an issue where they had thought of consulting a solicitor, but then decided against doing so. The majority of people answered 'no' to the question, but a minority (9%), drawn mainly from the professional and business communities, recognised that they had faced this dilemma. The issues involved were of a number of different kinds, including property, family, neighbour disputes, wills, debts, litigation, but invariably the other parties were closely connected to the respondent. The main reason given for not taking legal advice was that the problem was solved before this could be done, but other explanations were: that the issue was not worth consulting a solicitor about; that solicitors were too expensive; that there was internal dissension within the family about whether or not to take legal advice; and that there was a reluctance to do so because of previous experience of solicitors.

Whether or not a person takes legal advice is, of course, a

personal matter, but some of the issues involved were potentially very serious so that the decision not to proceed could have had important consequences. For instance, one man described how he had fallen off some scaffolding while at work and had wanted to claim compensation for physical injury from his employers, but had decided against doing so because he thought it would cost too much in relation to what he would have received. More than half of those who had decided against taking legal advice had not discussed the question with anyone else, but a number had taken a conscious decision to seek advice elsewhere. In the event this very often turned out to be somewhat unsatisfactory, as in the case of the man who had been in dispute with his neighbour about a hedge of fast-growing trees on his boundary. He had consulted a landscape gardener, who had described what the trees would look like when they were mature and how they might affect the foundations of his house, but this gave him no help in finding out what rights he had in the matter.

The most significant fact to emerge about this group of issues was that more than half were unresolved. In some cases it was a question of just putting off the evil day:

> I'll have to go to a solicitor eventually [about a divorce], but I keep putting it off because I have found them unhelpful. The CAB helped up to a point, but you have got to go to a solicitor in the end.

In other instances, however, the issue was circumvented:

> We have had a boundary dispute and didn't consult a solicitor, because it would be impossible to prove (we have had previous experience of this kind of problem). The issue was resolved by our moving house.

There is no way of knowing the extent to which the fact that the respondents in the survey lived in remote rural areas determined whether or not they took legal advice, but for virtually everyone it was clearly seen as a serious step and one that was likely to have significant consequences for their relationships with the other parties involved. For most people too it was a step into the unknown, for, even when they had had previous dealings with a solicitor, it had usually involved a routine matter and not a dispute. Undoubtedly, the fact that they lived a long way from the nearest solicitor and that they were unsure of questions like potential costs, were deterrents, which undermined their confidence and prevented them seeking professional legal advice.

IMPROVING ACCESS TO LEGAL SERVICES

Most people were pleased with the quality of the legal and the para-legal advice they had received (Jenkins *et al*, 1989, 1990). For CABx, on a four-point scale, 88 per cent of respondents were 'very pleased' or 'satisfied', and only 12 per cent were either 'not very satisfied' or 'very unhappy'. The picture was much the same for solicitors and, on the same scale, 77 per cent were 'very pleased' or 'satisfied' and only 23 per cent 'not very satisfied' or 'very unhappy'. However, the very limited previous knowledge of either informal or professional sources of legal advice which most people actually had meant that expectations were frequently unrealistic and suggestions for improvements to services somewhat vague and heavily biased towards the respondents' own personal concerns, with little appreciation of the practical constraints on the provision of legal and advice services in remote rural areas.

In order to test reactions to possible ways of extending legal services, opinions were sought on three schemes that are already operating elsewhere in the UK: a Freefone to an advice agency, enabling anyone to telephone the agency free of charge for advice; an official village link person, who would be a volunteer chosen by the local community and available to help anyone obtain appropriate advice; and a publicly funded law centre, staffed by professional lawyers offering a free legal service.

The idea of a Freefone scheme was generally welcomed, with most people claiming that, if it were available, they would use it themselves and that they could see others in their village doing so, not least because of the anonymity of such a scheme. Nevertheless, some respondents, all with telephones, questioned whether it would be a sensible use of resources, as the cost of making a telephone call never deterred anyone. The reaction from the minority of those without a telephone was very different:

> It's a bit of a pain going to a 'phone box. . . . First of all going to the post office for a pound of 10p coins and then going to the box and finding its jammed. It's a big thing making a 'phone call when you haven't much money.

> Phone calls cost quite a lot and it takes so long to get through and then you get through to someone and they put you through to someone else.

Reactions to a link person were more mixed. On the one hand, a number of respondents were suspicious, feeling that it could never be fully confidential in a village environment and that it would be a recipe for gossip:

> I doubt if you'd get anyone to go. . . you only need to blow your nose here and everyone knows. . . no one would believe it would be confidential.

> It depends on who the person is; in villages it's quite a close community, I'd feel she might 'phone up her friend up the road.

> I wouldn't want anyone to know I'd got problems.

On the other hand, others thought that it would be much more convenient to have an initial contact in the village and that it would formalise advice-seeking arrangements that already existed. However, strong views were expressed as to who the link person should be. Men were preferred to women, particularly retired professionals or businessmen already holding positions in the village, such as parish councillor or school governor. A number of people were strongly in favour of someone who had lived in the community for some time, but who had also lived and worked elsewhere in the past. Finally, great emphasis was put on the person being approachable and entirely trustworthy.

There was a cautious welcome from most respondents for the idea of a law centre, but, as no one had any direct experience of such a service, there was great uncertainty about how helpful it might prove to be. There was also a feeling that public funds would never be available for such a costly service in a rural area with a small and scattered population. The likely frequency of visits also caused concern, several respondents commenting that the lawyers might well not be contactable at the crucial time they were urgently required.

All three schemes would, of course, have to be paid for, but only a small minority of respondents thought that the users should finance them directly. Most were in favour of central or local government, or charities, footing the bill. One person, reacting to the suggestion of there being a law centre, summed up pithily a widely held view:

The main thing is it's free.

BARRIERS TO JUSTICE

People living in rural areas have to contend with a number of special difficulties, which inhibit the ease with which they are able to gain access to, and use, all kinds of services, including legal advice, whether it be from solicitors and other professional lawyers or from para-legal agencies such as CABx. For the most part these difficulties stem from the intrinsic remoteness of the countryside, which dictates that people have to expend more time, money and energy, if they are to benefit from any of the services that are ordinarily available to those living in towns and cities. It follows that any of those groups in rural society that are short of one or more of these commodities is in danger of being deprived.

In part isolation from legal and other services is a price that people have chosen to pay for the benefits of being able to live in rural surroundings, but by no means everyone living in country villages does so from choice. The young have usually grown up there, and the elderly grown old there, through force of circumstance, rather than as a result of any deliberate choice on the part of the individuals concerned. In any case, it seems unjust that anyone should be permanently penalised for a decision that was almost certainly taken under quite different circumstances at a different stage in their life.

It also needs to be remembered that access to legal services in rural areas is not just limited by the physical distance from better-provided towns and cities. Away from the urban areas sources of information are more restricted and there are fewer opportunities to find out from libraries and the like about what it is that legal advice has to offer. The close-knit nature of many rural communities often makes people reluctant to take a course of action which many believe may seriously disrupt fragile personal relationships with friends and neighbours (Melton, 1983). Many others are seriously concerned about the cost of legal advice and have no easy way of obtaining information.

Some of these 'barriers' are in reality relatively trivial and easily overcome, but they do inhibit and deter people. While there is no evidence that those in urgent need of legal advice systematically fail to obtain it, there is evidence of deprivation. For example, general ignorance about the law and the low level of familiarity with legal services, especially among those groups that do not have to transact routine business over property, create formidable barriers to seeking and obtaining legal advice when they are combined with the problems caused by the physical remoteness of rural areas. Local information facilities are necessary not only to reduce the problems caused by physical isolation for the most vulnerable groups in society, but also to act as a means of raising the general level of awareness about what legal advice and legal services may have to offer in helping to smooth the difficulties which everyone has to face from time to time.

7. Delivery Systems for Rural Legal Services

Problems of access to legal services in rural areas are common to virtually all societies, because economic pressures always force governments, and lawyers in private practice, to deploy their resources so as to reach the greatest numbers of people. Indeed, the discrepancy between the core and the periphery is an issue that has manifested itself in a multitude of different guises and one that has been clearly recognised by regional economic planners for more than a generation (Friedmann and Alonso, 1964). Legal resources in both developed and developing countries tend as a result inexorably to be concentrated in towns and cities where demand is most buoyant (Rojas, 1988). Rural areas, if not totally ignored, are usually sparsely provided with services, even when special programmes have been developed to deal with their particular needs.

Nevertheless, the dangers are legion of making judgements about the nature of rural legal services that are too sweeping. There are significant national and often subnational variations arising from the development of legal, political and economic structures, which have produced marked differences in prevailing legal cultures. As we have already demonstrated in this book, the nature of, and demand for, legal services in Scotland are quite different from the rest of the UK (Paterson and Bain, 1986), a situation which stems directly from the fact that that country has always had its own legal system with its own unique laws.

Equally, heterogeneity in legal cultures also has its counterpart in a plethora of ruralities with sharply differentiated forms of social and economic organisation. Again within the UK, substantial variations in practice and in the demand for legal services arise from the widespread use of the Welsh language in much of rural Wales (Thomas, 1986). This is a particularly obvious example, but in all countries historically specific social and spatial factors, operating at both national and regional levels, have interacted to produce different sets of problems for people living in rural areas.

The barriers to justice and legal services that those living in rural areas have to face are, therefore, intractable and varied and there is absolutely no guarantee that the problems examined in such detail in Chapter 6 for those people living in the remotest parts of the counties of Cornwall and Devon will be the same in remote rural locations elsewhere in the world. There is no panacea for overcoming the difficulties caused by isolation from legal services; solutions must be sensitive to local circumstances and capable of accommodating a wide diversity of aspirations. The issue of remoteness and sparse provision of services in rural areas may be common to most countries, but this is not true of other factors. For instance, the way in which the legal profession is organised in each individual country and the extent to which it is required to respond to market forces is crucial in determining the extent to which services are available in remote areas. In theory, those countries which have developed publicly funded legal services should have largely overcome problems of access arising from where people happen to reside, but all too often the levels of remuneration for lawyers working in the public sector are too low to retain their services and state intervention to ensure equality of access to legal advice is neutralised for want of adequate financial support. Equally, there are often specific features of individual societies and cultures that are especially marked in rural areas and which colour the nature of the demands that people make on legal services. Minority languages and local customs, as already mentioned with respect to Wales, often require special forms of legal representation if problems of discrimination and persecution are to be avoided.

It would clearly be unrealistic to attempt to survey the whole global spectrum of rural legal provision, but this chapter does try to illustrate, through selected examples, the ways in which the particular problems of rural areas have been tackled in a range of different countries, with a view to placing the detailed empirical findings from our work in the UK into a broader context. For the most part, the examples are drawn from the developed world and from those countries that share the traditions of a common law legal system with the UK (see generally, Abel and Lewis, 1988), although more general lessons are drawn where appropriate.

THE UNITED STATES OF AMERICA

The United States is a highly developed and largely urban society in a vast rural setting. There are huge tracts of land right across the country that are extremely remote from the urban infrastructure upon which all sections of the population are so heavily dependent. As a result, the contrasts between styles of legal practice in urban and rural areas are particularly marked and there have been a number of important initiatives aimed at trying to minimise the differences in legal service provision for those living in remoter rural areas.

The wide variations in the ratios of lawyers to population in different parts of the United States and the way that these patterns have persisted since the middle of the nineteenth century are well documented (Halliday, 1986). The data reveal a chronic under-representation of lawyers in rural areas and lead to the almost inevitable conclusion that, as a result, the rural population is disadvantaged in terms of access to legal advice and services.

For the most part, however, the nature of this deprivation has not been examined further than to note the discrepancies in the levels of resource provision, though there are some notable exceptions. These include a study of the distribution of lawyers in the state of New York (Cox, 1977) and a sensitive and intricate account of legal practice in rural Missouri (Landon, 1982, 1985, 1990). In the latter, Landon develops some research which was initially undertaken into styles of practice among lawyers practising in Chicago (Heinz and Laumann, 1982) to investigate whether there are measurable differences in urban and rural areas. He has augmented the Chicago data with data about lawyers practising in the city of Springfield (population 150,000) in neighbouring Missouri and lawyers practising in Missouri towns of 20,000 or less. He suggests that the three data sets – metropolitan, urban and rural small town – correspond to three distinctly different practice settings and he examines, in detail, the ways in which the professional lawyers, or attorneys, interact with the client community in each type of locality. He acknowledges the long-standing and largely inconclusive debates about the intrinsic validity of drawing rural–urban distinctions, but, nevertheless, argues that what is important is that:

> people living in small towns presume a significant difference in the rural context and conduct of their lives. (Landon, 1985: 85)

He lays particular emphasis on the prevalence of what he terms 'multiplex' relationships in rural areas, by which he means the way in which people living in close-knit rural communities routinely interact with each other in a number of different social roles, and the significance of this for the work of rural attorneys.

Among the metropolitan lawyers their organisation is characterised by deep division and rigid stratification in terms of size of firm and specialisation, whereas the rural practitioners constitute a more conservative and homogeneous professional group. They are more deeply embedded in their local communities than their metropolitan and urban counterparts and are, therefore, more likely to encounter conflict between their professional and community roles. Landon (1982: 468) finds that:

> Small town lawyers are typically products of the settings in which they practise. Thus the 'moral notions of community' are likely to be internalized long before the small town citizen becomes a professional practitioner. The local ideological pattern includes a conception of the community, a set of preferences as to who (what principle) shall rule, a sense of what constitutes an appropriate method of allocating values. It may also involve a uniquely local sense of what constitutes (and doesn't constitute) a legal problem.

These findings reflect the view that legal professionals are necessarily dependent upon the primary economic and social structures of the societies in which they operate and can be seen as reacting to stimuli from within their specific communities. Local legal cultures exert strong influence over the ways in which lawyers organise and run their practices. Subsequently, Landon (1985: 83) has expanded upon the theme of the conflict between the professional and the community role of lawyers, looking specifically at the ways in which the professional ideal of 'zealous advocacy' is mediated through

the expectations of the local community, local clients and local colleagues in rural communities.

He shows how the adversary ethic, which lies at the heart of the United States' legal system, becomes systematically 'redefined under the practicalities of entrepreneurial practice in intimate rural settings.' (Landon, 1985: 111). In so doing, he goes some way towards illustrating how lawyers themselves constitute local legal cultures and, in particular, how they have historically determined degrees of litigiousness within specific communities. However, the exact processes and practices which serve to shape local legal cultures are extremely complex and are, as yet, by no means fully understood.

This work in the heart of the Midwest provides a fascinating comparison with the findings of the AJRBP study in the UK. The inhibitions among large sections of the rural population at adopting a legal solution to local disputes are strong in both countries, but it is clear that litigation is much more central to legal practice in the United States. In the UK the overwhelming importance of residential conveyancing, especially marked among the non-specialist firms that predominate in rural areas, gives solicitors an economic foothold in the life of communities and helps to cement their social role. At the same time, it also provides a cushion that has enabled solicitors to avoid the need to promote other, more contentious and litigious, types of legal work, though whether this should be seen as a benefit or a loss depends on who the potential client happens to be.

One of Landon's main conclusions is that the combination of local and professional ties in rural communities can lead to increased emphasis on dispute resolution through informal negotiation, rather than formal litigation. The whole question of 'dispute processing' or 'dispute transformation' (Cain and Kulcsar, 1981–82; Trubek, *et al.*, 1983) has been the subject of intense and widespread academic interest in recent years, although the spatial dimensions of the problem have received scant attention. However, one attempt to redress this situation is Daniels' work on civil litigation in Illinois trial courts, which has the subtitle 'an exploration of rural–urban differences' (Daniels, 1982). The work represents an ambitious attempt to relate litigation rates to environmental, socio-economic and political–cultural factors. Overall, he demonstrates that urban areas have higher litigation rates than rural areas and highlights some broad differences in the types of case being litigated, such as, for example, a higher rate of probate cases in rural areas. In addition, socio-economic factors are found to be more significant than political–cultural factors in determining rates and types of litigation in rural areas.

Disappointingly, Daniels' social development model of rural–urban differences is rather limited and his discussion little more than a simplistic application of the notions of *Gemeinschaft* and *Gesellschaft*, which have long been recognised as gross over-simplifications of the complex web of relationships in rural and urban areas respectively (Pahl, 1968; Cloke and Little, 1990). Little attempt is made to assess or account for difference between rural areas in the study and key questions are not asked, let alone answered. For example, are there simply fewer disputes in rural areas and, if so, why? Is it the case that rural disputes are resolved by different means and, if so, what are those means?

In some more recent work, Daniels has analysed patterns of case handling in trial courts over a 90-year period in two rural counties in Illinois (Daniels, 1985). Although the rural dimension receives some attention in this later study, the analysis is again rather simplistic with differences being attributed in a very generalised way to a lack of urbanisation, rather than any intrinsic qualities of the rural areas themselves.

The AJRBP studies have begun to answer some of these questions with respect to attitudes to the law in the rural areas of the UK. They have shown that constraints on accessibility, particularly to publicly funded legal services, as well as the social constraints imposed by close-knit rural communities, do affect attitudes to the law and the propensity of the more vulnerable groups to adopt legal remedies. However, none of the AJRBP studies looked at the way court work was handled in rural areas, so that more precise comparisons with Daniels' work in Illinois are not yet possible.

There has been some interesting work in the United States investigating the rural dimension to the delivery of public legal services (*Duke Law Journal*, 1969). The development of nationally organised public legal services in that country is a recent phenomenon, dating back to the mid-1960s. The first impetus came through the Office of Economic Opportunity (OEO), as part of President Johnson's 'War on Poverty', in the form of the OEO's legal services programmes. Prior to that, with the exception of cases taken on a contingent fee basis, poor people had been forced to rely on *pro bono* work, i.e. the charity of individual practitioners, a duty laid down in the American Bar Association's Model Code of Professional Responsibility, which states that it is the duty of individual attorneys to provide assistance to those unable to afford it.

In the early stages, programme funding was predictably concentrated in urban areas and it was not until the independent incorporation of the Legal Services Corporation (LSC) in 1974, and with it the allocation of increased resources, that significant attempts were made to extend public legal services to poor people living in rural areas. Unfortunately, the wider brief did not flourish for long. After 1980 the hostility of President Reagan's administration towards the LSC resulted in a 25 per cent reduction in funding in 1982 and the harshest effects of the cutback have been felt in rural areas (Britt, 1986; Cooper, 1983; Economides and Garth, 1984; Turner, 1982).

Nevertheless, in its brief period of activity in the rural United States, the LSC did succeed in raising awareness of the deficiencies in the systems for delivering legal services to poor people in rural areas. In a study published in 1979 under section 1007(h) of its act of incorporation, the LSC highlighted the importance of physical access as a significant barrier to the provision of legal services in rural areas, few of which have adequate public transport systems and nearly all of which experience harsh climates which make travel difficult at certain times of the year (LSC, 1979). The study also makes the crucial point that the poor are not a homogeneous group and their numbers embrace a very wide range of social disadvantage, in addition to poverty. In the rural United States, migrant farmworkers and those with limited English-speaking abilities are faced with especially difficult problems of gaining legal advice because they tend to be cut off, almost by definition, from the established channels of communication with official bureaucracy.

A number of specific legal problems that the residents of sparsely populated rural areas often find difficult to overcome are also identified in the LSC study. These include seasonal employment, dealings with public agencies providing gas and electricity, questions of housing and land tenure, and property repairs. The solutions to these problems suggested in the study include: extending 'circuit riding' whereby peripatetic visits are made by LSC staff members to isolated communities; community outreach and education programmes; mobile offices; techno-logically orientated delivery systems; and mixed delivery approaches involving local attorneys. It is noteworthy that most of these kinds of solution are common to many attempts to ameliorate the consequences of rural isolation from legal advice and services in other developed countries, but in the United States the emphasis is heavily on the use of professionally qualified lawyers, rather than a mixed system involving para- legal agencies as has happened in the UK.

In an attempt to evaluate the work of the LSC in rural areas, Britt (1986) has undertaken a selective analysis of the implementation of these measures, in which she charts their relative success. Although specific schemes have subsequently been abandoned because of reductions in funding, she, and others, argue that valuable lessons have been learnt about the potential of innovatory delivery systems. Encouragingly, they conclude that reduced funding alone need not necessarily result in impoverished provision (Britt, 1986; Warschawsky and Warschawsky, 1983). Mixed delivery systems involving local practitioners in public legal services' provision, such as that organised by the West Virginia Legal Services Plan (Martin, 1981, and 1983), appear to have met with considerable success. These conclusions also reinforce those of Brakel (1973: 553) in the light of his study of the attitudes of clients towards staffed offices and publicly funded judicare programmes in upper Michigan, Wisconsin and Montana:

> The rural poor as an *a priori* matter, mistrust the private profit orientation as well as the altruistic institutional (govern-

mental) orientation. . . . Any further consideration of legal services to the poor and especially the rural poor must begin with the recognition that the rural poor themselves prefer the judicare approach.

It should also be borne in mind, in the light of Landon's findings which have been discussed above, that the efficacy of local attorneys in potentially controversial cases involving local litigants must be open to question. This is a strong argument for an independent, publicly funded service, such as that which used to be provided by the LSC. However, against this approach must be set the clear evidence that programmes which have adopted more radical pro-active approaches towards the legal problems of the rural poor, such as the California Rural Legal Assistance Program, have met with considerable political animosity, which has severely limited their effectiveness (Allen, 1986; Cochran, 1984; Turner, 1982).

CANADA

Although the problems of delivering the service to the public are intrinsically much the same, there are significant differences between the way in which public legal services in the United States and neighbouring Canada are organised. Whereas the LSC in the United States is a federal body, the Constitution dictates that the administration of justice in Canada is the responsibility of individual provincial administrations. The first full-scale legal aid scheme in Canada was the Judicare plan introduced in the province of Ontario in 1967, which provided government funds to aid those of low means in retaining the help and advice of lawyers. Subsequently, the federal government has also made funds available for sharing the cost of criminal legal aid, and now some form of public legal service, covering criminal matters and some civil issues, has been introduced in all provinces.

The organisation of public legal services on a provincial basis has, however, resulted in variations in the type of delivery model adopted by individual provinces, ranging from Judicare, through mixed delivery systems, to public legal offices employing salaried lawyers (Garth, 1980; Snider, 1981, 1986; Zemans, 1985; Chouinard, 1989). Moreover, as Zemans has argued, this 'provincial funding base and structure has allowed Canada to avoid the political onslaught on public legal services which took place in the United States' (Zemans, 1985: 297).

The rural dimension to the provision of public legal services in Canada is important for reasons that are similar, in general terms, to those that apply in the United States. There is a widely scattered, and often extremely isolated, rural population dependent on the services and infrastructure of a small number of major cities, so that all manner of problems of access abound for anyone requiring legal advice and assistance outside the metropolitan centres. These problems are also often compounded by the kinds of legal problem that tend to arise. Much of the native Indian population of Canada lives in remote settlements, far removed from the country's urban areas, yet this section of society has to face particularly severe difficulties as a result of racial and linguistic discrimination and disputes over the validity of their traditional claims to land and other resources. All are problems for which legal advice is urgently required, a need which is slowly coming to be recognised by the provincial governments (Coyle, 1986; Hathaway 1982, 1984/85). Further difficulties also arise as a result of the sharp cleavage between the anglophone and the francophone traditions in bilingual Canada. It is a particular problem in the rural areas of Montreal and much of lower Ontario, where French- and English-speaking communities exist side by side, but are effectively insulated from each other by their distinct cultural heritages. Finally, in many of the rural areas in south-eastern Canada, where there are pockets of intensive agricultural production, there are also locally important concentrations of migrant farmworkers, who are frequently illegally exploited and require access to professional legal assistance if they are to avoid harassment.

Traditionally, the main vehicle for delivering legal services to the general public in rural areas has been the private Bar–lawyers in private practice who cater predominantly for the wealthy minority and who are usually part of the social élite in their local communities. Partly as a result of the publicly funded judicare programme, this has now begun to change and research in the mining region of Sudbury in Ontario has demonstrated how rapidly both the composition of the legal profession has been broadened and the range of clients dealt with has increased.

There are now lawyers drawn from all the major ethnic groups and, with the support from the Judicare programme, they are able to reach out to all sections of the community (Ribordy, 1982; 1988).

Elsewhere, the concept of legal aid clinics, which originated in the city of Toronto in the early 1970s as a means of offering protection to the poorest sections of society using the services of professionally qualified lawyers paid for by the government, has been extended to rural areas as well (Mossman, 1983; Chouinard, 1989). There are 65 such clinics in Ontario as a whole and at least six serve populations that are almost exclusively rural. For instance, the Simcoe Legal Services Clinic in the town of Orillia in lower Ontario, about 300 km from Toronto, provides advice on all kinds of legal matter to the residents of Simcoe County and, where appropriate, will actually represent clients and fight their cases through the legal system. Since the clinic is entirely dependent on public funds, it has to be selective as to which cases it chooses to fight and it tends to be most ready to accept those where there is either some particularly gross injustice involved, or there is a point of general legal interest. Indeed, the staff of the clinic see awakening people to their legal rights as being as important as reacting to specific problems that are brought to them. Despite the fact that there are only four lawyers on the staff, there are four branch clinics in small communities outside Orillia and these are used as bases from which awareness of the law among the population generally may be heightened, in addition to their function in helping to solve individual legal problems.

Although it has a relatively large rural population, there has been little critical work undertaken in Canada on the impact of the various legal services initiatives on rural communities. The most significant contribution is Snider's detailed study of legal services in a rural area extending across two counties to the north of Kingston, Ontario. The attraction of this particular rural area was the operation there of the Queen's Rural Legal Services (QRLS), an experimental project set up and run by students at Queen's University, Kingston who felt that the legal needs of people living in the area were not being met. Snider (1986: 11) describes some of the difficulties involved in studying rural communities in the following manner:

Such communities are never static. . . . There is in each county not one but 30 or 40 communities to be studied, each with its social stratification system, its own prejudices and its own needs. Settlements of 600 resent the 'centralizing ambitions' of neighbouring towns of 1,200, and the usual class, ethnic, religious and gender divisions cut across these geographic ones. In addition. . . . the various community élites were eager to make their views of the world known to us, whereas the marginal farmers, unemployed seasonal workers, the domestics and the old living in poverty and isolation were very hard to reach.

The study revealed considerable variations between and within specific communities as to perceptions of legal problems or needs and community problems. However, widespread conservatism manifested itself in resentment against the idea of free legal services, which were seen as 'helping the undeserving and driving free market lawyers out of the area' (Snider, 1986: 13). At the same time, the few private practitioners working in the area maintained that insufficient profitable business was being generated and that at least half of their income came through government in the form of legal aid. However, many of the problems identified by people living in these communities could have been considered 'legal'; community residents, and the local Bar, agreed on a 'non-legal' interpretation (Snider, 1986: 14). In view of these findings, questions are raised about the value of extending traditional legal services within the area. Snider concludes that there is little to be gained from such a straightforward extension, but argues that if these rural communities are to halt their decline, then they must act collectively. In practice, such action would involve redefinition of existing problems in 'legal' terms and Snider suggests that the law and lawyers could play a much more influential and pro-active role in articulating the needs of rural communities.

Australia and New Zealand

The North American experience has clear parallels in similar societies in other parts of the world. In Australia and New Zealand, for example, those living in remote rural areas are chronically deprived in terms of access to lawyers and legal services in general. In both countries, the problem is not the relative lack of lawyers in relation to the size of the population, but rather how to match the available resources to the widely scattered pattern of settlement.

In all but two states in Australia more than 80 per cent of practising lawyers are based in the state capital cities and even in the two exceptions, Queensland and Tasmania, the proportions are 56 and 58 per cent respectively. The problems of access in Australia are further compounded because of the highly decentralised nature of the legal profession itself, with each state or territory having its own powerful professional association (Weisbrot, 1988; 1989; 69–71). It means that, in effect, it is impossible for lawyers from one state to practise in another. Since important minorities, notably the native aboriginal peoples, still live predominantly outside the metropolitan centres, their special legal needs tend to be widely ignored and, in consequence, they suffer severe discrimination.

The situation in New Zealand is broadly similar, but with the added gloss of a wide discrepancy between the North and South Islands (Murray, 1988). In the South Island, except for the immediate hinterlands of the three cities of Christchurch, Dunedin and Invercargill, there is on average less than one lawyer for every 3,000 people and in large parts of the south-west and the north-east there are, to all intents and purposes, no legal services at all.

OTHER WEST EUROPEAN PERSPECTIVES

In Western Europe no government has so far been persuaded to the extent of that in the United States when it established the LSC in 1974, that there is a need for a specifically rural dimension to its provision of legal services. Most countries approach the whole issue of legal aid in similar fashion to the UK by relying on a mixed delivery system, mainly dependent on Judicare, but backed up to a much lesser extent by a freely available, salaried legal service.

As in the UK, however, research and the monitoring of *ad hoc* provision of free and enhanced legal services in rural areas have revealed that there is both unmet demand and a specifically rural dimension to the nature of legal services. It is clear that increasing distance from the point of supply of legal services progressively reduces the use that is made of them, both in terms of volume and the range of users. Schuyt, Groenedijk and Sloot (1976) have shown that, even in a country as small and highly urbanised as the Netherlands, the relative remoteness of rural areas means that people are less likely to avail themselves of specialist legal advice, particularly in areas such as employment law, relying instead on more local, but non-professional sources, in much the same way that Snider discovered in Canada. Obviously the issue is a complex one, not least because the availability of a free service might give a distorted impression of need, but if a legal service is not readily available it is bound to reduce the extent to which people rely on it.

In an attempt to go more deeply into the nature of the deprivation caused by the lack of legal services in rural areas, Johnsen (1978, 1980, 1987) organised a carefully structured and monitored extension to a long-running law-centre scheme operating in the city of Oslo to two groups of isolated rural communities near Tromso in the far north of Norway. In the first group, each household in two agricultural and fishing villages included was sent a questionnaire asking them about legal services and offering free advice on any legal problems which they might have and want to try to solve. The response was overwhelming: 93 per cent of the households replied and 60 per cent had an identifiable legal problem. The most important categories related to taxation and property law (15% each), followed by housing law (13%), social security (12%) and pension rights (11%). Overall, more than two-thirds of the queries were difficulties in dealing with official bureaucracy, and most of the respondents had been completely at a loss to know where to turn for independent advice.

One of the main limitations of the above approach as a means of measuring the demand for legal services was that it invited people to come and air their grievances and take advantage of a free service, thus artificially boosting the level of demand. In an attempt to compensate for this bias, those included in the second group of two communities – one an island just off the coast, the other a village inland – were simply informed through the local media that a free legal advice service would be available. On the island a bus (the *Jussbuss*) was fitted out and toured around, stopping at a series of prearranged and advertised locations; at the village an office was opened in the centre of the settlement. In both communities the response was predictably very much lower than with the questionnaire sent to the first group. Only 12 per cent of households on the island and 5 per cent of those in the village came forward, though interestingly certain types of enquiry seemed to be disproportionately affected. Family and social security issues were very much less in evidence, probably indicating that without prompting most people did not view these as essentially legal problems.

The most significant conclusion of the study was, however, the comparison with the long-established law centre in Oslo. In both groups of communities in Tromso the level of enquiries was significantly higher than in Oslo throughout the whole of 1974, indicating a disproportionately large, latent, demand for legal advice in rural areas.

Another experiment in Germany, in the rural parts of the *Land* Rheinland Pfalz, established 47 legal advice centres linked to magistrates' courts (*Amtsgerichte*), specifically to help meet the needs of those living in remote, rural, locations (Buschmann, 1979). The scheme is staffed entirely by volunteers, mostly retired lawyers and civil servants, and its primary aim is to identify legal problems and to point people to where they can best obtain professional advice, rather than attempting to try and solve the problems there and then. The initial emphasis is on open access and the non-professional nature of the advice is similar to the early experience of the CABx in the UK, though now the CABx have become much more part of a para-legal advice service in their own right.

The most interesting feature of the Rheinland Pfalz experiment is the mix of problems it has elicited, revealing a distinct undercurrent of specifically rural concerns. There have been a large number of enquiries relating to property rights and the rights of inheritance as they relate to agricultural property. There are also a large number of enquiries from people who have retired from the major urban centres, in particular the Ruhr, who seem unsure about the extent and nature of their rights in the unfamiliar rural surroundings. For instance, one newcomer wanted to know whether he could seek an injunction to stop his neighbour's cows bellowing!

The ways the values of peasant societies can conflict with the demands of modern legal systems have stimulated some interesting research in northern Italy (Cottino, 1983, 1986) and Sardinia (Ferrari, 1982). Both studies demonstrate forcefully, through analyses of court cases, how family loyalties tend to transcend legal obligations to society as a whole. On the other hand, similar work in north-west France shows no significant difference in the number of cases that go to the Court of Appeal between urban and rural areas (Loyer, 1985). The results indicate that the way in which societies are organised may be more important in deciding how the court system is used, than whether people live in the town or the country. However, these studies in Italy and France are all dealing with a very much narrower range of legal work than those in either Norway or Germany, so only very limited comparisons are possible.

Although the evidence from the West European mainland is fragmentary, a number of general features are, nevertheless, quite clear. Physical isolation and remoteness do cut people off from specialist legal advice, if not from the courts, and many lack the means to overcome these disadvantages, relying instead on generalist or completely lay advice closer to hand, or, more likely, taking no advice at all. There is also evidence that the nature of rural communities, with their heavy emphasis on land ownership and the importance attached to family ties, brings with it particular types of legal problems and also raises unfamiliar legal issues for the growing numbers of people moving from the cities to the countryside, especially on retirement.

LESSONS FOR THE UK

Both reports of the Royal Commissions into legal services in the UK, which dealt with England, Wales and Northern Ireland (RCLS, 1979) and with Scotland (Hughes, 1980) respectively, conceded that there were special difficulties to be overcome in delivering legal services to rural areas, although they differed about how such disadvantage should be combated. The

Commission chaired by Lord Hughes in Scotland favoured specific, publicly funded, provision, while the Commission chaired by Lord Benson covering the rest of the UK tended towards subsidies for the private profession to encourage them to offer a full service in remote rural areas with sparse and scattered populations.

The evidence from elsewhere in the world confirms unequivocally that people living in rural areas, especially if they are poor or otherwise disadvantaged, experience much greater difficulty in gaining access to legal services than their urban counterparts. Although the details of the way in which national provision is organised vary, potential clients generally appear to be strongly in favour of some form of public provision through Judicare, rather than relying totally on the private legal profession and market forces to cater for their needs.

The reasons for this preference, however, appear to be only partially governed by purely economic motives. Undoubtedly it is true, as we discovered in the AJRBP study (Ch. 6), that the fear of incurring unknown costs can be a powerful deterrent to seeking legal advice, but equally important is the widespread perception that poor people's law is different from that of the rich and the private profession is not particularly well qualified to deal with the needs of rural populations. In urban areas it is a similar sense of unease that has led to the establishment of publicly funded legal services and the only real difference in rural areas is that the scale of demand is much less. As the evidence of this chapter has shown, wherever attempts have been made to cater for the needs of rural areas, and our examples have ranged from North America, to Australasia and to mainland Western Europe, they have met with an overwhelming public response and uncovered a range of special issues for which legal remedies are often highly appropriate. We have also shown that demonstrable need on its own has never been sufficient to ensure the long-term survival of public rural legal services in the face of scarce economic resources and the widespread belief that pro-active lawyers seeking out potential disputes are an unnecessarily destabilising influence on society. Access to justice is clearly controlled, at least in part, by access to legal services and this is particularly obvious in rural areas.

8. The Reform of Rural Justice

THE NEED FOR CHANGE

A primary objective of this book has been the identification and measurement of gaps in the provision of UK legal services. Chapter 2, for example, presented a series of maps which revealed that solicitors were the only group that offered the public a service approaching comprehensive geographical coverage. Other providers, notably barristers, para-legal agencies such as CABx, courts and tribunals were shown to be concentrated in towns and cities, their distributions reflecting historical trends towards centralisation in the administration of justice which were clearly established by the late nineteenth century. And even solicitors, now responding to the latest political and economic pressures which are reshaping the nature and scope of professional practice, increasingly display centripetal tendencies. Mergers and amalgamations have become popular means to attain economic security, as well as a certain political influence, in what has fast become an uncertain world. Consequently, small-scale rural practice currently is being absorbed by urban-based medium-sized or 'mega-firms' which means, in geographical terms, sizeable gaps are likely to continue in the provision of contemporary legal services.

But does this really matter? The demise of village postal services, schools or shops must have an impact on the fabric of rural life which is far more immediate than the loss of the country lawyer. If lawyers are reorganising themselves in larger units of production based in the towns and cities does it follow that rural populations will suffer deprivation? This is a difficult question to answer but we might begin by noting the danger of attaching too much importance to the physical distribution of services. Gaps in the distribution of services are not only predictable, but also inevitable. It would be odd indeed to find large concentrations of lawyers in areas of remote wilderness! In this study we have sought to relate the distribution of legal services to both quantitative and qualitative data without which it would be difficult to make sense of crude physical distributions. Thus population densities and the expectations of rural inhabitants provide a context which help us to explain and assess rural legal services. Yet important as this context is, these services should also meet certain minimum standards laid down at the national level – either by central government or by the governing bodies of the professional and para-professional associations responsible for the establishment and oversight of practice rules and codes of conduct. The notion of 'rural justice' advanced in this study represents an attempt to reconcile national standards, such as they are, with local conditions which might be used to justify a departure from established norms.

National standards for legal services have, of course, never been static but recently there have been some interesting attempts to define 'quality' in the field of legal services. The National Consumer Council (NCC) (1986, 1989) has played a pioneering role in formulating performance indicators which purport to measure the quality of legal services. In setting standards, they argue, one has to consider both inputs and outputs and this means first setting *resource standards* which 'lay down the minimum level of staff and access points for a given level of population' and then developing *performance indicators* 'to measure the services actually offered to consumers' (NCC, 1989: 122). Similarly, in the course of developing its proposals for franchising Legal Aid, the Legal Aid Board has also sought to define and monitor the 'quality' of professional services in order that it can take decisions as to whether to grant firms a Legal Aid franchise (Orchard and Blake, 1989). Furthermore, in order to advance and safeguard practice standards in the future, both branches of the legal profession are presently overhauling training and professional standards. The Law Society, for example, is preparing criteria to help it decide which firms and teaching institutions will be 'authorised' to train the next generation of solicitors – in effect a 'training franchise' (Law Society, 1990: para. 7.3). Assuming such attempts to define quality are implemented, the application of national standards in a rural context is unlikely to be straightforward and here it is important that policy and planning are sensitive to local conditions. But such conditions could dictate the need for great change, or no change at all.

Rural populations are of course very diverse but, as we have seen, some sections may think little of travelling distances far in excess of those covered by the average urban commuter in order to reach those services they require. Does it follow that legal services should be located in an urban setting and that efforts at rural 'outreach' are futile? Moreover, we have encountered evidence which suggests that some rural communities uphold a cultural tradition resistant to many of the basic premises of the welfare state (see also Melton, 1983). To fall back on the assertion that 'rural rights' must always be enforced could, some might argue, smack of cultural imperialism, legal paternalism or a combination of both. It may be hard for the city-dweller to accept that rural inhabitants might prefer to order their lives without reference to legal norms or the services of lawyers and other professionals. This should not be the case, however, particularly since many urban inhabitants – including lawyers themselves as our research has shown – see the countryside as a kind of refuge from the pressures of urban life. To escape to the country retreat in pursuit of the 'rural idyll' would appear to be a popular solution for professionals who must cope with living or working in the city. Clearly, attitudes towards both lawyers and the law vary considerably in and between the rural regions, both in the UK and elsewhere, and to a large extent such attitudes determine whether and to what degree there is a need for change.

The problem of rural justice then is essentially one of central–local relations in which local legal practice is measured against, as well as contributes to, the evolution of national standards. Given that there is such great variation not only between but also within local conditions it would seem sensible to focus on the role of regional and central planning in guiding future national policy for rural legal services. Universal or blanket prescriptions for improving these services are unlikely to be successful if they have to cover both conditions of extreme deprivation as well as relatively high levels of prosperity. Furthermore, even to concentrate on just the 'deprived areas' is likely to be unsatisfactory, because of the danger of slipping into what is known as an 'ecological fallacy' (the assumption that key variables such as 'need' can be measured on a universal territorial basis, thus ignoring important differences between groups and individuals within the defined area) (Alker, 1969). What is needed is a more flexible approach which recognises that even within so-called 'prosperous areas' conditions of deprivation may exist. It is our contention that the absence of a coherent policy specifically designed for rural legal services has in the past contributed to the uneven development and unpredictable standards of legal work carried out in rural areas.

ALLOCATING SCARCE RESOURCES

Whatever the reluctance of people generally to seek their legal rights, whether they live in rural areas or anywhere else, the law confers rights and guarantees freedoms, so that it is of the utmost importance that all people, under any jurisdiction, are covered by it and have the opportunity of proper and effective access to legal services. In this book we have shown that in the UK and a wide variety of other democratic, Western, countries, those living in rural areas are inherently disadvantaged by the way in which legal services are distributed. The attempts that have been made to compensate for these inadequacies are, for the most part, insufficient for the size of the task and leave the discrimination against those living in rural areas almost untouched. It is, therefore, essential that those resources that are available are used to maximum effect, so that as many people as possible benefit from the limited legal services that do exist.

The general issue is well known and a whole family of theoretical models, known as location–allocation models, have been developed to suggest ways of matching resources to demand as efficiently as possible (Massam, 1980). The general location–allocation model identifies the best site for a facility such as a solicitor's office, a law centre, or a CAB, where 'best' is taken to mean the minimum total or average distance to the consumers. Similarly, route location problems can also be defined and solved, with the shortest route between a set of places being the best one.

The reason for using distance as the criterion for choosing between alternative sites or routes is that it acts as a convenient surrogate for cost, time, or the effort involved in travel, and since the minimum distance location is by definition the most accessible place, it will also certainly be the one that has the highest utility for consumers. In addition, there are also strong practical reasons for using the distance criterion, because the most readily available data are likely to relate to the location of potential clients, the availability of potential alternative sites, and the distances between sets of clients and sites.

In order to illustrate the applicability of these techniques to the planning and location of legal services, a location–allocation model developed at the University of Iowa (Goodchild and Noronha, 1983) was used, together with data on the location of CABx in the counties of Cornwall and Devon, to evaluate the extent to which the actual distribution of bureaux deviated from the 'best', or shortest path, solution. In general the fit was good, with the larger settlements where most of the CABx are actually located predictably emerging as the locations preferred by the model. It was noticeable, however, that the most significant deviations occurred in the remoter rural areas with more scattered populations. In south-east Devon, for example, the small town of Totnes emerged as a much more important centre than was apparent from the services that were actually located there. Equally, the model proved to be very efficient in selecting rural locations for new bureaux, homing in on the very isolated border region between north Cornwall and north-west Devon and selecting not one of the more obvious coastal settlements, such as Hartland or Clovelly, but the inland village of Bradworthy.

It would be foolish to make too extravagant claims about the value of such optimising techniques for selecting appropriate locations for legal services, but undoubtedly they do provide a powerful guide to the relationship between demand, in the form of the consumers, and supply, in the form of CABx, solicitors' offices, courts and the like (Thomas, Robson and Nutter, 1989). Investment decisions about the location of new services need to be properly informed and not the result of *ad hoc* guesses based on intuition or special pleading, not least because once an investment has been made it is very often difficult to relocate elsewhere if it is shown not to be at the most suitable location. Once a suboptimal decision has been made, it is almost certain that the people disadvantaged by it will remain so for a considerable time. In considering theory and practice, it is abundantly clear that the bulk of decisions about where both private and public legal services are located are not taken with the interests of the consumers primarily in mind. In the private sector the driving force has to be financial viability of the enterprise as a business; in the public sector a lack of information and rigorous analysis ensures that most decisions are opportunistic, rather than the result of careful, systematic, planning and analysis.

REGIONAL AND CENTRAL PLANNING

The need for regional and central planning in the field of legal services stems from imperfections in the market for these services. The limits of private practice mean that gaps in provision will always be present and, in the previous section, we have indicated that techniques are available for testing, and improving on, our intuitive understanding. From the standpoint of the provider, the objective must be to achieve both maximum accessibility and quality in the service which is on offer. In the words of the recent White Paper the government has stated that:

> The overall aims are to give the public as wide a choice as possible in the providers of legal services available to them, whilst at the same time maintaining the high standards of integrity and competence which are necessary for protecting the interests of the client and for the more general public interest in the administration of justice. . . . These aims will be met by creating a framework which encourages flexibility and diversity in meeting the clients' needs, yet maintains the necessary standards. (HMSO, 1989: paras 1–5).

This objective, under the Courts and Legal Services Act 1990, is now called a 'statutory objective' and Section 17 refers explicitly to the need to develop legal services 'by making provision for new or better ways of providing such services and a wider choice of persons providing them'.

Furthermore, Section 17 also refers to a 'general principle' whereby persons should be granted rights of audience or the right to conduct litigation only if they have appropriate qualifications and fall under the guardianship and control of some kind of professional body. In short, legal services policy must in the future provide a framework which clearly recognises that there is a place for people without a formal legal qualification in the provision of legal services: legal services are no longer to be equated with those services provided by the legal profession alone.

Government policy on legal services is thus opening up new possibilities and opportunities for those who provide legal advice and assistance to the public. The legal services industry is to be made more competitive and many archaic, even arcane, traditions are now under attack. 'Economy' and 'efficiency' dominate the private sector. The basic ingredients of legal professionalism, the notion of 'quality' in legal work and the nature and scope of legal skills, are now under close scrutiny, whereas previously professional values were simply assumed and almost never analysed. Similarly with legal services policy itself which, once the result of historical accident, now becomes the end-product of research and rational planning. In this new climate of reform a number of challenges confront those responsible for the formation of future policy on legal services.

These challenges, as we have seen, involve finding a balance between complementary components of legal services delivery: legal professionalism and para-professionalism; the private and public sectors; and urban and rural practice. The boundaries of legal professionalism and the question of 'standards' is at the heart of the debate created by the Green and White Papers and continuing with the passing of the Courts and Legal Services Act 1990. The boundaries of the market for legal services and the size of the public sector are issues of great importance which will determine the 'accessibility' of the legal system; the limits of private practice in turn define the need and scope for public sector services such as law centres and generalist advice from voluntary agencies such as CABx. Finally, the boundaries of law have an important spatial dimension whereby legal services and even certain aspects of substantive law may have only a limited impact in rural and remote areas. Policy on legal services must therefore reconcile local conditions with central or national standards – the central problem of rural justice.

What these challenges add up to is the need for a co-ordinated, or, what the Legal Aid Advisory Committee has called an 'integrated' approach (LCD, 1990: 100) to legal services:

> we believe it is essential that the implementation of proposals made by the Civil Justice Review, the White Paper on Legal Aid and now the White Paper on Legal Services should be coherent, consistent, and designed to produce a comprehensive and national distribution of legal services across the country.

As far as Legal Aid is concerned, the Advisory Committee recognises that what is needed is 'a flexible system of legal aid which was responsive to local conditions and which satisfied basic minimum standards' (LCD, 1990: 94). The problem which policymakers must address now is how to define, measure and monitor these standards.

In *Good Advice for All* the NCC grasped this nettle and drew attention to the particular problems of legal service delivery in rural areas (NCC, 1986). Unlike many previous reports which also recognised that there was a problem in getting access to legal advice in rural areas, the NCC formulated a set of concrete guidelines for policymakers concerning the minimum level of resources which are necessary to secure a basic level of advice to all members of a given community. For example, they were prepared to spell out actual (though in practice as we have shown unrealistically small) distances clients could be expected to travel in order to reach their legal advisers:

> In rural areas, other than those that are very sparsely populated, no-one should need to travel more than two miles to consult a generalist advice worker, nor more than five miles to consult a specialist advice worker. (NCC, 1986: 2.36/3.6)

It is interesting to note that certain parts of the country, such as those that are very sparsely populated, have population densities too low to support a separate advice centre (NCC, 1986: 2.29). These areas would, however, still require some form of provision which might take the form of 'outreach' such as 'a telephone advice service, mobile advice centre, outreach workers or village contacts' (NCC, 1986: 2.40). These outreach services should also conform to certain standards but again these cannot be applied rigidly in a rural context:

> It is not, however, possible to provide a blue-print for rural advice services. Each form of delivery has its own strengths and weaknesses which must be assessed against the particular needs of each community. It is also important that the different forms of delivery should not be seen as alternatives. The needs of large rural areas are only likely to be met in full by a range of different methods of delivery, supported by a full-time advice centre. (NCC, 1986: 2.84)

The value of the NCC's approach is that it offers a basis for the evaluation of advice services starting with an examination of the size of the catchment area served by various providers. While the emphasis of these proposals is on generalist advice by para-professionals we think the approach could also be carried over to the services offered by the private profession. Now that the Legal Aid Board has been set up there is much that can, and is, being done to monitor the work of private lawyers in rural areas, and indeed the Board recognises that it has a duty to do this in its current franchising proposals which will provide 'a mechanism whereby geographical areas that have no service can be identified and targeted and also areas where only a limited number of categories of work are available' (Legal Aid Board, 1989: para. 35). Professional and para-professional services need to be considered together in order that the totality of provision can be assessed in any given area. Given that current reforms in the Courts and Legal Services Act 1990 blur the boundaries between the legal professions, other professions and para-professionals, it becomes even more necessary to know which services are available at the local level. For practical and logistical reasons local services are best assessed at a regional level.

If the role of central policymaking is to set national minimum standards the role of regional policy is to review local resources and monitor local performance. In addition, regional policy must inform the continuing development of national standards which set the objectives which local providers must aim for – this should never be static as there will always be scope for improvement (see LCD, 1982: 123–4, paras 171–5). In our view regional development of legal services can best be nurtured by central government supporting legal services committees set up on the model of the North Western Legal Services Committee. Each of the regions of the UK should be served by such a committee which would have the responsibility to review local resources and performance as well as feed into the development of national policy. Regional legal services committees must therefore be guaranteed core funding (see generally, LCD, 1989: 101–2, paras 47–50).

If set up on a nationwide basis these regional legal services committees would be well placed to connect and possibly co-ordinate central and local policymaking for legal services. At the county (or its equivalent) level, each county town might be served with a local committee which monitored available resources (i.e. numbers of lawyers and their specialisms; generalist and specialist advice agencies) and their physical distribution. If gaps in provision were uncovered these might be tackled under the auspices of a 'County Legal Plan'. Such a plan might provide for importing the requisite resources or expertise (for example through the use of new technology); developing a 'referral network'; or creating new facilities such as the strategic location of a law centre. County solicitors might contribute to the development of these plans and would be assisted by local groups interested in the provision of legal services. There would obviously be a need for independent lawyers not beholden to vested interests locally to engage in the development of public advocacy, for example initiating legal action on behalf of disenfranchised sections of the rural community.

There is already ample evidence which demonstrates that deprivation exists in rural areas, even if it has low visibility as compared with the plight of the inner cities (Economides, 1982; Neate, 1981; McLaughlin, 1986; CPAG, 1987). Access to the land and rural housing are particular problems for the rural population which public advocacy might begin to challenge (Shoard, 1987; Winter and Rogers, 1988; Shucksmith, 1990). The formation of rural housing associations and tenants' associations could well be assisted by public interest lawyers working in rural areas. Simcoe legal services in the Canadian province of Ontario, which was described in Chapter 7, offers one model but others might also be imagined. Improving inter-agency co-operation locally in order to avoid unnecessary duplication and overlap is another possibility and one which has been tried with limited success at South Molton in Devon, as we have shown. While a range of alternative methods of legal services delivery can be imagined the real problem is to decide on which mix is best suited to conditions locally. It is our contention that such decisions are best taken not by central planners but by consumers and their representatives at the local level. The formation of a nationwide network of county and regional legal services committees would seem to be the key to developing future legal services policy for rural areas.

POLICY IMPLEMENTATION

Assuming it were possible to develop plans for the development of legal services at the national, regional and local levels in the UK, the implementation of such plans is likely to run up against a number of obstacles many of which have been highlighted by the evidence from the AJRBP surveys which we have discussed in this book.

In the first place legal services, and law reform generally, suffer from inertia. Legal professions in the past have not on the whole been quick to perceive the need for reform and have created the impression that lawyers are complacent – a fact that was clearly demonstrated by the 'fatalist' group of solicitors identified in Chapter 4. The image of the country lawyer is not so much that of a young idealistic lawyer fighting for the rights of the rural poor as of a middle-aged gentleman handing out homespun advice to locals. While the image is no doubt a gross distortion of reality it remains true that pro-active public interest lawyers serving rural communities are a rare breed. Although the private profession has taken certain steps to tackle the absence of legal advice in rural areas (Law Society, 1987: 8), it must be said that these efforts have not been determined and fall far short of the work that has been done on rural legal services by the generalist advice agencies. Part of the explanation must be that for so long solicitors were able to earn a stable living from residential conveyancing, thereby removing pressures on them to develop innovative methods of delivering their services. Now that the profession is being forced to come to terms with new commercial realities they are quickly abandoning their old-style complacency and adopting a more aggressive 'business ethic'. Unfortunately, for rural communities, these new models of legal professionalism appear to offer little in the way of an improved service to rural clients as the pursuit of profit more often than not takes place within large urban commercial centres. Ironically, the very inertia of the country lawyer is what has kept alive a professional presence in rural areas: to move with the times usually implies moving to the city.

This raises the second major obstacle which concerns the structure and intrinsic nature of rural society. As we have seen, rural communities may be remote, have small and scattered populations, poor communications and relatively low levels of service provision. In these circumstances the provision of any service, legal or otherwise, confronts major logistical problems which prevent that service achieving comprehensive geographical coverage, accessibility and high standards at reasonable expense. While many public services in rural areas are now in decline it also appears that efforts to stimulate competition in the private sector have failed to provide an adequate solution. As we have observed in the field of legal services, the most dynamic among the private lawyers drift towards the cities which also happens to be where the public sector in legal services are concentrated. While the relationship between the public and private sectors in the rural UK remains problematic (Bell and Cloke, 1989), as far as legal services are concerned, this relationship simply does not exist at present on any meaningful scale, given the absence of rural law centres. If law is to play a role in the future development of rural society this will require an investment not only of public and private finance, but also of political will. Rural legal services, whether public or private, are expensive as compared with servicing the legal needs of urban populations and unless the political will exists to find and implement solutions these services will remain either undeveloped or underdeveloped.

Now that the Legal Aid Board has been set up there would appear to be some hope that progress can be made with regard to developing rural legal services. The new franchising proposals at least create the possibility of introducing an element of planning in the private sector and the Board has clearly recognised that a problem exists with regard to rural legal services (Legal Aid Board, 1989: para. 34; Economides, 1991). In researching the nature of rural legal services delivery, levels of rural accessibility and in monitoring the quality of these services it is clear that the recently constituted Legal Aid Board will have a central role to play in ensuring that rural legal services remain on the political agenda in the UK. It is to be hoped that it will also develop new models for delivery, building, for example, on the ideas and experience of para-legal bodies, such as the CABx (see Ch. 5). This might well involve both the application of new technology and a thorough-going review of traditional styles and rules of practice, particularly in the area of preliminary legal advice based on the Green Form Scheme (Ch. 4). There are also useful lessons to be learnt from other countries which have had to contend with similar problems of delivery in rural areas, though each within the context of its own legal system (Ch. 7).

The Board is in a unique position to harness both public and private resources in implementing national, regional and local plans which are committed to defining and achieving the goals of rural justice, but as the NCC has been so careful to point out, the presence of legal services in an area is only a start, just as important are the quality of the advice on offer and the monitoring mechanisms which ensure that quality is maintained. It is vital, therefore, that we do not lose sight of the dialectic linking quality and access. Our message in this book is that the infrastructure in the rural UK, particularly that provided by solicitors in private practice, for the time being at least, is in good heart, but the challenge for the legal and para-legal professions, and for the government, is to see to it that the rapid changes now occurring in the organisation and financing of legal services are not made at the expense of rural areas.

Appendix 1   Research Methodologies

1. SOLICITORS' SURVEY

The survey of solicitors in Cornwall and Devon carried out in 1985 was based on a series of personal interviews using semi-structured questionnaires among a sample of solicitors in the two counties. The option of undertaking a postal survey was rejected because it is well known that postal surveys usually have a low response rate (Moser and Kalton, 1971: 262). This is especially true in cases where a wide variety of different types of data, involving a lengthy questionnaire, needs to be collected. Results of previous surveys of solicitors have shown that solicitors' responses to postal questionnaires can be poor. Faulkener and Saunders (1985) in a postal survey of 508 solicitors in the East Midlands, for example, had only a 20 per cent response rate: rates as low as this preclude unbiased results.

Before selecting the sample and devising a questionnaire, it was decided to make contact with the solicitors' professional body, the Law Society, in order to explain the aims of the project and seek advice as to the best means of implementation. In particular, the local law societies were contacted at an early stage in the project. Through the secretaries of these local law societies, it was possible to distribute a copy of a paper outlining the project to all their members in the two counties. These solicitors were invited to let the project directors know if they would be interested in attending seminars to discuss the project, or receiving further information. Thirty-one solicitors replied and said they would be interested in receiving further information about the project.

It was decided to hold two seminars in order to discuss a 'background paper' listing the hypotheses we intended to test. The first was held at the University of Exeter in June 1984, the second at the Institute of Cornish Studies, Camborne, in July 1984. About 15 people attended each seminar, half being solicitors and half members of the CAB and other interested individuals. The discussions formed a most valuable way of covering a wide variety of issues in a short time and were both a means of encouraging good relations with the local profession (Mungham and Thomas, 1981) and, more importantly, discovering areas which might be focused upon in the questionnaire.

The sample

The sampling frame used in the selection of solicitors for interview was *The Solicitors' and Barristers' Directory and Diary* for 1984. The problems involved with this source of data have been discussed in some detail elsewhere (Watkins, Blacksell and Economides 1984), but it is worth repeating here that the solicitors are listed in the *Directory* by firm and by town. The 1984 *Directory* was compiled by the publishers from returns sent in by solicitors in December 1983. It is generally considered that the *Directory* contains just over 90 per cent of solicitors with practising certificates, the 10 per cent deficiency being due to the lack of response of certain solicitors, or illegible replies. However, as Podmore (1980: 159) points out, 'despite this shortcoming, the method of listing solicitors [in *The Law List*] – under the firms with which they practise, and firms by the towns in which they are located – makes it a particularly useful source'.

It was first necessary to decide what was to be the unit of study. What was the population from which a sample had to be drawn? The unit could be the solicitors' *firm*, the solicitors' *office* (for many firms have a number of different offices) or the *individual solicitor*. In their study of Birmingham solicitors, Bridges *et al.* (1975) used the solicitors' firms and the offices into which they were divided as the unit of study, while Podmore (1980) in his later study used the individual solicitor. Using the 1973 *Law List* as a sampling frame, he divided up the solicitors' practices into nine groups based on three size classes of practice and three classes of location (urban, suburban and small rural towns). As individual solicitors could be included in the *Law List* a number of times if their firm had more than one branch, Podmore only included one branch from each firm in the sample. In seven cases, Podmore found that a solicitor selected for a firm of a particular location class actually worked at another of the firm's offices. This meant that his sample contained a greater 'spread' of towns than he had originally intended.

For the purposes of the present study it was decided to take a sample in a similar manner to that of Podmore, although the method had to be substantially modified in order to take account of the nature of the study and the differences between the format of the 1973 *Law List* and the 1984 *Directory*. The first step was to make a list of all solicitors in Devon and Cornwall by taking all those noted as 'in attendance' at particular offices. In order to make possible a breakdown of the sample into three size classes of firm, where a firm was made up of more than one office, the totals of solicitors 'in attendance' at each office were added together to form a 'grand total' for the firm as a whole. The size classification of firms chosen was based on Podmore's: small firms (one or two qualified solicitors); medium firms (three to five qualified solicitors) and large firms (six or more qualified solicitors). These three groups were further divided into 'urban' and 'rural' subgroups. Those firms whose office (or principal office) was in Exeter, Plymouth (including Plympton and Plymstock) or Torbay (Brixham, Paignton and Torquay) were classed as urban and the remainder were classed as rural. Six categories of firm were therefore produced, and the numbers of firms falling in these categories are given in Table A.1.

A list of solicitors was drawn up for each of the six categories, and random number tables were used to select the individual solicitors (Neave, 1978). Only one solicitor from each firm was included. Both the individual solicitors and their firms were randomly selected by this method, although within each size category there was a slight bias in favour of the larger firms. Only solicitors listed as partners or assistant solicitors in private practices were included in the lists. A disproportionate sampling fraction was used for the urban and rural subgroups in order to ensure sufficient sample numbers in the two 'domains of study'

(Moser and Kalton, 1971: 95). It was decided to take a sample of 102 solicitors (10% of the total number of 1,022) with 30 per cent being taken from the urban category and 70 per cent being taken from the rural category. This resulted in 10 solicitors being selected for each of the three urban subgroups and 24 for the three rural subgroups. The number and proportion of solicitors selected from the six categories are shown in Table A.1. Solicitors from a third (32%) of the 'urban' firms and 43 per cent of the 'rural' firms were selected.

Table A.1 The number of 'urban' and 'rural' solicitors and firms in Cornwall and Devon by size, class of firm and the number and proportion of solicitors and firms included in the sample.

No. of solicitors in firm	a	b	c	d	e	f
'Urban firms'						
1–2	54	10	19	40	10	25
3–5	111	10	9	28	10	36
6+	295	10	3	25	10	40
	460	30	4	93	30	32
'Rural firms'						
1–2	112	24	21	86	24	28
3–5	198	24	12	53	24	45
6+	252	24	10	27	24	89
	562	72	13	166	72	43
'All firms'						
1–2	166	34	20	126	34	27
3–5	309	34	11	81	34	42
6+	547	34	6	52	34	65
	1022	102	10	259	102	39

a = number of solicitors; b = number of solicitors selected;
c = percentage of solicitors selected; d = number of firms;
e = number of firms selected; f = percentage of firms selected.

Letters were sent to the chosen solicitors telling them that they had been selected for interview and that they would be telephoned in the near future so that an appointment might be made. The letters stressed that answers to the questionnaire would be confidential and a leaflet describing the project was enclosed. Of the 102 solicitors contacted, 12 (11.8%) were no longer practising in the study area. (One had died, one had left the country, one had retired, three were incorrectly listed in the 1984 *Directory* and six had left the area.) A further seven (6.9%) solicitors refused to be interviewed. The most frequent reason given for refusal was that they were too busy, although one wrote that 'I cannot see that your project serves any useful purpose other than to give some academics an appearance of being useful and I do not wish to have any part in it'! This attitude was most unusual, and the high response rate of 81 per cent was similar to the 83.4 per cent response achieved by Podmore (1980: 164) in his survey of private practice solicitors in Birmingham. Podmore noted that this response rate compares favourably with other recent surveys of the profession.

Table A.2 shows number of non-respondents by 'urban' and 'rural' subgroups. Solicitors from small firms had the highest non-response rate (29.4% as compared to 11.8% for solicitors from firms in the largest size group). This is probably because sole practitioner firms tend to have a relatively high turnover and are less likely to be able to spare the time to be interviewed. The locations of the chosen solicitors are shown in Table A.3 which also shows the number of solicitors from the different towns who were actually interviewed.

Table A.2 Reasons for non-response of solicitors

Subtype	Small (1–2)		Medium (3–5)		Large (6+)		Total	
	a	b	a	b	a	b	a	b
Rural	4	5	1	1	1	2	6	8
Urban	0	1	1	2	0	1	1	4
	4	6	2	3	1	3	7	12

a = refusal b = no longer practising in the study area.

Table A.3　The location of solicitors included in the main sample by size of firm.

Location	Small (1–2) a	b	Medium (3–5) a	b	Large (6+) a	b	Total a	c
Devon								
Barnstaple	2	1	2	–	3	–	7	6
Bideford	1	–	2	1	–	–	3	2
Braunton	–	–	–	–	1	–	1	1
Crediton	1	1	1	–	2	–	4	3
Cullompton	1	–	–	–	–	–	1	1
Dartmouth	–	–	1	1	1	–	2	1
Dawlish	–	–	–	–	1	–	1	1
Exeter	2	–	2	1	3	–	7	6
Exmouth	–	–	3	–	–	–	3	3
Honiton	–	–	–	–	1	–	1	1
Ilfracombe	–	–	1	–	1	1	2	1
Kingsbridge	–	–	1	–	–	–	1	1
Newton Abbot	–	–	1	–	2	1	4	3
Ottery St Mary	2	1	–	–	–	–	2	1
Plymouth	2	1	4	–	4	1	10	8
Sidmouth	–	–	–	–	3	–	3	3
Torbay	6	–	3	1	1	–	10	9
Torrington	1	–	–	–	–	–	1	1
Totnes	1	–	–	–	1	–	2	2
	20	4	21	4	24	3	65	54
Cornwall								
Callington	–	–	–	–	1	–	1	1
Camborne	–	–	2	–	–	–	2	2
Camelford	–	–	–	–	1	1	1	0
Falmouth	2	1	1	–	–	–	3	2
Hayle	1	–	–	–	–	–	1	1
Helston	1	1	1	–	1	–	3	2
Launceston	–	–	–	–	2	–	2	2
Lostwithiel	–	–	1	–	–	–	1	1
Newquay	1	1	–	–	–	–	1	0
Penzance	2	–	2	–	1	–	5	5
St Austell	–	–	1	–	3	–	4	4
St Columb	–	–	1	–	–	–	1	1
St Ives	1	1	–	–	–	–	1	0
St Mawes	1	–	–	–	–	–	1	1
Redruth	1	–	–	–	–	–	1	1
Truro	5	2	3	1	2	–	10	6
	15	6	12	1	11	1	38	29
	35	10	33	5	35	4	103	83

a = number of selected solicitors; b = solicitors not interviewed;
c = solicitors interviewed.

The questionnaire

The initial step in designing the questionnaire was to construct a simple list of questions, using previous surveys and the seminar transcripts as sources of information. This list was then transformed into a rough questionnaire suitable for pilot survey, the questions being grouped into five main sections. The first section dealt with the solicitor's career and contains questions about the respondent's education, employment, reasons for working in his current firm and membership of professional organisations and public bodies. The second section contained questions relating to the firm, including the history and development of the firm, the number of staff employed, whether the firm has branch offices and how these are organised. Information was collected on the numbers of partners, assistant solicitors, articled clerks, legal executives and other staff (including secretaries, cashiers and office juniors) employed by each firm.

The third section of the questionnaire dealt with the categories of work undertaken by the solicitors and their firms. In order to make comparisons between the firms possible, it was decided as far as possible to use the categories of work definitions employed by the Law Society (these are given in Appendix 2) and three questions about this categorisation were therefore included. Solicitors were asked, both for themselves and for their firms, to list in order of importance the first five categories of work which they undertook in terms of income and time. They were also asked to note which categories had increased or decreased relatively in importance over the last 10 years. Further questions in this section dealt with the way cases are handled within the firm, whether any types of work were considered uneconomic, how the firm was likely to be affected by the possible loss of the 'conveyancing monopoly', and whether the firm was going to react to the relaxation of advertising controls.

The fourth section contained questions about the firm's clients. Solicitors were asked to estimate how important different types of referral were to the firm and the proportion of their clients who were private individuals as opposed to business organisations. It included a number of questions about the operation of the Legal Aid Scheme and about the difficulties rural clients may have in reaching the solicitor's office.

In order to assess the range of problems dealt with by the solicitors interviewed and the types of client concerned, a diary of cases was left with each solicitor for him or his secretary to fill in. The solicitor was asked if he would put information in the diary about each client he interviewed during a single week. The following information was required: whether the client was new; where the client was met; the category(ies) of work concerned; whether the client was supported by Legal Aid or the Green Form Scheme; the client's occupation and where the client lived. The solicitor was also asked, for the same week, to note the number of hours each day spent meeting clients; dealing with other casework; in court; travelling on business and doing general administration. The completed diaries provided invaluable information about the type of work undertaken by the solicitors interviewed which backed up the data collected at the interviews and assisted in the assessment of solicitors' catchment areas.

The final section of the questionnaire contained a series of more general questions dealing with the duty solicitor schemes, the CABx, the local Bar and legal expenses insurance. It also contained some open-ended questions about the general provision of legal services in rural areas.

A pilot survey was carried out in November 1984. Letters were sent to 12 solicitors who had been randomly selected from the *Law List* and 9 agreed to be interviewed. The interviews took between an hour and an hour and a half to complete. Notes were made at the time of the interview of any comments that the respondents made in addition to answering the set questions. The fifth section of the questionnaire was also recorded on tape. On comparing the notes made for the final section of the questionnaire and the recording it was considered that the recording was unnecessary: it was possible to note down all the main comments at the time of the interview and it was felt that the tape recorder might inhibit the responses to certain questions.

The design of the questionnaire and the results of the pilot survey were discussed at a seminar held at the Institute of Advanced Legal Studies, University of London, in December 1984. This was attended by 10 people who had either carried out research in this area, or who represented interested organisations such as NACAB, the Law Society, LAG and the Lord Chancellor's Department. This proved to be a useful meeting, and a number of modifications were made to the questionnaire in response to the general results of the pilot survey and to points made at the seminar.

The main survey itself was carried out between January and May 1985. The letters were sent to the selected solicitors in four main batches: south and east Devon, north Devon, Plymouth and east Cornwall, and west and central Cornwall. This system enabled appointments to be made and grouped together so that travelling time could be reduced to a minimum. It was possible for one person to carry out two, or at most three, interviews per day. When the survey was completed, the questionnaire schedules were coded for analysis using the Statistical Package for the Social Sciences (SPSSx). Any explanatory or illustrative comments made by solicitors were transcribed from the questionnaire schedules in order to be used in the analysis together with the coded data.

2. THE CITIZENS' ADVICE BUREAUX SURVEY

In order to gather as much information as possible about the CABx, it was decided to interview the CAB managers, who in Devon and Cornwall are in most cases salaried, rather than a sample of the volunteers. There are 24 bureaux in the two counties, although a number have extensions which are 'managed' from a bureau, and all of the managers were interviewed.

The questionnaire

The questionnaire was designed in conjunction with the area office of the CAB. As the total population was so small, a pilot survey was dispensed with, but the extensive consultation with the CAB largely performed the same function. Moreover, the results of a survey of bureaux in south Wales carried out by Diana Beale (Beale and Stow, 1986) proved very useful in identifying and overcoming problems associated with such a survey.

The questionnaire itself was divided into six main sections. The first section dealt with general information about the bureau, including the number and type of staff working in the bureau, reasons for its location and site, and its structure (i.e. how it was managed and whether there were extensions). The next section dealt specifically with links between the bureau and the legal profession and in particular asked how the variety of schemes associated with the referral of clients to solicitors were operated, and what the manager thought of such schemes. The main schemes dealt with are: legal advice sessions held by solicitors within the bureau; the referral of clients to solicitors' offices for free interviews outside the Legal Aid Scheme; the straight-forward referral of clients to solicitors; the ringing up of solicitors by the bureau for instant advice; and finally the availability of an HLA, that is a solicitor in private practice who advises the bureau.

The third section was concerned with links between the bureau and the courts and tribunals. The respondent was asked whether any of the volunteers acted as representatives at tribunals and what they thought of the tribunal system, whether the volunteers were involved with the operation of the county court small claims procedure, and whether any of the bureau's rural clients had difficulty getting to any courts. The links between the CAB and other agencies were dealt with in the next section. The respondent was presented with a list of agencies and asked to estimate how important each is in terms of the number of referrals the bureau received from them, and then, with the same list, asked to estimate the importance of the different agencies in terms of the number of referrals the bureau made. Further questions dealt with overlap between the different agencies, informal and formal links between the bureau and private and public bodies, and the organiser's view of the funding arrangements.

The fifth section dealt with the relationship between the bureau and its clients. Questions covered methods of advertising the services offered, whether there were special arrangements for contacting people in rural areas, and whether there were special problems associated with dealing with people from rural areas. Finally, the sixth section contained a number of general questions dealing with the differences between 'urban' and 'rural' bureaux, the respondent's opinion about different ways of improving access to legal services, the relationship between the bureau and NACAB, the use of specialist sources of legal information and computers in the bureau, and lastly some information about the education of the manager and her reasons for joining the CAB.

3. THE FIRST PARISH SURVEY

The first two detailed surveys carried out as part of the AJRBP in Devon and Cornwall were of the solicitors' profession and of CAB managers. These surveys helped us to assess the range of legal services available in the two counties and the attitudes of solicitors and managers on a range of issues associated with such services. The third main survey was designed to assess the use of legal services by people living in remote areas of the south-west of England. The two earlier surveys dealt with the provision of legal services; the parish surveys considered the use of, and latent demand for, those services, and the attendant attitudes of the general public towards them.

The sample

Three remote parishes were chosen for study. Each had half of its area at least 10 miles (16 km) or more from a town with no more than two full-time solicitors' practices. Each parish had one relatively large village of the same name, and was surrounded by an outer area characterised by small hamlets and isolated farmsteads and cottages. Chulmleigh is in North Devon District, and is a large parish of 3,604 ha with a population of 1,163. The nearest market town, South Molton, which is about eight miles (13 km) distant, has four solicitors' offices. Chulmleigh itself also has two solicitors' offices, but these satellite offices of South Molton firms are only open two hours a week on Fridays. The nearest CAB is at South Molton, but this is only open 14 hours a week and the nearest full-time CAB is at Barnstaple. Hartland is also in Devon, but is a rather larger parish of 7,003 ha, with a population of 1,420 in Torridge District on the north-west coast of the county. Bideford, 12 miles (19 km) away, has six firms of solicitors and a CAB which is open 25 hours a week. The third parish chosen was St Keverne, which consists of 4,168 ha and has a population of 1,874. The parish is situated on the Lizard peninsula and the nearest town, Helston, which is 10 miles (16 km) away, has seven firms of solicitors and a CAB open 20 hours a week.

The sampling frame used to select individuals for interview was the electoral register for each parish. For Chulmleigh and Hartland the electoral register for the whole parish was used, but for St Keverne, the small separate ward including the hamlet of Coverack was excluded. The qualifying date for the registers used was 10 October 1985; the surveys themselves were carried out in June and July 1986. Random number tables were used to select 150 individuals aged over 18 from each of the parishes. This was just over 10 per cent of the population of each parish (but a considerably higher proportion of the adult population). Only one person was selected from each household.

In order to obtain a high response rate, it was decided to carry out a personal interview survey, rather than send out a postal questionnaire. A pilot survey of the questionnaire showed that there was a moderately high refusal rate even with a doorstep interview, and so it was further decided to write to each of the selected individuals. Each person selected was sent a letter giving brief details of the project, and explaining that someone would call round on one of two specified days to carry out a short interview.

The interviews were carried out by the authors with the assistance of a small group of students who each attended two training sessions. Each parish was visited on two days. As only the selected individuals within the households could be interviewed, it was often necessary to visit a house a number of times before the respondent could be found. The interviews were carried out in the afternoon and evening in order that people at work had an equal chance of being successfully interviewed. A number of people could not be contacted after two days interviewing, and it was decided to revisit each parish after a period of a month, in order to contact people who were away from home or on holiday. Overall, there was a high (79%) successful response rate, varying from 75 per cent in Hartland to 83 per cent in St Keverne. The refusal rate of 5 per cent was very low indeed and in St Keverne it was as low as 3 per cent. The bulk of the non-response, 10 per cent overall, was made up of those people who had moved away from the parishes in the six months or so between the qualifying date of the register and the date of survey. A further 5 per cent could not be contacted within the three days of interviewing allotted to each parish. The very low refusal rate suggests that there is little bias due to this cause in the results presented in this book.

The questionnaire

The questionnaire went through a number of drafts and helpful comments were received from a number of people, especially, Dr Paul Webley of the Psychology Department, University of Exeter, and Professor John Flood, then of the American Bar Foundation. A pilot survey was carried out in Winkleigh, a mid-Devon village. The final version consisted of four main groups of questions. These were designed to complement the questions dealing with clients in the surveys of solicitors and CAB managers. The first dealt with the use of solicitors, and questions were asked about the number of separate issues that had been dealt with by solicitors and the type of issue involved. Details were collected of the reasons for choosing the solicitors concerned, and problems involved in contacting them. Respondents were also asked how satisfied they were with the way they had been dealt with by solicitors, and whether they would use the same solicitor again. There were also general questions dealing with the distance that people were prepared to travel to visit solicitors of their choice; preference for male or female solicitors; the use of legal services of trade unions and whether or not people considered that they had a 'family solicitor'. The second group of questions dealt with the CAB and broadly similar questions were asked about this organisation as had been asked about solicitors.

The third section was designed to assess the extent to which people may have thought about consulting a solicitor over an issue, but then decided against doing this for some reason. If this situation had occurred, the respondents were asked if they had gone to anyone else for advice, and whether the issue had ever been resolved. The final group of questions was designed to assess various characteristics of the respondent, including length of residence in the parish, type of tenure, car-ownership, number of residents in the household and their occupation and ages. A final question asked for general comments about the provision of legal services in their area.

Characteristics of the respondents

Just over half the respondents (54%) were female. This is slightly higher than the figure (52%) for Devon and Cornwall as a whole. There were variations between the parishes in this respect: in Chulmleigh, for example, almost two-thirds (63%) of the respondents were female, while in St Keverne a small majority (52%) were male. In total, only 11 per cent of the sample were under 30 years old, almost a half (48%) were between 30 and 59, while a further 41 per cent were over 60 years old. The 1981 census shows that 22 per cent of the population of Cornwall and 23 per cent of the population of Devon were 'of pensionable age', and although the data from the surveys are not directly comparable, it is clear that there is a greater proportion of people over 60 in the three parishes than in the two counties. There were considerable differences between the parishes: Chulmleigh, for example,-had a very high proportion (49%) of respondents over 60 and a relatively low proportion of people under 30 (8%), while St Keverne had the highest proportion of respondents (55%) between 30 and 59 years old, and under a third (32%) over 60.

There was little difference between the parishes in the length of time that the respondents had lived there. The current high turnover of properties in these areas is indicated by the fact that just under a quarter (23%) of the respondents had been living in their parishes for five years or less. At the other extreme, the same proportion (23%) had been living in the parishes for more than 20 years, and a fifth (20%) had always lived in the parish. The parishes were characterised by a high proportion of owner-occupied property. In general, well over two-thirds (69%) of the respondents' houses were owner-occupied, and in Chulmleigh the proportion was over three-quarters (76%). These figures are considerably higher than the proportions for Devon

(63%), Cornwall (66%) or Great Britain (56%) given in the 1981 census.

The majority of households (62%) consisted of two adults. Only 14 per cent had a single adult, while 23 per cent had three or more adults. There was little difference between the parishes in terms of the number of adults in the household. When the occupation of the adults is considered, however, there are important differences. Over a third (37%) of all the respondents were retired, but this proportion was highest in Chulmleigh (43%) and lowest in St Keverne (31%). In contrast, St Keverne had the highest proportion of respondents (26%) who were employees, and also the highest proportion of housewives (14%). Hartland had the highest proportion (13%) of self-employed businessmen, while Chulmleigh had the highest proportion (6%) of professional people. The proportion of farmers and farmers' wives (11%) and the unemployed (4%) was similar in each of the parishes.

The proportion unemployed (4%) may appear very low, but is not, of course, equivalent to the standard 'unemployment' figures which usually give the proportion unemployed and claiming benefit as a proportion of the working population. In order to put the 'unemployment' figure from this survey into context, therefore, it is necessary to compare it to the proportion of the total population of Devon and Cornwall over 17 which is unemployed. The relevant figures were, for Cornwall in August 1986, 6.9 per cent, and for Devon in July, 5.8 per cent. Thus the rural parishes selected do have a significantly lower level of unemployment than the two counties as a whole.

The importance of car-ownership for people living in remote rural areas was shown by the very high proportion of respondents whose household had at least one car. In St Keverne as many as 84 per cent of the respondents' households had a car, while in Chulmleigh (81%) and Hartland (79%) the proportions were also remarkably high. These figures may be compared to the proportions of households with a car in Devon (66%), Cornwall (70%) and Great Britain (61%) given in the 1981 census.

4. THE SECOND PARISH SURVEY

This survey was a qualitative investigation of rural legality, based on the experiences of people living in three remote rural parishes in Cornwall and Devon in gaining access to, and using, legal and para-legal services. It complemented the more wide-ranging, mainly quantitative survey of the use of these services in the same three parishes. The parishes, Chulmleigh and Hartland in Devon and St Keverne in Cornwall, have all been chosen because of their remoteness from legal services: in each case one has to travel over 10 miles (16 km) to reach a town where there were more than two solicitors' offices open permanently during working hours.

There were four basic themes: advice-seeking, communication and travel, legal knowledge, and the expectations of those using legal services and possible improvements. Each was probed in depth in a detailed, follow-up, interview survey, which covered a small sample of those questioned in the first parish survey.

The questionnaire

Each person selected for interview in the follow-up survey had indicated, as part of their replies to the initial questionnaire that they would be willing to be reinterviewed. Letters were sent to all those chosen, explaining that we wished to interview them once again and that they would be telephoned in a few days' time to arrange an appointment. The interview was based on a semi-structured questionnaire with the interviewer making notes on the answers given. The whole meeting was also tape-recorded. Afterwards, a comprehensive reconstruction of the interview was compiled by the researcher who conducted the interview, using the notes and the tape-recording made at the time. All the interviews, which lasted approximately an hour, were conducted by Alison Dixon.

The interview began by explaining that this study formed part of a piece of research being undertaken at the University of Exeter into the provision of legal services in rural areas and that it was a follow-up to the earlier brief interview about the respondent's use of legal services. It was stated quite clearly that what was being sought was greater detail about their own experience of using legal services and also their views on other aspects of legal service provision in rural areas. It was emphasised strongly that all the answers would be treated in the strictest confidence and that no individual would be named or identified in any published document emanating from the survey.

Respondents were asked about the use they had made of solicitors or CABx. Those that had consulted a CAB were then asked when, why and where they had done so. We were only interested in particular types of issue but anyone who had consulted a CAB about a relevant issue was then asked to describe in detail: how they came to take the matter to the CAB, how they contacted the bureau in question, what advice was given, what action was subsequently taken, how they evaluated the service, and how they felt it might be improved. All those who had consulted a solicitor, including anyone who had also consulted a CAB, were then asked a similar set of questions about solicitors. The only substantial difference was the inclusion of a short section about whether or not they had had the potential costs explained to them and whether they had understood sufficiently clearly what action was proposed on their behalf. A further category of respondent was those people who had had a problem with potential legal implications but who had not consulted either a solicitor or a CAB. This group was asked to provide details of the issue, to explain how they had gone about resolving it, and from whom they had sought advice and with what success. Our aim here was to uncover any latent demand for legal services which might have existed in the rural communities under investigation.

The interviewer then went on to ask respondents about any improvements to legal services that they felt might usefully be instituted. This was followed by a series of detailed questions about their travel arrangements for visiting the CABx and solicitors respectively, with particular emphasis being placed on any difficulties which had to be overcome.

In order to find out more about individual levels of legal competence, the interview then sought to establish whether the respondent, or anyone among his or her immediate family and friends, had specific legal training. This was followed by a series of questions about any legal knowledge they may have gleaned from reading, television or radio. For the latter two, an open question was followed by a prompt, using a card listing the main programmes broadcast with a legal content.

Towards the end of the interview, respondents were asked for their reaction to three potential new developments in the delivery of legal services which have already been experimented with elsewhere: a village link person, a Freefone service, and a law centre. Finally everyone was asked to provide brief details about their family, educational and economic circumstances.

Table A.4 shows that 42 people were selected and 32 successfully interviewed, a response rate of 76 per cent. Response rates varied from 50 per cent in Chulmleigh, to 91 per cent in Hartland and 100 per cent in St Keverne. There is no obvious reason for the rather high level of refusals in Chulmleigh, but in any case the total numbers involved in each individual parish in the follow-up survey were too small to make separate analysis meaningful.

Table A.4 The sample for the second parish survey

	Chulmleigh	Hartland	St Keverne	Total
Sampled	18	12	12	42
Interviewed	9	11	12	32
Moved away	1	0	0	1
Ill/unable to contact	1	1	0	2
Refused	6	0	0	6
Response rate (%)	50	91	100	76

The Sample Population

From the outset it was accepted that, owing to resource limitations, it would only be possible to reinterview a small proportion of the 355 people successfully interviewed in the initial survey. Eventually, the length of, and the level of detail in, the final questionnaire limited this proportion to about 10 per cent. It was decided, therefore, to select respondents for reinterview according to three criteria: whether or not they had agreed to being reinterviewed when responding to the first questionnaire; the type of issue raised; and whether or not this had arisen during the previous three years.

Since only a small minority of the original sample had refused to be reinterviewed, it seemed counterproductive to attempt to include them in the follow-up. Equally, given the detail that was being asked for in the second questionnaire and the importance of accurate recall by the respondents, it was thought sensible to consider fairly recent issues, although the three-year deadline was chosen arbitrarily. It was agreed that to be included an issue would have to satisfy one or more of three basic criteria:

1. It should not be purely 'routine', involving only matters such as conveyancing, making a will, or probate;
2. There should be some element of initial doubt, however slight, as to whether the issue should be taken to a solicitor or a CAB;
3. It should be an issue involving an area of law on which our earlier study of solicitors (Blacksell, Economides and Watkins, 1987) suggested there might be difficulty in obtaining legal advice in a country district, such as welfare, housing, or consumer law.

The result was that everyone was included who had agreed to be reinterviewed in our initial survey, and who had consulted a solicitor or a CAB in the previous three years about an issue classified as: consumer, family, housing, welfare, employment, and litigation (this category covered a wide range of disputes, from accident claims, to industrial injury, and business debts). We also reinterviewed anyone who had considered taking an issue falling into any of these categories to a solicitor, but had eventually decided against it. Finally, we reinterviewed all those who had been in dispute with their neighbours, because there was frequently uncertainty about whether or not to seek legal advice.

A number of minor problems arose when we actually came to conduct the follow-up interviews, stemming mainly from developments that had occurred since the initial survey was undertaken. The most significant was that, in a few cases, new issues had emerged which fell within our designated categories. In all these cases we concentrated in the interview on the most recent relevant incident, since recall was much better and it was much more acceptable to those being interviewed to talk about more recent events.

Successful interviews were conducted with 32 people, 20 men and 12 women, ranging in age from a young man of under 20 to a woman who was over 70. Nine lived in Chulmleigh, 11 in Hartland and 12 in St Keverne, and all but three were married or cohabiting. Only three people had been living in their respective county for less than five years and only six had been in their present parish for less than five years. The majority were owner-occupiers (22), but there were four council-house tenants, three living in property tied to a job, and two living in privately rented accommodation. All the men but one, who was retired, were in employment, with just over half being self-employed. Four of the women were retired, though they had previously had paid jobs, only one was in full-time paid employment, although seven worked part-time. An estimate of the balance between the standard social classes was derived from these data, which demonstrated that there was a small majority (17 : 15) in non-manual, as opposed to manual occupations, and a predominance of people in Class 2 (professional and managerial) of the Registrar-General's classification of employment. The majority (23) had left school at 16 or earlier, 12 with no educational qualifications, and only four had remained in full-time education after the age of 18. There was a wide range of household income, ranging from four with under £5,000 a year to four with over £20,000. The largest category (12) were households with between £5,000 and £9,999 a year. All but two of the households owned either a car, a van or a motorcycle, though only 23 of those interviewed had unrestricted access to a car. All but three households had a telephone.

Appendix 2   The Law Society's Categories of Work

A   Agricultural Property
B   Bankruptcy and Insolvency
C   Business Affairs
D   Child Care and Wardship
E   Commercial Property
F   Consumer Problems
G   Crime – General and Motoring
H   Crime – Juvenile
J   Employment
K   Family
L   Housing, Landlord and Tenant
M   Litigation – Accidents, Injury, Criminal Injury Compensation
N   Litigation – Commercial
P   Litigation – General
R   Planning, Compulsory Purchase, Land Tribunal
S   Residential Conveyancing
T   Taxation – Business and Personal
V   Welfare Benefits
W   Wills and Trusts
Z   (other categories of work)

    a   Admiralty
    b   Banking Law
    c   Building Contracts
    d   Charity Law
    e   Copyright Patents, Designs and Trademarks
    f   Entertainment, Artists and Performers
    g   European Human Rights
    h   Housing Association Law

i   Immigration and Nationality
j   Insurance Law
k   Libel and Slander
l   Liquor and Betting and Gaming Licensing
m   Mental Health
n   Mines and Mineral Law
p   Pension Scheme
r   Race and Sex Discrimination
s   Rating Law
t   Road Haulage Licensing

BIBLIOGRAPHY

ABEL R L 1979 Socializing the legal profession: can redistributing lawyers' services achieve social justice? *Law and Policy Quarterly* **1**(1): 5–51

ABEL R L 1981 Conservative conflict and the reproduction of capitalism: the role of informal justice. *International Journal of the Sociology of Law* **9**(3): 245–67

ABEL R L (ed) 1982 *The Politics of Informal Justice* (2 vols) Academic Press, New York

ABEL R L 1985 Lawyers and the power to change *Law and Policy* **7**(1): 5–18

ABEL R L 1986 The decline of professionalism? *Modern Law Review* **49**: 1–41

ABEL R L 1988 *The Legal Profession in England and Wales* Blackwell, Oxford

ABEL R L, LEWIS P S C (eds) 1988 *Lawyers in Society: A Comparative Perspective* (3 vols) University of California Press, Calif

ABEL-SMITH B, ZANDER M, BROOKE R 1973 *Legal Problems and the Citizen* Heinemann, London

ACORA (Archbishops' Commission on Rural Areas) 1990 *Faith in the Countryside* Churchman Publishing, ' Vorthing, Sussex

ADAMSDOWN COMMUNITY TRUST 1978 Community need and law centre practice: an empirical assessment. Unpublished

ALKER H S 1969 A typology of ecological fallacies. In Dogan M and Rokkan S (eds) *Quantitative Ecological Analysis in the Social Sciences* MIT Press, 69–86.

ALLEN P 1986 Legal services distrust. *California Lawyer* **6**: 21–62

ANDREWS Sir R 1989 *Review of Government Legal Services* HMSO, London

BALDWIN J 1988 The role of Citizens' Advice Bureaux and law centres in the provision of legal advice and assistance *Civil Justice Quarterly* **8**: 24–44

BALDWIN J, HILL S 1986 Research on the Green Form Scheme of legal advice and assistance. *Civil Justice Quarterly* **5**: 247–59

BEALE D, STOW B 1986 *CAB and Access to Legal Services in South Wales* NACAB Occasional Paper, NACAB

BELL P, CLOKE P 1989 The changing relationship between the private and public sectors: privatisation and rural Britain. *Journal of Rural Studies* **5**(1): 1–15

BERMAN H 1983 *Law and Revolution. The Formation of the Western Legal Tradition* Harvard University Press, Cambridge, Mass

BERRY B J 1967 *Geography of Market Centres and Regional Distribution* Prentice-Hall, Englewood Cliffs, NJ

BLACKSELL M, CLARK A, ECONOMIDES K, WATKINS C 1988 Legal services in rural areas: Problems of access and local need. *Progress in Human Geography* **12**(1): 47–65

BLACKSELL M, CLARK A, ECONOMIDES K, WATKINS C 1990 Citizens Advice Bureaux: Problems of an emerging service in rural areas. *Social Policy & Administration* **24** (3): 212–25

BLACKSELL M, WATKINS C, ECONOMIDES K 1986 Human geography and law: A case of separate development in social science. *Progress in Human Geography* **10**: 371–96

BLACKSELL M, ECONOMIDES K, WATKINS C 1987 Country solicitors: their professional role in rural Britain. *Sociologia Ruralis* **25**: 181–96

BLACKSELL M, ECONOMIDES K, DIXON A 1989 *Knowledge and Opinion of Law and Legal Services in Remote Rural Areas* AJRBP Working Paper 15, University of Exeter

BLOMLEY N 1989 Text and context: rethinking the law–space nexus. *Progress in Human Geography* **11**(4): 512–34

BOURDILLON M 1945 *Voluntary Services: Their Place in the Modern State* Methuen, London

BOYUM K O 1979 A perspective on civil delay in trial courts. *Justice System Journal* **5**: 170–86

BRACEY H E 1959 *English Rural Life* Routledge & Kegan Paul, London

BRAKEL S J 1973 Free legal services for the poor – staffed office versus judicare: The client's evaluation. *Wisconsin Law Review* **2**: 532–53

BRASNETT M E 1964 *The Story of the Citizens' Advice Bureaux* National Council for Social Service

BRIDGES L, SUFRIN B, WHETTON J, WHITE R 1975 *Legal Services in Birmingham* Institute of Judicial Administration, University of Birmingham

BRITT C 1986 *The Delivery of Public Legal Services to Rural Areas: The American Experience* AJRBP Working Paper No 5, University of Exeter

BROGDEN G 1978 Welfare rights and access to information. In Walker A (ed) *Rural Poverty: Poverty, Deprivation and Planning in Rural Areas* CPAG Poverty Pamphlet 37: 100–6

BROOKE R 1972 *Information and Advice Services.* Bell & Cooper, London

BROOKS C W 1986 *Pettyfoggers and Vipers of the Commonwealth* Cambridge University Press, Cambridge

BRUSH J E, BRACEY H E 1955 Rural service centres in southwestern Wisconsin and southern England. *Geographical Review* **45**: 559–69

BURMAN S B, HARRELL-BOND B E (eds) 1979 *The Imposition of Law* Academic Press, London

BUSCHMANN W 1979 Rechtshilfe für die Leute auf dem Lande – das rheinlandpfalzisch Modell. In Rasehorn T (ed) *Rechtsberatung als Lebenshilfe* Neuweid, Luchterhand

BUTCHER H 1976 Information services for rural areas. In Brooke R (ed) *Advice Services in Welfare Rights* Fabian Research Series 329

BUTTEL F, NEWBY H (eds) 1980 *The Rural Sociology of the Advanced Societies* Croom Helm, London

CAIN M, KULCSAR K 1981–82 Thinking disputes: an essay on the origins of the dispute industry. *Law and Society Review* **16**(3): 375–402

CAPPELLETTI M (ed) 1978–81 *Access to Justice: A World Survey* (6 Vols) Sijthoff/Giuffrè, Leyden, London, Boston/Milan

CAPPELLETTI M, GARTH B 1978 Access to justice: the worldwide movement to make rights effective. A general report. In Cappelletti M (ed) *Access to Justice: A World Survey* Vol 1, Book 1: 5–124

CARR-SAUNDERS A M, WILSON P A 1933 *The Professions* Clarendon Press, Oxford

CHAMBERS G, HARWOOD S 1990 *Solicitors in England and Wales: Practice, Organisation and Perceptions* Law Society Research Studies Series No. 2

CHAMPION A G (ed) 1989 *Counterurbanisation: The Changing Face and Nature of Population Deconcentration* Edward Arnold, London

CHAMPION A G, WATKINS C (eds) 1991 *People in the Countryside: Studies of Social Change in Rural Britain* Paul Chapman, London

CHILD POVERTY ACTION GROUP 1987 *Poverty and deprivation in the South-west* CPAG, London

CHOUINARD V 1989 Transformations in the capitalist state. The development of legal aid and legal clinics in Canada. *Transactions of the Institute of British Geographers* (New Series) **14**: 329–49

CHURCH T W 1982 *Examining Local Legal Culture: Practitioner Attitudes in Four Criminal Courts* National Institute of Justice, Washington

CHURCH T W, CARLSON A, LEE J, TAN T 1978 *Justice Delayed: The Pace of Litigation in Urban Trial Courts* National Center for State Courts, Williamsburg, Va

CITRON J 1989 *Citizens' Advice Bureaux. For the Community, by the Community* Pluto, London

CLARK A, ECONOMIDES K 1989 The poverty of technology. Unpublished paper presented to the 4th Annual Conference of BILETA, *Bridging the Technology Gap: Academy to Practice* Institute of Advanced Legal Studies, April

CLARK A, ECONOMIDES K 1990 Technics and praxis: technological innovation and legal practice in modern society. *Yearbook of Law Computers and Technology* **4**: 16–37

CLARK A, ECONOMIDES K 1991 Computers, expert systems and legal process: towards a sociological understanding of computers in legal practice. In Narayanan A, Bennun M (eds) *Law, Computer Science, and Artificial Intelligence* Ablex Publishing Corporation Norwood, New Jersey: 3–32

CLARK A 1991 Advances in information technology and the growth of para-legal services. Unpublished Ph D dissertation (thesis), University of Exeter

CLARK G L 1985 *Judges and the Cities* University of Chicago Press, Chicago

CLARK G L 1989 The Geography of Law. In Peet R and Thrift N (eds) *New Models in Geography* (2 vols) Unwin Hyman, London

CLOKE P, PARK C 1985 *Rural Resource Development* Croom Helm, London

CLOKE P, EDWARDS G 1986 Rurality in England and Wales 1981: a replication of the 1971 index. *Regional Studies* **20**: 289–306

CLOKE P, LITTLE J 1987 The impact of decision-making on rural communities: an example from Gloucestershire. *Applied Geography* **7**: 55–77

CLOKE P, LITTLE J 1990 *The rural state? Limits to planning in rural society* Clarendon, Oxford

COATES B E, RAWSTRON E M 1971 *Regional Variations in Britain: Studies in Economic and Social Geography* Batsford, London

COCHRAN D 1984 Down and out in the valley. California Lawyer 4: 50–4

COLE J P, KING C A M 1968 *Quantitative Geography* Wiley, New York

COOKE P 1989a Cultural cosmopolitanism: urban and regional studies into the 1990's. *Geoforum* **20**: 241–52

COOKE P (ed) 1989b *Localities* Unwin Hyman, London

COOPER J 1983 *Public Legal Services: A Comparative Study of Policy, Politics and Practice* Sweet & Maxwell, London

COTTERRELL R 1989 *The Politics of Jurisprudence. A Critical Introduction to Legal Philosophy* Butterworths, Sevenoaks, Kent

COTTINO A 1983 Criminalità contadina e giustizia borghese: una ricerca sull'amministrazione della giustizia nelle campagne del cunese all'Inizio del secolo. *Sociologia del Diritto* **10**(3): 97–131

COTTINO A 1986 Peasant conflicts in Italy. *Journal of Legal Pluralism and Unofficial Law* **24**: 77–100

COYLE 1986 Traditional Indian justice in Ontario: a role for the present? *Osgoode Hall Law Journal* **24**(3): 605–33

COX K H 1977 Lawyers, population and society in New York: a study of the distribution of lawyers among rural metropolitan areas and its relationship to demographic, economic and political patterns. *Cornell Rural Sociology Bulletin* **86**: 11–78

DAMESICK P J 1986 Service industries in Britain: trends and issues. *Transactions of the Institute of British Geographers* (New Series) **11**: 212–26

DANIELS P W 1983 Service industries: supporting role or centre stage? *Area* **15**: 301–10

DANIELS S 1982 Civil litigation in Illinois trial courts: an exploration in rural–urban differences. *Law and Policy Quarterly* **4**: 190–214

DANIELS S 1985 Continuity and change in patterns of case handling: a case study of two rural counties. *Law and Society Review* **19**: 381–420

DEAR M 1981 The state: a research agenda. *Environment and Planning:A* **13**: 1191–6

Duke Law Journal 1969 The legal problems of the rural poor. *Duke Law Journal* 495–619

ECONOMIDES K 1982 Legal services and rural deprivation. *Bracton Law Journal* **15**: 41–78

ECONOMIDES K 1991 Franchising and rural legal services. *European Yearbook in the Sociology of Law* (forthcoming)

ECONOMIDES K, GARTH B 1984 The determination of legal services policy in the United Kingdom and the United States of America. *Environment and Planning C: Government and Policy* **2**: 445–60

ECONOMIDES K, WATKINS C, BLACKSELL M 1985 *Studying Rural Lawyers: Research Strategy and Context* AJRBP Working Paper No 4, University of Exeter

ECONOMIDES K, BLACKSELL M, WATKINS C 1986 The spatial analysis of legal systems: towards a geography of law? *Journal of Law and Society* **13**: 161–81

ECONOMIDES K, BLACKSELL M 1987 Access to justice in rural Britain: final report. *Anglo–American Law Review* **16**(4): 353–75

ECONOMIDES K, BLACKSELL S, BLACKSELL M 1991 *Referrals to Solicitors in Rural Areas with Particular Reference to Cornwall and Devon.* Law Society Research Study Series, London

ELLIOTT D K 1984 *Rural Rights* NACAB North East Area Office, Mea House, Ellison Place, Newcastle upon Tyne

ENGEL D M 1980 Legal pluralism in an American community: perspectives on a civil trial court. *American Bar Foundation Research Journal* 425–54

ENGEL D M 1984 The oven bird's song: insiders, outsiders, and personal injuries in an American community. *Law and Society Review* **18**(4): 551–82

ENGEL D M 1987 Law, time, and community. *Law and Society Review* **21**(4): 605–37

EXETER DISTRICT LAW CENTRE STEERING GROUP 1981 (EDLCSG) A proposal for a rural law centre. Unpublished, University of Exeter

FAULKENER T M, SAUNDERS R N S 1985 Are the professions entering the small business sector? Paper presented at the 7th National Small Firms Policy and Research Conference

FERRARI V 1982 Diritto e dispute: osservazione empiriche in una piccola communitá. *Sociologia del Diritto* 9: 25–76

FOSTER K 1973 The location of solicitors. *Modern Law Review* 36: 153–66

FRANKENBURG R 1966 *Communities in Britain* Penguin, London

FRIEDMANN J, ALONSO W 1964 *Regional Development and Planning* The MIT Press, London

GALANTER M 1980 Legality and its discontents: a preliminary assessment of current theories of legalisation and delegalisation. In Blankenburg E *et al* (eds) *Alternative Rechtsformen und Alternatives zum Recht* Oplanden Westdeutscher Verlag 11–26

GARDEN J (ed) 1978 *Solving the Transport Problems of the Elderly: The Use of Resources* Department of Adult Education, University of Keele

GARTH F B 1980 *Neighborhood Law Firms for the Poor: A Comparative Study of Recent Developments in Legal Aid and the Legal Professions* Sijthoff & Noordhoff, Alphen aan den Rÿn

GEERTZ C 1983 *Local Knowledge. Further Essays in Interpretive Anthropology*. Basic Books, New York

GILG A W 1985 *An introduction to rural geography* Edward Arnold, London

GOAD T W 1989 *Just a Country Solicitor* Dalesman, Lancaster

GOODCHILD M F, NORONHA V T 1983 *Location–Allocation for Small Computers* Monograph 8, Department of Geography, University of Iowa

GRIFFITHS J 1977 The Distribution of Legal Services in the Netherlands *British Journal of Law and Society* 4: 260–86

HALLIDAY T C 1986 Six score years and ten: demographic transitions in the American legal profession, 1850–1980. *Law & Society Review* 20(1): 53–78

HARDMAN G W 1961 The qualities of the country practitioner *Law Society's Gazette* 58: 77

HARPER S 1989 The British rural community: an overview of perspectives *Journal of Rural Studies* 5(2): 161–84

HARRIS D, GENN H, 1984 *Compensation and Support for Illness and Injury* Clarendon Press, Oxford Socio–Legal Studies

HARRIS F 1989 Dispute resolution and the courts in south-west England: Towards an empirical enquiry. Paper presented at the 25th Anniversary Meetings of the Law and Society Association, Madison, Wisconsin

HARRIS F 1991 *The development of court architecture: its effect on utilisation of the law courts, with specific reference to the court houses of Truro, Cornwall* AJRBP Working Paper 16, University of Exeter (forthcoming)

HARVEY D 1973 *Social Justice and the City* Arnold, Leeds

HARWOOD S 1989–90 *Law Society Annual Statistical Report* Research and Policy Planning Unit, The Law Society, London

HATHAWAY J C 1982 *Legal Aid in New Brunswick: An Empirical Evaluation* Department of Justice, Ottawa

HATHAWAY J C 1984/85 Native Canadians and the criminal justice system: a critical examination of the native courtworker program *Saskatchewan Law Review* **49**(2): 201–37

HAGGETT P 1965 *Locational Analysis in Human Geography* Edward Arnold, London

HEINZ J P, LAUMANN E O 1982 *Chicago Lawyers: The Social Structure of the Bar* Russell Sage, New York

HENRY F S 1983 *Private Justice. Towards Integrated Theorising in the Sociology of Law* Routledge & Kegan Paul, London

HMSO 1989 *Legal Services: A Framework for the Future* Cm 740

HOGGART K 1988 Not a definition of rural *Area* **20**(1): 35–40

HOOKER M B 1975 *Legal Pluralism: An Introduction to Colonial and Neo–Colonial Laws* Oxford University Press

LORD HUGHES 1980 *Report of the Royal Commission on Legal Services in Scotland* (2 vols) HMSO Cmnd 7846, London

JEFFERIES R 1880 *Hodge and his Masters* (2 vols) Smith, Elder & Co

JENKINS J, SKORDAKI E, BAKER L 1990 *Independent Legal Advice* Research Study No 3, Research and Policy Planning Unit, The Law Society, London

JENKINS J, SKORDAKI E, WILLIS C 1989 *Public Use and Perception of Solicitors' Services* Research Study No 1, Research and Policy Planning Unit, The Law Society, London

JOHNSEN J T 1978 *Rettshjelp i utkantstrok* (Legal aid in the outskirts) Oslo, Institute for Sociology of Law, University of Oslo

JOHNSEN J T 1980 Problems in planning legal services. In Blankenburg E (ed) *Innovations in the Legal Services* Verlag Anton Hain, Konigstein: 19–27

JOHNSEN J T 1987 *Retten til juridisk bistand. En rettspolitisk studie* (Right to Legal Counselling. A Legal Policy Study). Oslo: Tano (with an English summary)

JOHNSTON R J 1984 *Residential Segregation, the State and Constitutional Conflict in American Urban Areas* Academic Press, London

JOHNSTONE Q, FLOOD J 1982 Paralegals in English and American Law Offices. *Windsor Yearbook of Access to Justice* 2: 152–90

JONES B D 1986 Political geography and the law: banishing space from geography. *Political Geography Quarterly* 5: 283–7

JOSEPH A E, HALL G B 1985 The locational concentration of group homes in Toronto. *Professional Geographer* 37: 143–54

JOSEPH A E, PHILLIPS D 1984 *Accessibility and Utilisation: Geographical Perspectives on Health Care Delivery* Harper & Row, New York

KEMPSON E 1981 *On the Road: A Guide to Setting up and Running a Mobile Advice Centre* Library Association, London

KEMPSON E 1989 *Legal Advice and Assistance* Policy Studies Institute, Pinter, London

KIRK H 1976 *Portrait of a Profession* Oyez Longman Publishing Co, London

KNORR–CETINA K 1988 The micro–social order: towards a reconception. In Fielding A J (ed) *Action and Structure* Sage, London

KRITZER H M 1988 *Political Culture and the 'Propensity to Sue'* Dispute Processing Research Program Working Paper 9:1. Institute for Legal Studies, University of Wisconsin, Madison

LANDON D D 1982 Lawyers and localities: the interaction of community context and professionalism. *American Bar Foundation Research Journal* 459–85

LANDON D D 1985 Clients, colleagues and community: the shaping of zealous advocacy in a country law practice. *American Bar Foundation Research Journal* 81–111

LANDON D D 1990 *Country Lawyers. The Impact of Context on Professional Practice* Praeger, London

LAW CENTRES FEDERATION 1980 Statement on the development of law centres in areas of scattered populations. 2 August, unpublished

LAW CENTRES FEDERATION (LCF) 1989 *The Case for Law Centres* 3rd edn Law Centres Federation

LAW SOCIETY 1987 *New Directions in Legal Aid Practices* November

LAW SOCIETY (TRAINING COMMITTEE) 1990 *Training Tomorrow's Solicitors: Proposals For Changes to the Education and Training of Solicitors* The Law Society, London

LEGAL AID BOARD 1989 (May) Second stage consultation on the future of the Green Form Scheme. Unpublished

LEGAL SERVICES CORPORATION (LSC) 1979 *Special Legal Problems and Problems of Access to Legal Services – Overview of Section 1007(h): Summary of Conclusions, Recommendations and Methodology* Legal Services Corporation, Washington DC

LEWIS P S C 1973 Unmet legal needs. In Morris P *et al* (eds) *Social Needs and Legal Action* Martin Robertson, London

LORD CHANCELLOR'S DEPARTMENT (LCD) 1982 *32nd Legal Aid Annual Reports* (1981–82) HMSO, London

LORD CHANCELLOR'S DEPARTMENT (LCD) 1983 *33rd Legal Aid Annual Reports* (1982–83) HMSO, London

LORD CHANCELLOR'S DEPARTMENT (LCD) 1986a *35th Legal Aid Annual Reports* (1984–85) HMSO, London

LORD CHANCELLOR'S DEPARTMENT (LCD) 1986b *Legal Aid Efficiency Scrutiny* (2 vols) June LCD

LORD CHANCELLOR'S DEPARTMENT (LCD) 1989 *38th Legal Aid Annual Reports* (1987–88) HMSO, London

LORD CHANCELLOR'S DEPARTMENT (LCD) 1990 *39th Legal Aid Annual Reports* (1988–89) HMSO, London

LOVELOCK D 1984 *Review of the National Association of Citizens Advice Bureaux* Cmnd 9139, HMSO, London

LOYER L 1985 *Justice et Justiciables* Centre de Documentation Juridique de l'Ouest, Rennes

McLAUGHLIN B 1986 Rural policy: the revival of the rural idyll. *Journal of Rural Studies* **2**: 81–90

MARKS P 1984 Law Society Annual Statistical Report. *Law Society's Gazette* **81**: 2607–9

MARKS P 1985 Law Society Annual Statistical Report. *Law Society's Gazette* **83**: 2903–17

MARKS P 1986 Law Society Annual Statistical Report. *Law Society's Gazette* **83**: 3257–62

MARKS P 1987–88 *Law Society Annual Statistical Report* Research and Policy Planning Unit, The Law Society

LADY MARRE 1988 Report of the Committee on the Future of the Legal Profession (Chairman: Lady Marre). *A Time for Change* Report to the General Council of the Bar and the Council of the Law Society, July 1988, London

MARSDEN T 1989 *Commoditisation of the Labour Process: Farm Households and British Agriculture* Sociology of Agriculture (IRSA), Working Paper No 2

MARSDEN T, MURDOCH J 1990 *Restructuring rurality: key areas for development in assessing rural change* ESRC Countryside Change Initiative, Working Paper No 4

MARSDEN T, WHATMORE S, MUNTON R 1987 Uneven development and the restructuring process in British agriculture: a preliminary exploration. *Journal of Rural Studies* **3**: 297–308

MARTIN J P 1981 Judicare: one component of a diversified delivery system. *Clearinghouse Review* **15**: 501–5

MARTIN J P 1983 Private attorney involvement in rural legal services delivery. *Clearinghouse Review* **17**: 260–4

MARX K, ENGELS F 1970 *The German Ideology* International Publishers Edition, New York

MASSAM B 1980 *Spatial Search: Applications to Planning Problems in the Public Sector* Pergamon, Oxford

MASSEY D 1984 *Spatial Divisions of Labour: Social Structures and the Geography of Production* Macmillan, London

MATTHEWS R (ed) 1988 *Informal Justice?* Sage, London

MAYHEW L, REISS A 1969 The social organisation of legal contacts *American Sociological Review* **34**: 309–27

MELTON G B 1983 Community psychology and rural legal systems. In Childs AW, Melton GB (eds) *Rural Psychology* Plenum Press, New York 359–80

MILES M 1986 A haven for the privileged: recruitment into the profession of attorney in England 1709–1792. *Social History* **11**(2): 197–210

MINGAY G E 1963 *English Landed Society in the Eighteenth Century* Routledge & Kegan Paul, London

MOSELEY M 1979 *Accessibility: The Rural Challenge* Methuen, London

MOSELEY M, PACKMAN J 1982 *Mobile Services in Rural Areas* University of East Anglia, Norwich

MOSER C A, KALTON G 1971 *Survey Methods in Social Investigation* Heinemann, London

MOSSMAN M J 1983 Community legal clinics in Ontario. *Windsor Yearbook of Access to Justice* 3: 376–402

MUMFORD L 1961 *The City in History. Its Origins, its Transformations and its Prospects* Peregrine, Hitchin, Herts

MUNGHAM G, THOMAS P 1981 Studying lawyers: aspects of the theory, method and politics of social research. *(British) Journal of Law and Society* 8: (1) 79–96

MURPHY M 1989 Civil legal aid eligibility. *Legal Action* October: 7–8

MURRAY G 1988 New Zealand lawyers: from colonial GPs to the servants of capital. In Abel R and Lewis P (eds) *Lawyer in Society: The Common Law World* Vol 1, University of California Press, Berkeley: 318–68

NACAB 1987 *Annual Report* NACAB, London

NATIONAL CONSUMER COUNCIL (NCC) 1977 *The Fourth Right of Citizenship. A Review of Local Advice Services* Robendene, London

NATIONAL CONSUMER COUNCIL (NCC) 1983 *Information and advice services in the United Kingdom: Report to the Minister of State for Consumer Affairs* NCC

NATIONAL CONSUMER COUNCIL (NCC) 1986 *Good Advice For All. Guidelines on Standards for Local Advice Services* NCC, Oxford

NATIONAL CONSUMER COUNCIL (NCC) 1989 *Ordinary Justice. Legal Services and the Courts in England and Wales: A Consumer View* HMSO, London

NATIONAL CONSUMER COUNCIL/NATIONAL COUNCIL OF SOCIAL SERVICE (now NCVO) (NCC/NCSS) 1978 *The Right to Know. A Review of Advice Services in Rural Areas* Bedford Square Press, London

NEATE S 1981 *Rural Deprivation: An Annotated Bibliography of Economic and Social Problems in Rural Areas* Geo Abstracts, Norwich

NEAVE H R 1978 *Statistics Tables* George Allen & Unwin, London

NELKEN D 1986 Beyond the study of 'law and society'? *American Bar Foundation Research Journal* 323–38

NEWBY H 1980 *Green and Pleasant Land? Social Change in Rural England* Pelican, Harmondsworth

NEWBY H 1986 Locality and rurality: the restructuring of rural social relations. *Regional Studies* **20**: 209–16

NIEMEYER B 1978 *De invloed van afstand op het gebruik van kostelose juridische dienstveriening bij het Buro voor Arbeidsrecht te Groningen* (The effect of distance on the use of free legal services at the trade union legal service office in Groningen), unpublished, Groningen

NUTLEY S D 1984 Planning for rural accessibility provision: welfare, economy and equity. *Environment and Planning A* **16**: 357–76

ORCHARD S, BLAKE A 1989 Franchising: the next steps. *Law Society's Gazette* **46**: 12–14

PAHL R 1968 The rural–urban continuum. In Pahl R (ed) *Readings in Urban Sociology* Pergamon, Oxford 263–97

PARTRIDGE B 1940 *Country Lawyer* Harrap, London

PATERSON A, BAIN S 1986 *Access to Legal Services in Scotland* AJRBP Working Paper No 13, University of Exeter

PATERSON A, FARMER L, STEPHEN F, LOVE J 1988 Competition and the market for legal services. *Journal of Law and Society* **15**(4): 361–73

PATERSON A, NELKEN D 1984 Evolution in legal services: practice without theory? *Civil Justice Quarterly* **3**: 229–44

PHILLIPS D, WILLIAMS A 1984 *Rural Britain – A Social Geography* Blackwell, Oxford

PODMORE D 1980 *Solicitors and the Wider Community* Heinemann, London

RHYS D G, BUXTON M J 1974 Car ownership and the rural transport problem. *Journal of the Chartered Institute of Transport* **2**: 109–12

RIBORDY F X 1982 Les Services d'aide juridique à Sudbury. *Canadian Legal Aid Bulletin* **5**(4): 18–31

RIBORDY F X 1988 Socio–economic history of the Bar of Sudbury. Paper presented at Canadian Law and Society Conference, Windsor, Ontario, June 7–8

RICHARDS J 1989 *Inform, Advise and Support. 50 years of the Citizens' Advice Bureau* Lutterworth Press

ROBERTS 1978 Rural legal services: A report by the liaison lawyer of the National Association of Citizens Advice Bureaux. Devon and Cornwall area, unpublished paper

ROJAS F 1988 A comparison of change–oriented legal services in Latin America with legal services in North America and Europe. *International Journal of the Sociology of Law* 16: 203–56

ROYAL COMMISSION ON LEGAL SERVICES (RCLS) 1979 *Final Report* Cmnd 7648 HMSO, London

ROYAL COMMISSION ON THE POLICE (Sir Henry Urmston Willick) 1962 *Final Report* Cmnd 1728 HMSO, London

RURAL ADVICE AND INFORMATION COMMITTEE (RAIC) 1984 *At Your Convenience?* RAIC

RUSSELL A 1984 *The Clerical Profession* SPCK, London

SARAT A 1981 Book review of *Access to Justice. Harvard Law Review* 94: 1911–24

SAYER A 1989 The new regional geography and problems of narrative. *Society and Space* 7: 253–77

SCHUYT K, GROENENDIJK K, SLOOT B 1976 *De weg naar het recht* (The road to justice) Kluwer, Deventer

SCHUYT K, GROENENDIJK K, SLOOT B 1977 Access to the legal system and legal services research. *European Yearbook in Law and Sociology* 98–120

SCOTTISH CONSUMER COUNCIL (SCC) 1982 *Consumer Problems in Rural Areas* Scottish Consumer Council

SCOTTISH CONSUMER COUNCIL (SCC) 1983 *A Call For Advice. An Evaluation of Two Rural Advice Experiments in Scotland* Scottish Consumer Council

SEARLE G 1982 *Coordinating Public Transport in Rural Counties: Summary of the Lewes Study Approach* Department of Transport

SERON C 1990 Managing entrepreneurial legal services: the transformation of small-firm practice. In Nelson R L, Trubek D M, Solomon R L (eds) *Lawyers' Ideals and Lawyers' Practice* Cornell University Press, Ithaca, New York

SHOARD M 1987 *This Land is our Land* Paladin, London

SHUCKSMITH M 1990 *Housebuilding in Britain's Countryside* Routledge, London

SLATTER M, MOSELEY M 1986a *Access to Legal Services in Rural Norfolk* AJRBP Working Paper No 7, University of Exeter

SLATTER M, MOSELEY M 1986b M'rural friend. *New Law Journal* 136: 626–8, 641

SMALLCOMBE J 1991 *Representation by Solicitors in Magistrates' and Crown Courts* Law Society Research Study Series, London

SMITH R LLOYD BOSTOCK S 1990 *Why People go to law: An Annobated Bibliography of Social Science Research* Centre for Socio-legal studies Oxford

SNIDER D L 1981 *Legal Services in Rural Areas: An Evaluation Report Prepared for the Department of Justice, Ottawa and the Faculty of Law, Queens University* Department of Justice, Ottawa

SNIDER D L 1986 Rural justice in Canada: theoretical and empirical issues. Paper presented to Annual Meeting of the Law and Society Association, Chicago

SPRING D 1963 *The English Landed Estate in the Nineteenth Century: its Administration* Baltimore

STOCKFORD D 1978 Social service provision. In Walker A (ed) *Rural Poverty* Poverty Pamphlet 37, Child Poverty Action Group: 50–56

SUGARMAN D (ed) 1983 *Legality, Ideology and the State* Academic Press, London

TARLING R 1979 *Sentencing Practice in the Magistrates' Courts* HMSO, London

TAYLOR P J 1977 *Quantitative Methods in Geography: An Introduction to Spatial Analysis* Houghton Mifflin Co, Boston

THOMAS P 1986 *Access to Legal Services in Southwest Wales* AJRBP Working Paper No 11, University of Exeter

THOMAS R W, ROBSON B T, NUTTER R D 1989 *County Court Workloads: A Location–Allocation Analysis* Working Paper 7, Centre for Urban Policy Studies, School of Geography, University of Manchester

TRUBEK D M 1984 Where the action is: critical legal studies and empiricism. *Stanford Law Review* **36**: 575–622

TRUBEK L G, TRUBEK D M 1981 Civic justice through civil justice: a new approach to public interest advocacy in the United States. In Cappelletti M (ed) *Access to Justice and the Welfare State* Sijthoff, Alphen aan den Rijn: 119–44

TRUBEK D M, GROSSMAN J B, FELSTINER W L F, KRITZER H M, SARAT A 1983 *Civil Litigation Research Project: Final Report* (2 vols) Disputes Processing Research Program, University of Madison Law School, Madison

TURNER A F 1982 President Reagan and the Legal Services Corporation. *Creighton Law Review* **115**: 711–32

UNGER R 1976 *Law in Modern Society. Toward a Criticism of Social Theory* Free Press, New York

WARSHAWSKY R, WARSHAWSKY J 1983 Legal services in rural areas: decline and opportunity. *Social Development Issues* **7**: 68–73

WATKINS C, BLACKSELL M, ECONOMIDES K 1984 *The Use of the Law List to Assess the Distribution and Characteristics of Solicitors in England and Wales* AJRBP Working Paper No 1, University of Exeter

WATKINS C, BLACKSELL M, ECONOMIDES K 1988 The distribution of solicitors in England and Wales. *Transactions of the Institute of British Geographers* (New Series) **13**: 39–56

WATKINS C, ECONOMIDES K, BLACKSELL M 1986 *The Use of Legal Services in Three Remote Rural Parishes* AJRBP Working Paper No 14, University of Exeter

WEISBROT D 1988 The Australian legal profession. From provincial family firms to multinationals. In Abel R and Lewis P (eds) *Lawyers in Society – The Common Law World* Vol 1, University of California Press, Berkeley 244–317

WEISBROT D 1989 *Australian Lawyers* Longman, Cheshire

WIBBERLEY G P 1972 Conflicts in the countryside. *Town and Country Planning* **40**: 259–65

WILLIAMS R 1973 *The Country and the City* Hogarth Press, Longman

WILLIAMS R, BLOAR M, HOROBIN G, TAYLOR R 1980 Remoteness and disadvantages: findings from a survey of access to health services in the Western Isles. *Scottish Journal of Sociology* **4**: 105–24

WILLIAMS W M 1963 *A West Country Village: Ashworthy* Routledge & Kegan Paul, London

WINTER M, ROGERS A (eds) 1988 *Who can Afford to Live in the Countryside? – Access to Housing Land* Centre for Rural Studies Occasional Paper No 2. Royal Agricultural College, Cirencester

ZEMANS F H 1985 Recent trends in the organisation of legal services. *Anglo–American Law Review* **14**: 283–335

Index